BEYOND ROSIE

Ms. Clemons

Beyond Rosie

*A Documentary History of Women
and World War II*

EDITED BY

JULIA BROCK,
JENNIFER W. DICKEY,
RICHARD J. W. HARKER,
AND CATHERINE M. LEWIS

The University of Arkansas Press
Fayetteville
2015

To all the American women who
served in World War II, overseas or on the home front.
Our nation owes a debt of gratitude that we can never repay.

CONTENTS

Acknowledgments   ix

Introduction   xi

CHAPTER 1
Into the Factories   1

CHAPTER 2
New Opportunities, New Challenges   55

CHAPTER 3
Women's Auxiliary Services   89

CHAPTER 4
"Make Do and Mend":
Women and the Home Front   123

CHAPTER 5
The Secret War   175

Appendix 1   229

Appendix 2   233

Appendix 3   235

Annotated Bibliography   241

About the Museum of History
and Holocaust Education   248

Index   249

About the Editors   261

ACKNOWLEDGMENTS

This project has been a collaborative effort in the best sense of the word. The editors are faculty and staff members of the Museum of History and Holocaust Education (MHHE), which is part of the Department of Museums, Archives, and Rare Books at Kennesaw State University, Georgia. In 2012, the MHHE curated a traveling exhibition entitled *Beyond Rosie: Women and World War II*, which has proven very popular among area schools, universities, and museums. After hearing from teachers, museum professionals, and students, we realized that the exhibition was not enough, so this documentary collection was born. A number of books have been published on women and World War II, but there is no single collection of primary documents focused on this topic. We assembled a team of historians and got to work.

We have so many colleagues to thank at institutions throughout the United States, including Eileen Hurst (Burritt Library at Central Connecticut State University), Rachel Mears and Megan Harris (Veterans History Project, American Folklife Center, Library of Congress), Karen V. Kukil (William Allan Neilson Library, Smith College, Massachusetts), Alexandra Levy (Atomic Heritage Foundations), Niki Denison (University of Wisconsin Alumni Association), Vivian M. Santangelo (Meredith Corporation), Evora Swoopes (*Science News*), Tomi Yoshikawa (Japanese American National Museum), Nathaniel Wiltzen (National Archives Boston), Shane Bell and Nathan Jordan (National Archives Atlanta), Sara Logue (Manuscript, Archives, and Rare Book Library, Emory University, Georgia), Susan Snyder (Bancroft Library, University of California, Berkeley), Lisa Marine and Mary K. Huelsback (Wisconsin Historical Society), Nancy Ireland (Eleanor Roosevelt Literary Estate), Sara Duke (Prints and Photographs Division, Library of Congress), Jack Eckert and Jessica Murphy (Countway Medical Library, Harvard Medical School), John Garofolo, India Artis (*The Crisis*), Adam Watson (Florida Memory Project), Matthew Herbison (Legacy Center: Archives and Special Collections, Drexel College of Medicine, Pennsylvania), Stephanie George (Center for Oral and Public History, California State University, Fullerton), and Tom Leatherman (Rosie the Riveter—World War II Home Front National Historic Park).

We would like to extend a warm thanks to Dr. Ouida Dickey for her valuable edits to the introduction as we were completing the manuscript. Many others at Kennesaw State University deserve recognition, especially Patricia Mosier for helping us prepare the manuscript. Dr. Randy Hinds and the staff and faculty in the Department of Museums, Archives, and Rare Books provided much encouragement and patience as we finished this manuscript.

Julia is grateful to her family for their support and encouragement. She could not have finished the book without the intellect and humor of her fellow coeditors or the staff of the Museum of History and Holocaust Education. She would like to thank Mark Greenberg for his contagious interest in women photojournalists during the war.

Jennifer would like to express her appreciation to Dr. Ouida Dickey and Kathy Knapp for their encouragement, support, and patience while she worked on three book projects simultaneously.

Richard wishes to thank his parents, Barbara and Graham Harker, for imparting their love of learning, education, and history, and his siblings and their significant others, who continually challenge him to think about the world and its history in different and new ways and strive to be creative: Dr. Chris Harker and Dr. Sonya Sharma, Lucy Harker and Tom Hemming, and Tricia, Chris, and Poppy Turner. He owes a special debt of gratitude to Sue Gloor, who has lived and breathed this book with him and has been a continual source of love and support. Richard dedicates this book to his grandmother, Marjorie Mullen, who was a wartime nurse in London during the Blitz and is a truly remarkable woman.

Catherine owes a special debt to Dr. Leslie Schwalm and Dr. Linda Kerber, who years ago at the University of Iowa guided her through the study of US women's history. Their wisdom and curiosity have helped shape a generation of scholars. She would also like to thank her husband, John Companiotte, daughter, Emma Lewis Companiotte, and father, Dr. J. Richard Lewis, who have supported and assisted her throughout the research and writing of this book.

Finally, the editors owe quite a debt to the editorial staff at the University of Arkansas Press, formerly led by the ever-cheerful Larry Malley. The press's staff, including Mike Bieker and Brian King, have been great partners in this book, and we are thankful for their wisdom and help bringing it to fruition.

INTRODUCTION

More so than any war in history, World War II was a woman's war. Women, motivated by patriotism, the opportunity for new experiences, and the desire to serve, participated widely in the global conflict. Within the Allied countries, women of all ages proved to be invaluable in the fight for victory. Rosie the Riveter, a fictional American character, became the most enduring image of women's involvement in World War II. Rosie, however, tells only a small portion of a complex story. As wartime production workers, enlistees in auxiliary military units, members of voluntary organizations or resistance groups, as wives and mothers on the home front, as journalists, and as USO performers, American women found ways to challenge traditional gender roles and stereotypes. This documentary collection explores the diverse experiences of women during World War II. It also serves as a companion volume to the Museum of History and Holocaust Education at Kennesaw State University's traveling exhibition, *Beyond Rosie: Women in World War II.*

Beyond Rosie offers readers an opportunity to see how American women's roles changed during the war and the numerous contributions they made to the fight against the Axis powers. The primary documents (newspapers, propaganda posters, cartoons, excerpts from oral histories and memoirs, speeches, photographs, and editorials) collected here are organized into five chapters and represent cultural, political, economic, and social perspectives on the diverse roles women played during World War II. They have also been selected to highlight both the top-down and bottom-up motivations for the creation and re-creation of these roles.

This introduction functions as an overview of the main issues related to women and World War II and is followed by five chapters that provide multiple perspectives on this complex era. The editors, all faculty and staff members at Kennesaw State University (KSU), working with the Museum of History and Holocaust Education, have prepared brief headnotes to introduce each document and provide information about it or the context necessary to interpret it. We created this volume to be useful for upper-division high school, undergraduate, or graduate history courses in women's studies, American studies, ethnic studies, political science, legal studies, criminal justice, or sociology. We also hope it will appeal to museum educators, library professionals, and community members interested in this topic, especially those who host KSU's *Beyond Rosie* exhibition. The volume's appendices include "Timeline," "Questions and Assignments" (a section to offer readers an opportunity to expand their understanding of this important moment in history), and "Classroom and Research Activities." In addition, there is an annotated bibliography.

Understanding World War II

World War II affected American women in unprecedented ways that would not become obvious until after the bombing of Pearl Harbor in 1941, but the war began much earlier. In the 1930s, Imperial Japan and Nazi Germany set the stage for one of the most destructive conflicts in world history. Germany invaded Poland on September 1, 1939, as part of Adolf Hitler's plan to create *lebensraum* (or living space) for the Aryan master race. Two days after the invasion, Britain and France (allies of Poland, which had largely appeased Hitler to this point) declared war on Germany. Using *blitzkrieg* (lightning war) tactics, Germany quickly conquered Poland, Denmark, Norway, the Netherlands, Belgium, Luxemburg, and France. With the fall of France in the summer of 1940, Great Britain and members of the Commonwealth stood alone in Europe against Germany. Germany, Italy, and Japan created a formal alliance and became known as the Axis powers with the completion of the Tripartite Pact on September 27, 1940. Though allied with Germany, Japan fought a different war to gain power and influence throughout Asia. Japan had been at war with China since the 1930s and shared with Nazi Germany the dream of territorial expansion.

Isolationism dominated US politics, and despite numerous public pleas for help from Great Britain, the United States was reluctant to join another international conflict. Congress passed three separate neutrality laws in 1935 and 1937, intending to allay public fears of entry into a potential war. As Japan and Germany began to rearm and increase their militarization, however, pacifist sentiment began to wane. On March 11, 1941, President Franklin D. Roosevelt signed "An Act to Further Promote the Defense of the United States," more commonly known as the Lend-

Lease Act. Under the pretense of neutrality, the United States supplied Allied nations with materiel beginning in 1941. America's neutrality ended on December 7, 1941, when Japan bombed Pearl Harbor. The next day, President Roosevelt delivered his now famous "A Date Which Will Live in Infamy" speech to Congress. Shortly afterward, Congress passed a formal declaration of war on Japan, bringing the United States into the conflict. Germany and Italy quickly declared war on the United States, which, in turn, issued a declaration of war on the remaining Axis powers. In an alliance that became known as the Allied powers, the United States joined Great Britain and members of the Commonwealth, along with European and African countries occupied by Germany and the Soviet Union, against the Axis powers. In the European Theater, the war raged until Allied victories at Stalingrad (1942–1943), in North Africa (1943), and in Normandy (1944) began to turn the tide. A Soviet offensive in 1945 helped secure an Allied victory; and on May 7, 1945, a week after Hitler's suicide, Germany surrendered.

In the Pacific Theater, the Allies faced a war unlike anything they had ever witnessed. The Japanese army, battle-hardened by their invasion of China, sought to exact victory over the Allies on the many small islands in the Pacific Ocean. At Midway Atoll in June 1942, the US Navy turned the tide of the war. Despite this important victory, it would take three more years and brutal battles on Pacific islands, such as Guadalcanal and Iwo Jima, for the Allies to declare victory over Japan. In August 1945, the United States dropped atomic bombs on Hiroshima and Nagasaki, decimating the cities and prompting the Japanese surrender on September 2, 1945. When World War II was over, 55 million people were dead and many millions more wounded, making it the most destructive conflict in history. Yet, the impact of this global conflict was not limited to the men who served on the battlefield. Women contributed to and were transformed by World War II. This book, focused on the experience of American women, tells some of those stories.

Into the Factories

Women worked in the United States long before the start of World War II, and wartime necessities often brought them expanded opportunities for work. During the Revolutionary War and Civil War, for example, women took over men's jobs. Katharine Wormeley started a factory during the Civil War in Newport, Rhode Island, to make shirts for Union soldiers and hired only women workers. *Harper's Weekly*, on July 20, 1861, published an etching by Winslow Homer of women filling cartridges for the US Arsenal in Massachusetts. During World War I, women served as clerks, railroad workers, machinists, and streetcar conductors. But these examples do not compare to the mobilization of American women during World War II.[1]

Even before the United States entered the war, President Roosevelt called for an increase in military production. On December 29, 1940, he delivered a speech to Congress, calling the United States "a great arsenal for democracy." In March 1941, Congress passed the Lend-Lease Act, which required a mobilization of US industry that helped bring women into the workforce. Many Americans, however, were not aware of growing threats in Europe and Asia throughout the late 1930s and early 1940s. Eileen Hughes of Narragansett, Rhode Island, recalled: "Before Pearl Harbor, I didn't realize how serious the war in Europe was. I think it seemed very, very far away. We were also far from Japan as well as Germany. It was horrible what was going on in Europe, but I don't think I realized how close it was going to hit us until Pearl Harbor."[2] The United States may not have been prepared for war, but that would quickly change. As head of the War Production Board, Donald Nelson noted, "For nine years before Pearl Harbor, Germany, Italy, and Japan prepared intensively for war, while as late as 1940 the war production of peaceful America was virtually nothing. Yet two years later that output of our war factories equaled that of the three Axis nations combined."[3]

After Pearl Harbor was attacked, war production increased dramatically as factories were transformed to build airplanes, ships, and troop supplies and to manufacture munitions. Large production quotas and the development of new industries created labor shortages that were exacerbated by the millions of American men leaving to join the armed services beginning in 1942. As historian Brenda Ralph Lewis argued, "It took a catastrophe like Pearl Harbor to shift traditional thinking about what was and was not 'women's work,' beginning a new era in which American women participated in national life as never before."[4] This new reality required creative solutions, and government and industry officials began to see women as a largely untapped resource in manufacturing and agriculture.[5] By 1943, government officials and industry leaders looked to women workers to contribute to the production needs created by war. Secretary of War Henry L. Stimpson acknowledged, "The War Department must fully utilize, immediately and effectively, the largest and potentially the finest single source of labor available today—the vast reserve of woman power."[6] Early recruitment efforts by the US government, however, did not bring large numbers of women into the workplace. In 1943, the US government sought a different approach.[7]

Propaganda, largely coordinated by the Office of War Information (OWI) and supported by voluntary associations such as the War Advertising Council (WAC), played a critical role in influencing women's participation in the war effort. These bureaus created posters and pamphlets, screened newsreels at movie theaters, and used radio broadcasts and newspaper advertisements to appeal to women's patriotism and create energetic support for and participation in the war. The image of Rosie the Riveter remains the lasting symbol of these propaganda efforts, though many different images and slogans were used to mobilize American women by a range of organizations and individuals.[8] Rosie was the ideal woman worker: loyal, efficient, patriotic, and pretty.[9] Redd Evans and John Jacob Loeb composed a song entitled "Rosie the Riveter" that was issued by Paramount Music Corporation of New York and released in early 1943. The song was popular and featured in two films, *Follow the Band* (1943) and *Rosie the Riveter* (1944).[10] The first two stanzas indicate the kind of "girl" Rosie was and, by extension, what American women should strive to emulate:

> While other girls attend their fav'rite cocktail bar
> Sipping Martinis, munching caviar
> There's a girl who's really putting them to shame
> Rosie is her name.
>
> All the day long whether rain or shine
> She's a part of the assembly line
> She's making history, working for victory
> Rosie the Riveter
> Keeps a sharp lookout for sabotage
> Sitting up there on the fuselage
> That little frail can do more than a male will do
> Rosie the Riveter.

Rosie was perhaps most famously popularized in images. In late 1943, Westinghouse Company's War Coordinating Committee hired graphic artist J. Howard Miller to create a series of posters, including the now famous "We Can Do It!" image of a the highly stylized female war worker. Miller supposedly based his work on Geraldine Doyle, a Michigan factory worker, but the poster was not immediately associated with Rosie the Riveter. Today, Miller's image is the iconic symbol of Rosie, but during the war, a depiction by Norman Rockwell was more popular. Rockwell created his famous illustration for the cover of the *Saturday Evening Post* (May 29, 1943). Mary Doyle (no relation to Geraldine), a nineteen-year-old telephone operator in Arlington, Vermont, was said to be Rockwell's model, and Rockwell's illustration soon became the first widely publicized pictorial representation of Rosie.[11] She is portrayed as both a muscular and feminine figure with her foot on Adolf Hitler's book *Mein Kampf.* The *Post* loaned the image to the Treasury Department, which in turn used the image to promote bond sales. Rosie was only one of many images created to inspire the recruitment of women to wartime work. Newspapers regularly printed headlines encouraging women to join the workforce, and radio stations endlessly broadcast appeals that sought the same outcome.

Propaganda campaigns made wartime jobs and services appear fashionable and glamorous while also emphasizing that women would earn more money supporting the war effort than in other professions. Photographer David Conover captured Norma Jeane Baker Dougherty working on a drone aircraft, and that photo was published in *Yank* magazine, which wanted to publish "morale boosting shots of pretty girls doing their bit to help the war effort." This photograph, and others, helped launch the career of nineteen-year-old Dougherty, who became Marilyn Monroe.[12] Due in part to the success of these efforts, 6 million women joined the workforce and another 350,000 joined military services between 1941 and 1945. Although most propaganda used positive language and images, women were also seen as potential threats to the success of the Allied war effort. Government images and slogans, for example, warned women against "loose talk" and admonished them to practice self-censorship.

Women went to work during World War II in jobs that they had not traditionally held before in factories, plants, and on farms. Some were surely motivated by patriotism; others embraced the opportunity to learn new skills, contribute to the public good, gain financial independence, and prove themselves in jobs thought of exclusively as men's work.[13] Margarita Salazar traded a job in a beauty shop for one in an aircraft factory and explained her decision: "Sure, the money was in defense. You worked more hours, and the more hours you worked, the more money you made. And it was exciting. You figured you were doing something for your country—and at the same time making money!"[14] In Mobile, Alabama, a waitress could make fourteen dollars per day, compared to a shipyard worker who made thirty-seven dollars.[15] Money was an important motivating factor for women to pursue wartime work.

Age, race, class, sexual orientation, marital status, and children also shaped women's decisions to enter the workforce and their wartime, working lives. Many working-class women, especially immigrants and African Americans, were already in paid labor because of necessity. Some benefited from giving up traditionally female jobs in favor of higher-paying factory positions. At first, unmarried women without children were the targets of government recruiting efforts; then, as the labor shortages grew, married women without children were also included in recruitment campaigns. Eventually, even women with small children were targeted, despite government fears that women's work would lead to a rise in juvenile delinquency.[16] African American men and women were at first denied access to high-paying defense jobs, just as African American soldiers were assigned to segregated units and given low-status jobs. To resist this treatment, men and women activists launched a civil rights campaign, later known as the Double V campaign, which focused on victory against fascism abroad and victory against racism at home. As part of this effort, in 1941, labor organizer A. Philip Randolph threatened to lead a march on Washington of fifty thousand protestors to force the US government to address the issue of segregation. In response, President Roosevelt issued Executive Order 8802, banning discrimination in industries with government contracts.[17] While an important step, the executive order did not stop discrimination in these workplaces, especially for women of color.

Wartime jobs for women brought not only new opportunities, but also unforeseen challenges. Many families had to relocate for work, and defense housing in communities from Seattle to Mobile became necessary to accommodate workers. The huge influx of war workers left these communities with inadequate housing, transportation, childcare, sanitation, and schools.[18] Additionally, the women who entered defense jobs were frequently snubbed by men who were disdainful about working alongside them. Fellow workers and unions were often suspicious of women, and managers often denied women positions of power because they saw them as temporary workers or less qualified than their male counterparts. Ely Campbell of Portland, Oregon, worked for the Progress Department of the Kaiser Shipyard and remembered the initial hostility of male coworkers: "The guys obviously made a pact not to talk to us . . . to freeze us out. . . . We were friendly, doing the job, and after a couple of weeks they not only thawed out but actually enjoyed us—and we enjoyed them."[19]

Industrial jobs were dangerous; women were injured and even killed on the job. The *New York Times* reported on January 21, 1944, "Industrial casualties (women and men) between Pearl Harbor and January 1st of this year aggregated 37,500 killed, or 7,500 more than the military dead, 210,000 permanently disabled, and 4,500,000 temporarily disabled, or sixty times the number of military wounded or missing."[20] Peggy Terry, who worked at a plant filling artillery shells with powder, remembered: "Our hair was streaked orange. Our hands, our face, our neck just turned orange, even our eyeballs. We never questioned. None of us ever asked, 'What is this? Is it harmful?' We simply didn't think about it. This was just one of the conditions of the job."[21] Without modern-day workplace safety standards, women regularly put themselves at risk in defense work.

Women also faced challenges in receiving equal wages. Most companies paid women a fraction of what male workers received. In 1942, the War Labor Board adopted the concept of equal pay for equal work, and some companies adjusted their pay levels, including the Huntsville Chemical plant, which paid men $5.76 and women $4.40 per day. But change was slow, and most men working in US factories during the war made an average of $54.65 per week, compared to women's $31.21.[22]

In addition to facing discrimination on the job, women faced the challenge of the "double shift," in which a job outside the home was added to their family responsibilities. Childcare became a significant problem for wartime workers, and many had to cobble together creative solutions to keep their jobs and raise a family. Mindful of women's experiences, First Lady Eleanor Roosevelt wrote in *Reader's Digest* in 1944: ·

> Some of the married women workers are not doing their best because we haven't taken into consideration their personal problems. Their homes must still go on. Their children must be cared for. Day nurseries are being established, but they are not always properly organized. . . . I was told of one nursery which was five blocks from a bus stop and meant that a woman had to walk 20 blocks every day. To a tired woman carrying a child, those blocks seem very long.[23]

Women helped to sustain the booming industrial and agricultural sectors—a crucial factor in helping the Allies win the war. By 1945, as historian Penny Colman explained, "America's wartime production record included 296,429 airplanes, 102,351 tanks and self-propelled guns; 372,431 artillery pieces; 47 million tons of artillery ammunition; 87,620 warships; and 44 billion rounds of small-arms ammunition. *Time* magazine called America's wartime production a miracle."[24] That miracle depended on American women, and the presence of women in industry challenged traditional views of women's work in dramatic ways. But overall, most American women remained at home during the war. As visible as war workers were, the average American family was not led by a factory worker.

When the war ended, so did many women's jobs. William Mulcahy, a supervisor, reflected on the change:

> Unfortunately, when the war ended, despite the skill and patriotism the women had displayed, we were forced to lay them off. I will never forget the day after the war ended. We met the girls at the door, and they were lined up all the way down Market Street [in Camden, New Jersey] to the old movie theater about eight blocks away, and we handed them a slip to go over to personnel and get their severance pay. We didn't even allow them in the building, all these women with whom I had become so close, who had worked seven days a week for years and had been commended so many times by the Navy for the work they were doing.[25]

Despite being pushed out of defense work at the war's conclusion, women proved in a very visible way that their capabilities extended beyond traditional roles as wives and mothers.

New Opportunities, New Challenges

Women found work in industrial settings—where few skilled jobs had existed before—but also began moving into professional work. These jobs, which included work in the legal, medical, and academic fields, had always contained a small number of women, but the war brought about new opportunities to find training and paid positions. As historian Anne Firor Scott remembered, "Many American women . . . found open doors where once they would have encountered brick walls" in white-collar work.[26] Women made new gains during the war, only to feel stymied in the postwar years, when "Americans in general were experiencing considerable confusion about what women could and should be doing."[27]

True to Scott's words, the number of women who sought professional training in the legal and medical fields doubled during the war.[28] Women filled the positions in graduate training left open by men who left for the battle theaters. Simply receiving training, however, did not necessarily mean placement in a paid position, though the need for practicing professionals allowed women to find work more easily.

Though women had been practicing law for decades before World War II (there were 4,187 women lawyers in 1940), the war created urgency for law firms whose associates went to the front lines.[29] Constance Cook, a law student at Cornell University during the war, remembered, "Pearl Harbor came and just decimated our class." A young professor at Cornell persuaded the school to begin admitting more women, who then found jobs in firms that previously had not hired them. "Women with marvelous qualifications had been graduating from law school for seventy-five years," Cook recalled, "and [law firms] never took any of them. There's no question. [Firms] were desperate for help."[30] When legal firms acted out of need, women proved that they could ably fill the positions of men.

Women physicians had been on the decline in the 1930s; in the early part of the twentieth century, through the Great Depression, they made up a small percentage of the medical profession. Still, there were eight thousand female doctors in the United States in 1943; a large number were pediatricians, obstetricians, and gynecologists.[31] First-class medical training was largely unavailable to women. Harvard did not open its doors to female students until 1945, and, even though enrollment dropped in medical programs as men went to war, most medical schools kept their quota for female students at 5 percent.[32]

The military was in need of medical workers, but women doctors encountered strong resistance from the military and medical establishments, which kept them from enlisting. Though they did not need any legal action to back commissions in the military (the Army Medical Corps was permitted to commission women), women doctors such as Dr. Emily Barringer lobbied Congress to support their efforts in building the number of women doctors in the army and navy. Congress responded by passing the Sparkman Act, an "act to provide for the commission of female physicians and surgeons in the Medical Corps of the Army and the Navy," which Roosevelt signed into law on April 16, 1943.[33] Nonetheless, the army and navy largely refused to take advantage of the many eligible women doctors.

Women also served at home in other roles. "Government girls" were women who served as temporary federal employees to cover for men who served overseas. They mainly worked in clerical positions in places such as the War Department and Social Security Administration. By 1944, women comprised more than a third of civil service jobs, many holding clerical positions in Washington, D.C.[34] Additionally, nearly one hundred thousand women served in unpaid positions in local rationing boards.[35] Photographers employed by the Farm Security Administration (FSA) during the Depression also helped document home-front activities for the Office of War Information in the 1940s. Marjory Collins and Dorothea Lange used their cameras to illustrate how the war transformed daily life. The photographs were used to promote the mobilization of workers and bond sales and presented a story of sacrifice and national unity to an anxious US public.

Women journalists became more numerous during the war. Though they had commonly populated society pages in the past, serious female journalists found new need for their work as news coverage became more robust during wartime. In the 1930s, they found a ready ally in Eleanor Roosevelt, who had begun a weekly all-women press conference to pressure news organizations to hire women.[36] By wartime, women were employed as war correspondents by more than twenty-five newspapers, dozens of magazines, eight wire services, and five radio stations. Fewer than one hundred women acted as war correspondents—a small minority in a male-dominated field—and had to fight against discrimination from military leaders and male reporters, as well as the dangerous physical conditions of wartime reporting.[37]

Margaret Bourke-White became perhaps the most famous female war correspondent. Bourke-White had already made a name for herself by photographing the lives of tenant farmers during the Great Depression and for having her photo on the cover of the debut issue of Henry Luce's *Life* magazine in 1936. She traveled to the Soviet Union in 1941 on an assignment for *Life* and, while there, witnessed the disintegration of the Non-Aggression Pact between Germany and Russia and the bombing raids of Moscow.[38] Her images of the attacks became famous and began her career as a war correspondent.

Bourke-White remembered that her subsequent commission in the US Army Air Corps prompted the creation of the first uniform for women war correspondents (made by Abercrombie and Fitch): "the basic pattern of an officer's uniform except that women would have skirts as well as slacks."[39] The women correspondents were given the same rank in the army as their male counterparts, at first as lieutenants, then captains, and, finally, at the end of the war, lieutenant colonels. Though they shared rank with men, female correspondents did not share open access to the battlefield in order to do their job. Bourke-White remembered:

> "To be a woman in a man's world," as people often phrase it is usually—I have found—a distinct advantage. There are a few exceptions, and [being a woman war correspondent] was a classic example. In a combat situation, men tend to overprotect, and no overprotected photographer, male or female, can get pictures by remote control.[40]

Bourke-White was denied access to air-bombing raids in England when she first began her assignment. It was only when she left for the Allied invasion of North Africa and sought the influence of an old friend, General Jimmy Doolittle, commanding general of the Eighth Air Force, that she was given permission to shoot the invasion from the front lines.[41]

Nonetheless, women journalists were crucial in documenting the war, and their work left a record of military life, of battle, and of the scarred remains of the landscape and the travesty of human loss wrought by the war. Bourke-White was with the Allied forces at the liberation of the Dachau concentration camp—her photos were some of the first to provide witness to the horrors of the Third Reich. Some women war correspondents went on to acclaimed careers in photojournalism after the war. Dickey Chapelle, who acted as war correspondent for *National Geographic,* photographed the US Marines in battle in the Pacific Theater, including at the battle of Iwo Jima. She continued to work as war correspondent after World War II, until November 4, 1965, when she became the first war correspondent killed on the front lines in Vietnam.[42]

Though gains in professional careers for women came slowly, wide growth occured in clerical work. Historians Kim England and Kate Boyer point out, "The booming war economy meant women in white-collar workplaces were given positions of responsibility formerly only available to men: not only as bank tellers, but also auditors, bookkeepers, and occasionally accountants or supervisors (of women), although women managers (even temporarily) remained rare."[43] Bank tellers were almost invariably men before the war, but by 1950, 45 percent of tellers were women. Similarly, women bookkeepers grew to 78 percent by 1950, from 63 percent in 1930. Clerical work continued to expand after the war because, as England and Boyer note, men chose not to return to these jobs. Women were able to hold onto their wartime clerical work, though they remained underpaid compared to the salaries men had made in the same positions. The feminization of clerical work, which began during the war, continued to be a dominant trend in the twentieth-century labor force.[44]

Women in the Military Auxiliary Services

Nearly 350,000 women assisted the armed forces during World War II in auxiliary units: the Women's Army Auxiliary Corps (WAACs, later renamed the Women's Army Corps), the Navy Women's Reserve (WAVES), the Marine Corps Women's Reserve, the Coast Guard Women's Reserve (SPARS), the Women Airforce Service Pilots (WASPS), the Army Nurses Corps, and the Navy Nurse Corps. As radio operators, mechanics, and ordnance specialists, women served with distinction. Although male superiors often doubted the effectiveness of their new recruits, by the end of the war the performance and skill of these women was celebrated in popular culture and by military leaders, including Eisenhower, who declared, "The contribution of the women of America, whether on the farm or in the factory or in uniform, to D-Day was a sine qua non of the invasion effort."[45] Women in the Army Nurse Corps often served near the front lines; 16 were killed by enemy fire and 1,600 were decorated for bravery. Nurses arrived in Normandy four days after D-day, and in the Philippines sixty-eight women were taken prisoners of war.[46]

Women played significant roles in the leadership of the auxiliary forces during the war, most notably, Oveta Culp Hobby. Before becoming a state legislator and the first secretary of the Department of Health, Education, and Welfare in 1953, Hobby was an army colonel and the director of the Women's Army Auxiliary Corps, later the Women's Army Corps, during World War II. A native of Texas, she attended the University of Texas Law School, served as parliamentarian for the Texas House of Representatives, and was the assistant to the city attorney in Houston. She married William P. Hobby, the former governor of Texas, who was president of the *Houston Post-Dispatch*. When in 1941 General David Searles asked Hobby to direct a woman's initiative in support of the army, she moved to Washington to lead the Women's Interest Section in the War Department's Bureau of Public Relations. After Pearl Harbor and the passage of a law establishing the Women's Army Auxiliary Corps, US representative Edith Nourse Rogers (R-MA) recommended Hobby to head the organization. Hobby described women's new roles: "The gaps our women will fill are in those noncombatant jobs where women's hands and women's hearts fit naturally. WAACs will do the same type of work which women do in civilian life. They will bear the same relation to men of the Army that they bear to the men of the civilian organizations in which they work." Framing women's work as traditional and nonthreatening to men helped generate broad public support for the WAACs. Hobby was a tireless leader and advocate for the women under her command. She told the first WAAC officer candidate class: "You are the first women to serve. . . . Never forget it. . . . [Y]ou have a debt and a date. . . . A debt to democracy, a date with destiny."[47] In 1943, the WAAC's name was changed to the Women's Army Corps (WAC). The women under Hobby's command served with distinction in Europe, the South Pacific, and the China-India-Burma Theater.

The Women's Auxiliary Ferrying Squadron (WAFS) was led by Philadelphia native Nancy Harkness Love. Having flown since she was a teenager, Love was an accomplished pilot. She married Air Corps Reserves officer Robert Love in 1936, and together they created an aviation company in Boston. In 1940, Love suggested to Lieutenant Colonel Robert Olds, who oversaw the Ferrying Command within the Army Air Forces, that skilled female pilots could contribute to his effort. By 1942, her suggestion came to fruition, and she became the director of the WAFS, with twenty-five experienced female pilots. In 1943, the WAFS merged with a women's pilot training program. Noted aviator Jackie Cochran led the combined unit, known as the Women's Airforce Service Pilots, or WASPs. Love continued to oversee WASP ferrying operations, and after the war she received an Air Medal for service to her country.[48]

The women who joined the auxiliary services faced similar obstacles to those who took defense jobs. They were not always welcomed by male peers and faced discrimination based on race, class, and sexuality. African American women served in the auxiliary services, but in segregated units, reflecting America's Jim Crow policies.[49] They were often given low-level positions with little chance for advancement. Lesbian women had to deny their sexuality to serve. Women who served in the auxiliary services also did not enjoy the same pay and pensions as male soldiers, further complicating their wartime experiences. Despite these challenges, Hobby noted, "Women who stepped up were measured as citizens of the nation, not as women. This was a people's war and everyone was in it."[50]

Women who served in the auxiliary services during World War II are often remembered for their heroic sacrifice. This was, as Brenda Ralph Lewis documents, not always the case:

> It was not easy for women to enlist in the military. . . . There was a lot of resistance, not necessarily to women's entering a "man's world" but to protect them from doing so. . . . In at least one instance, a man physically attacked recruiting personnel in charge of enlisting women. GI mail, read by censors, included numerous letters to female relatives objecting to their joining up. Some women were threatened with divorce or being disowned by their families. . . . Angry GIs and other men bombarded President Roosevelt, Secretary of War Henry Stimpson, and members of

congress with letters and telegrams demanding the immediate release of their women from service. . . . One Massachusetts bishop regarded women in the military as "opposed by the teachings and principles of the Catholic Church."[51]

In some cases, women who joined were deemed immoral. Five hundred WACs in North Africa, for example, were accused of sexual misconduct. The rumors were so persistent that Congress held hearings and found that, "compared to women, male noncombatants were 89 times more prone to going absent without leave, 85 times more likely to get drunk, and 150 times more likely to breach military rules or commit a criminal offense. Venereal disease proved rife among men in the military, virtually non-existent among women."[52] In spite of these challenges, "by the summer of 1945, 57,000 Army nurses and 11,000 Navy nurses were on duty, together with 1000,000 in the Women's Auxiliary Army Corps (WAAC), 86,000 Women accepted for Volunteer Emergency Service (WAVES), 1,800 women Marines, and 11,000 in the Coast Guard Reserve (SPARS)."[53] In these units, women's skills were not always valued. Some WACs worked as babysitters, and one female journalist who spoke fluent Japanese served as a cook. As a result, nearly a third of the women who reenlisted when the WAAC became the WAC returned to civilian life soon after because of the hostility and disrespect they endured.[54]

After the war, many women who had joined the auxiliary services hoped to remain in these jobs, but they were often forced to leave their positions to make way for returning soldiers. Female veterans also advocated for the same benefits extended to their male counterparts, including those offered by the Servicemen's Readjustment Act of 1944 (the GI Bill), which women willingly embraced.[55] Veterans who served for more than ninety days and were not dishonorably discharged were given access to low-cost mortgages, low-interest loans to start a business or farm, cash payments of tuition and living expenses to attend college, high school or vocational education, and one year of unemployment compensation. Despite the recognition of their service, the United States was not necessarily ready for a cadre of female soldiers and veterans in public life.

Women also served in support of the troops in other capacities that were not associated with the military. They filled the roles of food and beverage distributors and nurses and performed many other jobs in the Red Cross, the United Service Organization (USO), the American Women's Voluntary Services (AWVS), and other service organizations during World War II. Driven by patriotism and a desire to assist troops, hundreds of thousands of women embraced these new nonmilitary jobs, often as unpaid volunteers. In some voluntary positions, women went into the very heart of combat and challenged the assumption that they were neither brave nor capable of facing the horrors of war. Red Cross food and service vendors, such as Captain Elizabeth A. Richards, distributed hot food and drinks to soldier foxholes on the front lines. By 1945, sixteen women had been awarded Purple Hearts for wounds received in battle, thereby dispelling myths about women's capabilities to serve their country during the war.

Make Do and Mend: Women on the Home Front

In addition to filling the labor shortage left when millions of men joined the armed forces, women were required to maintain order and stable conditions. *Business Week* reported four months after Pearl Harbor on the growing list of goods and staples that were becoming scarce, including sugar, rubber, heating oil, and coffee, foretelling "the rapidly approaching exit of life-as-usual."[56] When the government introduced rationing in response to commodity shortages, women had to do more with less. The list of items in short supply kept growing; soon it included zippers, batteries, waffle irons, tea, vacuum cleaners, bicycles, and toys. The shortages were the result of numerous factors. Ships carrying items such as coffee from South America began being used to move troops. The importation of rubber from Asia became impossible because of hostilities with Japan. Iron and steel were used to make tanks, explosives, and armaments.[57] In order to ensure that military personnel were adequately supplied on the front lines, a spirit of "make do and mend" swept the nation. The Office of Price Administration and Civilian Supply Management (OPA) created a rationing system, focusing primarily on twenty items, such as shoes, butter, sugar, and gasoline. Citizens were given ration books to control the flow of goods. Airplane worker Charlcia Neuman, who relied on her family to do the shopping and navigate the complex rationing system, recalled, "I had a daughter who was very capable. She took the ration books and she figured that all out. She was in junior high at the time. It helped make her a stronger person, I'm sure."[58]

Although wartime life was challenging, women as the heads of households embraced frugality and conservation and reinvented the way that they fed, clothed, and cared for their families. Propaganda campaigns encouraged US women to save newspapers, tin and aluminum cans, bacon grease, and razor blades. The War Production Board (WPB), established in January of 1942, had official stations and drives to collect these materials. Whole communities became involved in the effort. For example, the city of Griffin, Georgia, donated an antique fire engine, while students at City College in New York collected tinfoil from gum and cigarette packages. The female alumni members of the New York Vassar Club collected silk stockings to be made into glider plane towropes and parachutes.[59]

Although the responsibilities were overwhelming, women participated in a variety of activities to further conservation and support home front defense initiatives. The government encouraged them to grow produce in their own backyards to stabilize the output of goods going overseas. These "victory gardens" brought families together and provided produce that was not otherwise available. Families were also asked to buy war bonds for $18.75 each to help finance the war, with the understanding that in ten years the value would grow to $25.00. Bond drives were quite popular, and women played a critical role in helping to sell them at grocery stores, movie theaters, and schools.[60] Women also participated in civil defense activities, ranging from assisting emergency medical personnel to spotting enemy aircraft. Local councils were created to assist the Office of Civil Defense, and a large number of women volunteered to support their initiatives.[61]

Women in the Secret War

The sheer scope and complexity of World War II resulted in secret operations that were not widely publicized to the general public. Some American women served as spies and in resistance groups that engaged in sophisticated activities of deception and sabotage against the Axis powers during World War II, and others served in work that was even hidden from them, such as in the Manhattan Project. But this was dangerous work, as Brenda Ralph Lewis explained: "For men and women alike, every day in enemy territory was potentially their last. The slightest slip or wrong word could blow their cover and reveal them for what they were. Betrayal, too, was an ever-present threat."[62]

The Office of Strategic Services (OSS) recruited women and expected their agents to "cheat, lie, kill silently, perform acts of sabotage, use guns and explosives, keep their secrets when under torture and face the very likely chance of an early, violent death."[63] American Amy Thorpe, who worked for Britain's Special Operations Executive (SOE) and the OSS, wrote in her diary, "Life is but a stage on which to play. One's role is to pretend and always to hide one's true feelings."[64] Women were perceived to have a unique advantage as spies and saboteurs because they were considered less obvious than men and could often pass undetected through enemy lines. They could walk a baby carriage full of explosives or a basket with clandestine maps past German soldiers without a second glance, as few expected women to embrace these roles. Women were also assumed to use their sexuality to manipulate the enemy and extract important secrets. These stereotypes should not undermine the skill and bravery that women brought to the secret war. Of the thirteen thousand soldiers in the OSS in 1944, nearly forty-five hundred were women, one-third of whom were assigned overseas.[65]

Three Americans reflect the varied ways women served in the secret war. Amy Thorpe was selected to infiltrate the German, Italian, and Vichy embassies in Washington, D.C., prior to the United States' entry into the war. Prior to the war, Thorpe, whose husband was a diplomat stationed at the British Embassy in Warsaw, Poland, had experience in espionage. She was hired by MI6, the British spy agency, in 1937 and discovered that Polish mathematicians had broken the German Enigma codes used to encipher and decipher secret messages. With this information, the British persuaded the Poles to give them the code and a replica Enigma machine, invented by the German engineer Arthur Scherbius. This meant that by the start of the war in 1939, the British were already reading German transmissions. When Thorpe left her husband, she returned to the United States and began infiltrating the embassies, passing codes used by the Italian navy. In 1941, Thorpe began working for the OSS and had an affair with Charles Emanuel Brousse, a French diplomat disenchanted with the Vichy government (the French government that collaborated with the Nazis after the fall of France). In the summer of 1942, Thorpe and Brousse stole code books from the French embassy safe, copied them, and passed these confidential Vichy government plans to the OSS, the US spy agency.[66]

A second woman, Virginia Hall, worked for the British Special Operations Executive and OSS and became a target of the Gestapo. Hall began working for the US State Department in 1931, serving in Warsaw, Estonia, and Turkey. After losing her leg as the result of a hunting accident while in Turkey, Hall abandoned her plans of becoming a diplomat and resigned from the State Department in 1939.[67] She remained in Europe, however, and began working for the SOE in 1941. Posing as a journalist for the *New York Post*, Hall entered Nazi-occupied France in 1941. Her job was to coordinate SOE agents, but she had to flee the country in 1943 and began working for the OSS. In 1944, she returned to France, posed as a milkmaid, trained three hundred agents for sabotage operations, and radioed German troop movements to London at least thirty-seven times. Despite the Gestapo's best efforts to capture Hall, she remained evasive. After the war, Hall continued to work for the OSS (now the CIA) and was given the Distinguished Service Cross by President Harry Truman. One of her fellow agents, Denis Rake, wrote of Hall, "Virginia Hall in my opinion . . . was one of the greatest women agents of the war."[68]

A third woman, Mildred Fish-Harnack, was the only American woman executed for conspiring against the Nazis during the war. A native of Milwaukee, Wisconsin, Harnack met Arvid Harnack, a German Rockefeller scholar, while studying literature at the University of Wisconsin in Madison. After moving to Germany in 1929, Harnack taught American literature in Berlin. She befriended Martha Dodd, daughter of US ambassador William E. Dodd, and others interested in the German resistance movement. Mildred and her husband joined a Berlin-based group known as the Red Orchestra, which assisted in the escape of German Jews and political dissidents and provided economic and military intelligence to both Washington and Moscow. As the result of a Soviet blunder, members of Harnack's group were arrested and tortured. In December 1942, Harnack's husband was hanged at Ploetzensee, a detention center outside Berlin. On February 16, 1943, Mildred was guillotined.[69]

But the "secret war" also had a different and, in some cases, darker connotation, as the US government turned on its own citizens by interning those of Japanese descent. Although World War II opened doors for many women, Japanese Americans were not among that group. In 1942, the US government interned 120,000 Japanese Americans in assembly centers and then "relocation" camps, primarily in the western United States. Considered a possible threat to national security because of their ethnic background, these women and their families—most of whom were US citizens—were detained in the camps until 1945. In 1990, the US government began issuing reparations to surviving internees for the loss of their property, livelihood, and civil liberties. A number of memoirs have been written about Japanese internment, including *Farewell to Manzanar*, the story of Jeanne Wakatsuki, who was seven years old in 1942 when her family was uprooted from their home and sent to the Manzanar War Relocation Center in California.[70]

Another part of the secret war focused on technology. With assistance from Great Britain and Canada, the US government launched the Manhattan Project, the secret US effort to develop the atomic bomb, largely out of public view. Women played complex and often hidden roles in both civilian and military capacities. The Women's Army Corps (WAC) provided administrative manpower, while civilian women occupied a range of jobs from engineers to typists.[71] Several hundred women worked at the highest levels as scientists, mathematicians, engineers, and technicians. Physicist Leona Woods Marshall Libby "participated in the experiment on December 2, 1942, in which the first self-sustaining nuclear chain reaction took place, releasing nuclear energy and establishing the feasibility of moving ahead toward designing and developing nuclear weapons." Another notable member of the project team was Maria Goeppert Mayer, a native of Germany who won the Nobel Prize in physics with Eugene Wigner and J. Hans D. Jensen in 1963. Her research during the war focused on thermodynamic properties of uranium hexafluoride gas and photochemical reactions for isotope separation.[72] Long after the war had ended, women's contributions to the Manhattan Project remained hidden from history, as Denise Kiernan's recent book, *The Girls of Atomic City: The Untold Story of the Women Who Helped Win World War II*, documents.[73]

Interest in new technologies had an added benefit for women.

During the war, the US Office of Education promoted a nationwide effort to train scientists. The program spread to 277 colleges and focused on courses in engineering, physics, and mathematics. An important provision of the program was that "no trainee shall be discriminated against because of sex, race or color." The result was that women were encouraged to consider careers in these fields, something quite rare before the US entry into the war.[74]

The Legacy of Women at War

World War II allowed women to make significant gains in occupations that had previously been closed to them. They found independence in steady salaries and adventure in their new roles outside the home, excelled at managing wartime rations and food shortages, and maintained stable homes in the absence of husbands, brothers, and fathers. Allied governments were quick to recognize the power of women, in contrast to both Japan and Germany. After the war Albert Speer, Hitler's architect and Minister of Armaments and War Production for the Third Reich, reflected in a conversation with Lieutenant-General Ira C. Eaker: "How wise you were to bring your women into your military and into your labor force. Had we done that initially, as you did, it could well have affected the whole course of the war. We would have found out as you did, that women are equally effective, and for some skills, superior to males."[75]

By joining organizations such as the Women's Auxiliary Army Corps and the Women's Air Force Service Pilots, US women proved their effectiveness in the male-dominated military. In 1948, President Harry Truman signed the Women's Armed Service Integration Act, opening the door for women to serve full-time in the armed forces, though not in active combat roles.

After the Allied victory in 1945, women were expected to give up their jobs in factories to the returning soldiers and resume their roles as wives and mothers. Although many women continued to work in waged labor, an ideal of domestic life reemerged that cast men as the breadwinners and women as the bread makers. Some women voluntarily left their positions, but others felt they had earned their jobs and were not prepared to leave. Ottilie Juliet Gattus, a worker at the

Grumman Aircraft Engineering Corporation, wrote to President Harry Truman at the war's end, "I happen to be a widow with a mother and son to support. . . . I would like to know why, after serving a company in good faith for almost three and a half years, it is now impossible to obtain employment with them. I am a lathe hand and was classified as skilled labor, but simply because I am a woman I am not wanted."[76] The Women's Bureau of the Department of Labor surveyed women workers in 1946 about their future plans. Nearly three-fourths of the surveyed group revealed that they wanted and needed their wartime work to continue. As the report noted, "postwar job openings as cafeteria bus girls, for example, are not apt to prove attractive to women who are seeking work as screw-machine operators."[77]

During the war women comprised 36 percent of the workforce, but by the 1950s that number had dropped by 10 percent.[78] While female war workers became iconic symbols of womanhood in the 1940s, they were replaced in the 1950s by other fictional characters, such as June Cleaver, the mother made famous on the television sitcom *Leave It to Beaver*, which began in 1957. The model postwar family was popularized in 1950s and 1960s television sitcoms such as *The Donna Reed Show*. Though women continued to pursue new opportunities outside of the home after the war, it was not until the late 1960s that society began publicly to revisit and reconsider the importance of women's rights and equal access to employment. Rosie's daughters would join other female activists to fight that battle.

Notes

1. Penny Colman, *Rosie the Riveter: Women Working on the Home Front during World War II* (New York: Crown Publishers, 1995), 100.

2. Eileen Hughes, quoted in Brenda Ralph Lewis, *The Women in World War II, at Home, at Work, on the Front Line* (New York: Reader's Digest, 2002), 20–21.

3. Donald Nelson, quoted in Colman, *Rosie the Riveter*, 21.

4. Lewis, *The Women in World War II*, 16.

5. Aja Sorensen, "Rosie the Riveter: Women Working during World War II," World War II National Historical Park, accessed July 23, 2012, http://www.nps.gov/pwro/collection/website/rosie.htm.

6. Henry L. Stimpson, quoted in Emily Yellin, *Our Mothers' War: American Women at Home and at the Front during World War II* (New York: Simon and Schuster, 2004), epigraph.

7. Leila Rupp, *Mobilizing Women for War: German and American Propaganda, 1939–1945* (Princeton: Princeton University Press, 1978), 98.

8. In 1998, the American Rosie the Riveter Association was established, and Congress authorized the Rosie the Riveter World War II Home Front National Historic Park in San Francisco. The park was dedicated in October 2000. See Lewis, *The Women in World War II*, 30.

9. Yellin, *Our Mothers' War*, 43.

10. The Pop History Dig, "Rosie the Riveter," accessed July 23, 2012, http://www.pophistorydig.com/?tag=rosie-the-riveter-song.

11. Norman Rockwell Museum, accessed July 1, 2013, http://www.norman rockwellvt.com/rosie_riveter_story.htm.

12. Colman, *Rosie the Riveter*, 91.

13. Susan Hartmann, *The Home Front and Beyond: American Women in the 1940s* (Boston: Twayne Publishers, 1982), 79.

14. Margarita Salazar, quoted in Lewis, *The Women in World War II*, 70.

15. Lewis, *The Women in World War II*, 70.

16. Aja Sorensen, "Rosie the Riveter: Women Working during World War II," World War II National Historical Park, accessed March 28, 2013, http://www.nps.gov/pwro/collection/website/rosie.htm.

17. Colman, *Rosie the Riveter*, 28.

18. Ibid., 56–57.

19. Ely Campbell, quoted in Lewis, *The Women in World War II*, 75.

20. *New York Times*, in Colman, *Rosie the Riveter*, 86.

21. Ibid., 87. Peggy Terry, quoted in Studs Terkel, *The Good War: An Oral History of World War II* (New York: New Press, 1997).

22. Lewis, *The Women in World War II*, 65.

23. Quoted in Lewis, *The Women in World War II*, 81.

24. Colman, *Rosie the Riveter*, 19.

25. William Mulcahy, quoted in Colman, *Rosie the Riveter*, 21–22.

26. Anne Firor Scott, "One Woman's Experience of World War II," *Journal of American History* 77, no. 2 (September 1990): 556.

27. Ibid., 556.

28. Ibid.

29. Ibid.

30. Constance Cook, quoted in Cynthia Grant Bowman, "Women in the Legal Profession from the 1920s to the 1970s: What Can We Learn from Their Experience about Law and Social Change?" *Cornell Law Faculty Publications*, Paper 12 (2009): 6, accessed August 6, 2012, http://scholarship.law.cornell.edu/facpub/12.

31. Yellin, *Our Mothers' War*, 299.

32. Doris Weatherford, *American Women during World War II: An Encyclopedia* (New York: Routledge, 2010), 347.

33. Ibid.

34. National Women's History Museum, "Partners in Winning the War: American Women during World War II," accessed August 1, 2013, http://www.nwhm.org/online-exhibits/partners/12.htm.

35. Ibid.

36. Yellin, *Our Mothers' War*, 292.

37. Nancy Caldwell Sorel, *The Women Who Wrote the War* (New York: HarperCollins Publishers, 1999), xiii–xiv.

38. For more information about her wartime experiences, see Margaret Bourke-White, *Portrait of Myself* (New York: Simon & Schuster, 1963).

39. Ibid., 197.

40. Ibid., 202.

41. Ibid., 203.

42. Dickey Chapelle, Wisconsin Historical Society, accessed August 1, 2013, http://www.wisconsinhistory.org/topics/chapelle/.

43. Kim England and Kate Boyer, "Women's Work: The Feminization and Shifting Meanings of Clerical Work," *Journal of Social History* 43, no. 2 (Winter 2009): 317.

44. Ibid., 318.

45. Dwight D. Eisenhower, quoted in Stephen Ambrose, *D-Day, June 6, 1944: The Climactic Battle of World War II* (New York: Simon and Schuster, 1995), 489.

46. National World War II Museum, "American Women in World War II on the Homefront and Beyond," accessed March 24, 2013, www.nationalww2museum.org/education/for.../women-in-w.pdf.

47. Women in Military Service for America Memorial Foundation, Inc., "Oveta Culp Hobby," accessed June 23, 2013, http://www.womensmemorial.org/H&C/History/hobby.html.

48. Public Broadcasting Corporation, American Experience, "Nancy Harkness Love," accessed March 28, 2013, http://www.pbs.org/wgbh/amex/flygirls/peopleevents/pandeAMEX03.html. Love held more speed, altitude, and distance records than any other pilot in the history of aviation.

49. Laurie Lee Weinstein and Christie C. White, *Wives and Warriors: Women and the Military in the United States and Canada* (Westport, CT: Greenwood, 1997), 212.

50. Nancy Harkness Love, quoted in Senator Kay Bailey Hutchison, "Women's History Month: 'Oveta Culp Hobby,'" *Humanities Texas*, March 2012, accessed March 26, 2013, http://www.humanitiestexas.org/news/articles/womens-history-month-oveta-culp-hobby-senator-kay-bailey-hutchison.

51. Lewis, *The Women in World War II*, 21–22.

52. Ibid., 24.

53. Ibid., 15.

54. Ibid., 27.

55. Women in Military Service for America Memorial Foundation, "History Highlight—Women Veterans and the WWII GI Bill of Rights," accessed July 1, 2013, http://www.womensmemorial.org/H&C/History/historyhl.html.

56. Colman, *Rosie the Riveter*, 8.

57. Ibid., 8–9.

58. Charlcia Neuman, quoted in Colman, *Rosie the Riveter*, 10.

59. Colman, *Rosie the Riveter*, 11.

60. Ibid., 13.

61. National Women's History Museum, "Partners in Winning the War," online exhibit, accessed March 29, 2013, http://www.nwhm.org/online-exhibits/partners/40.htm.

62. Lewis, *The Women in World War II*, 143.

63. Ibid., 146.

64. Amy Thorpe, quoted in Lewis, *The Women in World War II*, 146.

65. Amy Downs, Amy Grenier, Holly Kearl, and Linda McCarthy, "Clandestine Women: Spies in American History," National Museum of Women's History online exhibition, accessed March 29, 2013, http://www.nwhm.org/online-exhibits/spies/14.htm.

66. Lewis, *The Women in World War II*, 159–60.

67. Weatherford, *American Women during World War II*, 196–96.

68. Denis Rake, quoted in Lewis, *The Women in World War II*, 151.

69. See Shareen Blair Brysac, *Resisting Hitler: Mildred Harnack and the Red Orchestra* (London: Oxford University Press, 2002).

70. Jeanne Houston and James D. Houston, *Farewell to Manzanar: A True Story of Japanese American Experience during and after the World War II Internment* (San Francisco: San Francisco Book Company, 1973).

71. See Caroline L. Herzenberg, "Women of the Manhattan Project," accessed June 3, 2012, http://www.geocities.com/cherzenberg/Manhattan_Project_women.html; Caroline L. Herzenberg and Ruth H. Howes, "Women of the Manhattan Project," Technology Review 96, no. 8 (November/December 1993): 32–40; Ruth H. Howes and Caroline L. Herzenberg, *Their Day in the Sun: Women of the Manhattan Project* (Philadelphia: Temple University Press, 1999); Ruth H. Howes and Caroline L. Herzenberg, "Women in Weapons Development: The Manhattan Project," in *Women and the Use of Military Force*, edited by Ruth H. Howes and Michael R. Stevenson (Boulder, CO: Lynne Rienner Publishers, 1993); Richard Rhodes, *The Making of the Atomic Bomb* (New York: Simon & Schuster, 1995); Margaret W. Rossiter, *Women Scientists in America: Before Affirmative Action, 1940–1972* (Baltimore: Johns Hopkins University Press, 1995).

72. AP College Board, "Women Scientists of the Manhattan Project," accessed February 2, 2013, http://apcentral.collegeboard.com/apc/members/courses/teachers_corner/31784.html.

73. See Denise Kiernan, *The Girls of Atomic City: The Untold Story of the Women Who Helped Win World War II* (New York: Touchstone, 2013).

74. See Rita Halle Kleeman, "The College Girl Goes to War," *Independent Woman* (January 1943), 18–19.

75. Albert Speer made this observation in a discussion with Lieutenant-General Ira C. Eaker, quoted in *Air Force Magazine* (December 6, 1976), 54; National Women's History Museum, "Partners in Winning the War," temporary exhibit, accessed March 29, 2013, http://www.nwhm.org/online-exhibits/partners/40.htm.

76. Ottilie Juliet Gattus, quoted in Colman, *Rosie the Riveter*, 97–98.

77. Department of Labor, Women's Bureau, *Women Workers in Ten War Production Areas and Their Postwar Employment Plans*, Bulletin 209 (Washington, DC: US Government Printing Office, 1946), quoted in *America's Working Women*, ed. Rosalyn Baxandall, Linda Gordon, and Susan Reverby (New York: Vintage Books, 1976), 310–12.

78. National Women's History Museum, "Partners in Winning the War," temporary exhibit, accessed March 29, 2013, http://www.nwhm.org/online-exhibits/partners/40.htm.

CHAPTER 1

Into the Factories

When men left to serve in the armed forces during World War II, their absence created a labor shortage throughout the United States. By 1943, government officials and industry leaders looked to women workers to contribute to the production needs created by war. Nearly six million American women took jobs that they had not traditionally held before: in factories and plants and on farms. Work in wartime production allowed women to express patriotism and gain financial independence. In these positions, women helped to sustain the booming industrial and agricultural sectors—a crucial factor in helping the Allies win the war. The documents in this section show how the presence of women in industry challenged traditional views of women's work. Though most lost their jobs when soldiers returned from war, women proved in a very visible way that their capabilities extended beyond traditional roles as wives and mothers. After the war, women were expected to give up their jobs in factories to the returning soldiers and resume their roles as wives and mothers. Although in reality many working-class women continued to work in wage labor, an ideal of domestic life re-emerged that cast men as the breadwinners and women as the bread makers. The model postwar family was popularized in television sitcoms such as *Leave It to Beaver* and *The Donna Reed Show*. Though women continued to pursue new opportunities outside of the home, it was not until the late 1960s that society began to publicly revisit and question the importance of women's rights.

DOCUMENT 1

Photograph, *Women Assembling Hand Grenades*, ca. 1918, from the Army Industrial Service Section, Women's Branch, US War Department

Courtesy of the Library of Congress, LC-USZ62-116444.

Though women joined the industrial workforce in unprecedented numbers during World War II, smaller numbers held manufacturing jobs during World War I. This image shows women immersing bouchon assemblies (or enclosures) for hand grenades in Vatudrip (a liquid to prevent rust) at Gorham Manufacturing Company in Providence, Rhode Island. Gorham was a major metals manufacturer that supported the war effort during World War I. Few female industrial workers remained on the job after hostilities ended in 1918.

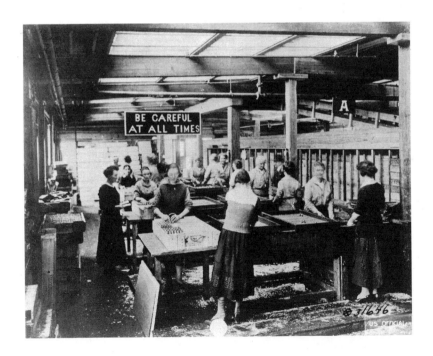

DOCUMENT 2

Poster, US Department of Labor, "Minimum Standards for Employment of Women in Industry," 1940

Courtesy of the US Department of Labor.

The US Department of Labor's Women's Bureau created this poster before the bombing of Pearl Harbor and the United States' entry into the war. The poster lists twenty standards that were intended to "promote the welfare of wage-earning women."

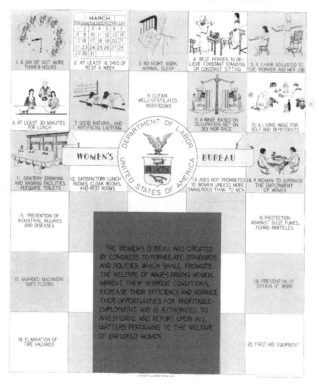

DOCUMENT 3

Franklin D. Roosevelt, "Executive Order 8802—Reaffirming Policy of Full Participation in the Defense Program by All Persons, Regardless of Race, Creed, Color, or National Origin, and Directing Certain Action in Furtherance of Said Policy," June 25, 1941

As the United States began to prepare for war, millions of jobs were created in defense industries. Yet African American workers were largely excluded from industrial work. A. Philip Randolph, president of the Brotherhood of Sleeping Car Porters, and other leaders began the March on Washington Movement in 1941 in an effort to eliminate discrimination in the war industries and the armed services. Randolph threatened to bring "ten, twenty, fifty thousand Negroes on the White House lawn" if their demands were ignored. The threat of a march on the nation's capital led President Roosevelt to issue Executive Order 8802 to end discrimination in defense industries. This order, which also established the Fair Employment Practices Committee to investigate incidents of discrimination, impacted women throughout the United States.

WHEREAS it is the policy of the United States to encourage full participation in the national defense program by all citizens of the United States, regardless of race, creed, color, or national origin, in the firm belief that the democratic way of life within the Nation can be defended successfully only with the help and support of all groups within its borders; and

WHEREAS there is evidence that available and needed workers have been barred from employment in industries engaged in defense production solely because of consideration of race, creed, color, or national origin, to the detriment of workers' morale and of national unity:

NOW, THEREFORE, by virtue of the authority vested in me by the Constitution and the statutes, and as a prerequisite to the successful conduct of our national defense production effort, I do hereby reaffirm the policy of the United States that there shall be no discrimination in the employment of workers in defense industries or government because of race, creed, color, or national origin, and I do hereby declare that it is the duty of employers and of labor organizations, in furtherance of said policy and of this Order, to provide for the full and equitable participation of all workers in defense industries, without discrimination because of race, creed, color, or national origin;

And it is hereby ordered as follows:

1. All departments and agencies of the Government of the United States concerned with vocational and training programs for defense production shall take special measures appropriate to assure that such programs are administered without discrimination because of race, creed, color, or national origin;

2. All contracting agencies of the Government of the United States shall include in all defense contracts hereafter negotiated by them a provision obligating the contractor not to discriminate against any worker because of race, creed, color, or national origin;

3. There is established in the Office of Production Management a Committee on Fair Employment Practice, which shall consist of a Chairman and four other members to be appointed by the President. The Chairman and members of the Committee shall serve as such without compensation but shall be entitled to actual and necessary transportation, subsistence, and other expenses incidental to performance of their duties. The Committee shall receive and investigate complaints of discrimination in violation of the provisions of this Order and shall take appropriate steps to redress grievances which it finds to be valid. The Committee shall also recommend to the several departments and agencies of the Government of the United States and to the President all measures which may be deemed by it necessary or proper to effectuate the provisions of this Order.

Franklin D. Roosevelt
The White House,
June 25, 1941

DOCUMENT 4
Speech, President Franklin D. Roosevelt, "A Date That Will Live in Infamy," December 8, 1941

On December 7, 1941, the day of the Japanese attack on Pearl Harbor, President Franklin D. Roosevelt met with military advisors and dictated to his secretary, Grace Tully, a request to Congress for a declaration of war. He composed the speech in his head and revised a typed draft, notably changing the first and most famous line. The next afternoon, Roosevelt addressed a joint session of Congress, which was broadcast to the nation via radio. The Senate responded with a vote to support the war, and later that afternoon Roosevelt signed the official declaration of war. The reading copy of the speech, which Roosevelt left behind in the House chamber, was misfiled and "lost" for forty-three years. It was discovered in a file by a National Archives staff member in 1984. This declaration put into motion one of the largest mobilizations in US history, one that directly affected millions of women.

Yesterday, Dec. 7, 1941—a date which will live in infamy—the United States of America was suddenly and deliberately attacked by naval and air forces of the Empire of Japan.

The United States was at peace with that nation and, at the solicitation of Japan, was still in conversation with the government and its emperor looking toward the maintenance of peace in the Pacific.

Indeed, one hour after Japanese air squadrons had commenced bombing in Oahu, the Japanese ambassador to the United States and his colleagues delivered to the Secretary of State a formal reply to a recent American message. While this reply stated that it seemed useless to continue the existing diplomatic negotiations, it contained no threat or hint of war or armed attack.

It will be recorded that the distance of Hawaii from Japan makes it obvious that the attack was deliberately planned many days or even weeks ago. During the intervening time, the Japanese government has deliberately sought to deceive the United States by false statements and expressions of hope for continued peace.

The attack yesterday on the Hawaiian islands has caused severe damage to American naval and military forces. Very many American lives have been lost. In addition, American ships have been reported torpedoed on the high seas between San Francisco and Honolulu.

Yesterday, the Japanese government also launched an attack against Malaya.
Last night, Japanese forces attacked Hong Kong.
Last night, Japanese forces attacked Guam.
Last night, Japanese forces attacked the Philippine Islands.
Last night, the Japanese attacked Wake Island.
This morning, the Japanese attacked Midway Island.
Japan has, therefore, undertaken a surprise offensive extending throughout the Pacific area. The facts of yesterday speak for themselves. The people of the United States have already formed their opinions and well understand the implications to the very life and safety of our nation.
As commander in chief of the Army and Navy, I have directed that all measures be taken for our defense.
Always will we remember the character of the onslaught against us.
No matter how long it may take us to overcome this premeditated invasion, the American people in their righteous might will win through to absolute victory.
I believe I interpret the will of the Congress and of the people when I assert that we will not only defend ourselves to the uttermost, but will make very certain that this form of treachery shall never endanger us again.

Hostilities exist. There is no blinking at the fact that our people, our territory and our interests are in grave danger.

With confidence in our armed forces—with the unbounding determination of our people—we will gain the inevitable triumph—so help us God.
I ask that the Congress declare that since the unprovoked and dastardly attack by Japan on Sunday, Dec. 7, a state of war has existed between the United States and the Japanese empire.

DOCUMENT 5

Flyer, "If Hitler Came to Mobile," 1942, Office for Emergency Management, War Manpower Commission

Courtesy of the National Archives,
NRCA-211-WMC11-WMJOBFLYER.

The War Manpower Commission was created in April 1942 to reg-
ulate the use of labor during the war. This flyer, which was distributed by the War Manpower Commission in Mobile, Alabama, told
women that they were "needed in the war jobs and other essential civilian jobs directly aiding the war effort in Mobile NOW."
The flyer boldly declared, "Hitler and his hordes will not come if
women help to build ships."

IF HITLER CAME TO MOBILE—
Every woman would defend her home with a gun, a knife or her bare fingers.
BUT—
Hitler and his hordes will not come if women help to build ships, more ships
to transport our men, tanks, planes and munitions to the battle lines on other
Continents—or if women take other jobs directly aiding the war effort.
This folder tells every Mobile woman not now in a war job how she may help
win the war. Read it carefully and pass it to your neighbor. It is an official
statement from the War Manpower Commission.
Remember February 22 is an important day in Mobile.

TO THE WOMEN OF MOBILE
You are needed in the war jobs and in other essential civilian jobs directly
aiding the war effort in Mobile NOW. Manpower has been practically exhausted.
Housing available at this time will not permit the bringing into Mobile of the
thousands of additional workers required for the shipyards and other war and
essential industries. We must depend on you—upon womanpower. There are
idle machines in war plants which you can operate. There are idle jobs in the
shipyards which you can fill. There are jobs in stores, offices, transportation,
restaurants, hospitals in which you can render essential war service.
Hitler will not come to our shores if we build the ships which can transport
our soldiers and our war material overseas. We are training the armies, we are

building the airplanes, tanks, guns and trucks, to do the job that must be done. But they will be of little use if we do not build the ships that can transport them to the battle zone.

Many of you already in war jobs are rendering essential service to our common country in the hour of need. We do not ask that you give up one essential job to take another. We do appeal to you, however, to take a job in which you can aid the war program. Those of you who are not engaged in war work or essential civilian employment, we do urge you to take the training which will equip you for such a job, or if you have the training to take the job NOW without delay.

Women have responded nobly to the call to war service through the Nation. Many are employed in the shipyards of Mobile now. Many are at Brookley Field. Still others are in plants which are producing the war supplies essential to victory. Women who have never worked before are employed in stores and other necessary business establishments. Women have proved their efficiency in war work. Through our country they are doing work which many believed could be done only by men.

In many war plants women make up more than 50 percent of the workers. In some war plants, they constitute 70 percent of the employment list. In one war plant every employee is a woman. In another plant, where before the war the hiring policy was "No Women," women are in 25 percent of the jobs and are now being hired as fast as they can be found. In the Norfolk navy yards 500 women are employed as mechanics. They operate lathes, serve as drill press operators and shapers, assemble engines, repair radios, generators and electric starters, and are expert welders. The United States Employment Service, after long study, has reported that, "It can hardly be said that ANY occupation is absolutely unsuitable for the employment of women. Women have shown that they can do or learn to do almost any kind of work."

Four million women are now employed in America's war industries. Fifteen million women are employed in other jobs which have released men for the armed services and other essential war work. But this is not enough. SIX MILLION ADDITIONAL WOMEN MUST GO INTO JOBS ESSENTIAL TO MAXIMUM WAR PRODUCTION. Every housewife should ask herself and answer this question: "Can I be of greater service in my home or in a war plant?" If she finds that her children can be cared for in a nursery or by a home nurse, relative or friend, then she should take the training which will equip her for a job in a war plant or an essential civilian industry.

A recent survey of Mobile shows that approximately 6400 women are unemployed and available for war work. This does not include women who have come into Mobile with their husbands in recent months. Many of them might serve. It does not include women whose daily presence is required in their home.

Every woman in Mobile who is willing to take an essential job can get the training and can be referred to a job as soon as she completes a short training course. There are idle training machines in Mobile. One is waiting for you. You may get training in welding, machine shop practice, drafting and tracing, sheet metal, and ship electricity. Every business in Mobile has a training program, either in its plant or in a training course elsewhere. You may select your course. Supervisors will recommend courses which you can readily master and which will lead to war jobs, without delay. The United States Employment Service, 107 Government Street, will be glad to tell you about them.

If you can't take a permanent job, you are needed for essential volunteer service by the Mobile Council of Defense. You can fill many jobs in the civilian defense program. Every woman in Mobile in can render an essential service as a worker in a war plant, in an essential civilian industry or in the civilian service program of the Council of Defense.

You now have an opportunity to register for an essential job or a training course. REGISTRATION BOOTHS WILL BE OPENED BY THE UNITED STATES EMPLOYMENT SERVICE AT PUBLIC SCHOOLS AND MANY OTHER PLACES IN MOBILE AT 9 A.M. MONDAY, FEBRUARY 22. THEY WILL BE OPEN FROM 9 A.M. TO 8 P.M. EACH DAY THROUGH SATURDAY, FEBRUARY 27. Women volunteers, who have been trained to fill out the registration cards used by the United States Employment Service, will be in charge of the booths.

Every woman in Mobile who can take an essential job or training for a job is urged at this time of national crisis as a good American to register with the United States Employment Service during this Woman's Registration Week. Remember: EVERY WOMAN WHO TAKES A JOB HASTENS THE DAY OF VICTORY FOR AMERICAN ARMS—AND PEACE.

Help bring them back alive!

War Manpower Commission United States Employment Service
Register for War Jobs at the United States Employment Services Office or at a Woman's Booth February 22 to 27.

DOCUMENT 6
Photograph, *Pearl Harbor Widows*, August 1942

Courtesy of the Library of Congress, LC-DIG-fsac 1a34888.

Women who had been married to armed forces personnel killed in the attack on Pearl Harbor were known as "Pearl Harbor widows." Howard Hollem took this photo for the Office of War Information of two such widows working at the Naval Air Base in Corpus Christi, Texas. The caption for this image reads: "Pearl Harbor widows have gone into war work to carry on the fight with a personal vengeance, Corpus Christi, Texas. Virginia Young (*right*), whose husband was one of the first casualties of World War II, is a supervisor in the Assembly and Repairs Department of the Naval Air Base. Her job is to find convenient and comfortable living quarters for women workers from out of the state, like Ethel Mann, who operates an electric drill."

DOCUMENT 7

Excerpt, Oral History, Evelyn Duran and Rosa Silvas, 2002

Courtesy of Rosie the Riveter World War II American Homefront Oral History Project, University of California, Berkeley, Regional Oral History Office, the National Park Service, and the City of Richmond, California.

Sisters Evelyn Duran and Rosa Silvas migrated from Phoenix, Arizona, to the Bay area in California to work in wartime industries in 1942 and 1943. Their experiences highlight the important role Latina women played in wartime work. For the complete transcript, visit http://digitalassets.lib.berkeley.edu/roho/ucb/text/duran_silvas.pdf.

Duran: But people all worked together. You couldn't tell one from the other unless you saw their welding outfit, or you had a torch.

Silvas: They had burners, welders—

Washburn: You're saying you couldn't even tell who was a man and who was a woman?

Duran: Really, lots of times you didn't.

Silvas: The welders—we had to use leathers.

Duran: Burners did too. We had to have these heavy leather outfits.

Silvas: I used to have—

Duran: The goggles.

Silvas: —you know, the welder's—outfit and hood.

Duran: What do they call that?

Washburn: The face shield kind of thing?

Duran: Yeah, it had a name, but I forget.

Washburn: So did you work as a burner for the whole time you were at the shipyards?

Duran: Mostly, I would say.

Silvas: And I worked as a welder, all the time.

Washburn: You came in as a welder? Evelyn came in in '42 and Rosa, you came in in '43.

Silvas: Mm-hmm.

Washburn: Did you move into the same house that Evelyn was staying at?

Silvas: No, I didn't. I went to live with Albert, the other brother.

Washburn: Albert had gotten his own place?

Silvas: Mm-hmm.

Duran: Albert and I came with Frank together, with his family first.

Washburn: With Frank's wife and—

Duran: Kids.

Silvas: I was with Albert—

Washburn: So Albert got his own place?

Silvas: —and his wife.

Washburn: So where was your place?

Silvas: Right there, right next to Frank, on the other side of the street.

Duran: On B Street, just across the street.

Washburn: So how did you come into the shipyards as a welder?

Silvas: I went to school. I was supposed to be in school for a whole week, but they needed welders so bad that I was in school only two days and they put me in yard one. I started tacking—what you call tacking steel—in place, before the welders come in and weld the whole works. Then they put me in the plate shop. In the plate shop, I was welding those big rails that are inside the bottom of the Liberty ships. Rails as big as this house, with those big rods. Size eleven rod. I stayed there. They kept me there. We were about six girls and two men—our crew. One year, they had a competition, who would put more work out. We won. Our crew won the competition, so they put our names in the paper. I have the picture of all the welders with my leaderman when we won. That's why they took a picture, because we won. We made most of the work. We did more work than any of the two others groups.

Duran: It was a competition between the shipyards.

Washburn: Tell me about the competition between the three yards.

Silvas: Whoever put out more work, and we did it.

Washburn: You put out more work than other people?

Silvas: That's why they put our pictures in the paper. I have that picture.

DOCUMENT 8

Photograph, Mary Withrow, Bell Bomber Plant, Marietta, Georgia, 1942

Courtesy of Kennesaw State University Archives.

Bell Aircraft Corporation opened the Bell Bomber plant in Marietta, Georgia, in 1942. The plant spurred explosive growth in the small town of Marietta, making it an industrial center throughout the war. In the spring of 1943, assembly lines were fully functional, and Bell employees built the Boeing-designed B-29s. At the height of its production, the Bell Bomber plant employed nearly forty thousand people, including six thousand women. The Bell Bomber plant closed at the end of the war but was acquired by the Lockheed Corporation (later Lockheed-Martin) in 1951. This image shows Mary Withrow spot welding at the Bell Bomber plant.

DOCUMENT 9

Excerpt, "Your Questions as to Women in War Industries,"
Bulletin No. 194 of the Women's Bureau, 1942

Courtesy of the US Government Printing Office.

This report, written by Mary Elizabeth Pidgeon (chief of the
Women's Bureau's Research Division), focused on the employment of women in war industries and was, as Secretary of Labor
Frances Perkins explained, "made in response to an insistent and
widespread demand for current information on many phases of
this subject."

What Kinds of Work Are Women Doing in War Plants?

Field investigators of the Women's Bureau of the United States
Department of Labor are finding that women workers in war factories
now operate some of the heavier machine tools formerly new to them,
such as millers, lathes, automatic screw machines, grinders, profilers,
and precision tappers. Where conditions warrant, women are setting
up these machine tools and working to great precision. Thousands
of other women are skillfully doing work requiring a delicate touch,
manipulative dexterity of a high degree, as well as extreme accuracy in
measurement. In addition, large numbers perform repetitive processes.

Women are at work in Government arsenals turning out small-
arms ammunition, in such processes as trimming bullet jacket and case,
annealing case parts, and assembling bullet cartridge. They are doing
shell and bag loading in artillery-ammunition plants. They are making
gas masks, balloons, rubber life-rafts, and parachutes. They are making blankets, uniforms, tenting fabrics, aircraft instruments, wire for
the Signal Corps. They are working as overhaul and repair mechanics,
assembling and disassembling machine guns for testing, and disassembling wrecked airplanes. A major airfield is employing them on maintenance work, cleaning spark plugs and painting luminous dials.

In airplane plants women operate hand drills and hand screw
machines, turret lathes, power sewing machines, and light rivet guns;

at the drill presses they change and sharpen their own drills; they install fittings and equipment in fuselages on the assembly line; they splice and prepare assemblies of light cable, assemble and prepare electrical systems, and install the radio in the plane; in the woodworking department they operate band saws, sanding belts, and do nailing and gluing of small wooden parts; they do wiring, light grinding, profiling, sheet-metal cutting, spot and arc welding, spray painting, and all types of bench work. Several large aircraft companies have women on production jobs throughout the plant.

In plants making lenses, bomb sights, precision instruments, and fire-control instruments, women work as assemblers, grinders, honers, operates of drill and punch presses, solderers, cementers, welders, engravers, polishers, testers, and inspectors. In the making of electrical machinery women are assemblers, winders, inspectors, power-press operators, and X-ray technicians. The Women's Bureau has many further details as to industrial jobs women are doing, and is continually making recommendations in various industries as to particular types of work suitable for women.

Women are performing many technical processes that require considerable training. Some ferry planes from plant to training field; at Army training schools they are instructors in flying and ground mechanics. By the end of 1941 there were 92 women journeyman instructors, though women are no longer admitted to Government courses for pilot training. Women are medical-social and recreational workers at United States military hospitals here and with Army units abroad, sailing under sealed orders. A few women are in unique positions, such as testing durability of aircraft paints, testing alloys, directing a corps of women helping to build ship and plane instruments, specializing in X-ray of metals, managing a company making cable grips for battleships, electrical engineering in aircraft.

Are Women Replacing Men?

In war industries expansion has permitted women to work side by side with men on the same jobs without taking over the jobs held by men. This is true today, though as more and more men go into the specific war services actual substitution of women on men's jobs in war industries is likely to increase. Women have replaced men primarily in civilian services for which men are not deferred from the Army, often in types of work women long have done, though from day to day some new type of work is engaging women.

In large and small places Women's Bureau agents find women at work as elevator operators in hotels, stores, and office buildings; as telegraph messengers and in other messenger services; as clerks, cashiers, soda-fountain girls, and pharmacists in drug stores. Women are serving as taxi drivers and filling-station attendants. They are being hired as men are drafted from shoe, electrical-supply, and food plants. They are replacing men as finger-print classifiers. A large industrial company began to take on a few women technicians in their laboratories, a type of work women formerly have done elsewhere. Women are serving at airports as reservation supervisors, dietitians, passenger-service superintendents, and dispatch clerks. Women are reported as machine-shop instructors, as mechanics, and mechanics' helpers. They service typewriters, act as bank tellers and assistants, and are reported at work in brokerage offices, and as stock-exchange floor employees. They are serving as guards at industrial plants, with police power. At least one of our largest cities has supplemented the traffic police force with women, who direct traffic at school and church crossings and at municipal parking lots, in the latter locations also guarding the parked cars. Another city has a woman managing a municipal airport.

The United States Employment Service has listed over 460 industrial jobs as suitable for women, though 40 percent of these would require some rearrangement of the processes if women are to perform them. At the time this list was compiled women worked in only a small proportion of these occupations.

DOCUMENT 10

Poster, "Rosie the Riveter: We Can Do It," 1943, by J. Howard Miller, Produced by Westinghouse for the War Production Coordinating Committee

Courtesy of the National Archives.

Rosie the Riveter was a fictional character created to entice American women into the workforce and became the most enduring image of their involvement in World War II. Norman Rockwell's Rosie (published on May 29, 1943, in the *Saturday Evening Post*) was more popular at the time, but J. Howard Miller's version, shown here, has become the iconic image of female war workers. A song, "Rosie the Riveter," written by Redd Evans and John Jacob Loeb, was popular during the war. The first stanza details Rosie's dedication to her job: "All the day long, whether rain or shine / She's a part of the assembly line / She's making history, working for victory / Rosie, brrrrrrrrrrr, the riveter."

DOCUMENT 11
Excerpt, Summary Report, April 29, 1943

Courtesy of the National Archives, Records of the National War Labor Board, ARC Identifier: 596504.

President Franklin D. Roosevelt established the National War Labor Board (NWLB) in January 1942 to mediate wartime labor disputes. Women asked the NWLB that they be paid equal wages for equal work, and this summary report sets forth provisions for women's wages. This entry is an excerpt of a report involving General Motors Corporation and two of its unions.

April 29, 1943
Cases No. 125 and 128
In the Matter of:
General Motors Corporation
and
United Automobile, Aircraft and Agricultural Implement Workers of America–C.I.O.
and
United Electrical, Radio and Machine Workers of America, C.I.O.

SUMMARY REPORT OF THE BOARD'S SPECIAL
REPRESENTATIVE
RETROACTIVE DATE FOR WOMEN'S PAY ADJUSTMENTS

1. Subject to the following qualifications it is recommended that wage rate adjustments, if any, which may be made by agreement or decision of an Arbitrator appointed by the War Labor Board and which result from application of the "equal pay for equal work for women" clause of the September 26, 1942 Directive Order shall be made effective as of April 5, 1943 or at the beginning of the payroll period most closely approximating that date.

2. If local agreements should already provide a retroactive date or dates, the April 5th date shall not supersede any such agreement.

3. If unsettled grievances exist in cases of rate alleged to have been established unilaterally by Management on jobs or operations formerly performed by men and where women perform exactly the same job with equal pay and quantity of work, and if such is found to be the case by agreement or by decision of the Umpire or Arbitrator, the April 5 date is not necessarily compelling.

4. The April 5th date does not apply to jobs or operations for which the Union has not submitted a completed Form #1 on or before June 1, 1943 or within thirty (30) days after the forms are made available by Management whichever date is later.

5. If it can be proven that the Union is responsible for other unreasonable delays, the retroactive date may be established later than April 5th by agreement or by decision.

William E. Simpkin
Special Representative

Special Representative's Report
Retroactive Date for Women's Pay Adjustment

INTRODUCTION

The Director Order of September 26, 1942 contains the following provisions respecting wage rates for women:

> "Wage rates for women shall be set in accordance with the principle of equal pay for comparable quantity and quality of work on comparable operations.
> "Any dispute arising as to the question of quality, quantity or comparability as herein defined, shall be subject to final determination by an Arbitrator appointed by the National War Labor Board; provided, however, that any such dispute which involves an alleged violation of a local wage agreement shall be settled within the procedural framework of the grievance provision in the agreement."
> "The parties shall include in the new Agreement the above provision and in their application shall be guided by the opinion of the Board in this case."

These provisions were incorporated in the October 19, 1942 Agreement between the Corporation and the UAW-CIO and in the November 2,

1942 Agreement between the Corporation and the U.E.R.M.W.A.—CIO. To both agreements is affixed as an exhibit the text of the Board's opinion on Wage Rates for Female Employees as written by George W. Taylor, Vice-Chairman. The Board action on this part of the General Motors case was unanimous.

DOCUMENT 12
Letter from Thomas Johnstone to the National War Labor Board, June 8, 1943

Courtesy of the National Archives, Records of the National War Labor Board, ARC Identifier: 595878.

This letter, sent from the United Automobile, Aircraft, Agriculture Implement Workers of America, presents the unions' response to the National War Labor Board's rulings on women's pay.

Dr. George W. Taylor, Vice Chairman
National Labor Relations Board
Washington, D.C.

Dear Sir:

We are in receipt of a letter signed by Mr. Davis, Chairman of the Board, relative to the principle of equal pay for equal work as respects women and the effect of Executive Order No. 9328 upon General Order No. 16, if any.

At a recent hearing in Washington in your office on May 26, I believe you spoke of this letter and requested our comments after we had reviewed it. I recollect that you stated this was not a new position on the part of the Board but represented their unanimous viewpoint and one which had been held since their adoption and publication of the principle.

There appear to be three categories into which the question of women's rates fall.

1. Situations where women are employed to replace men on jobs which are not changed.

2. Situations where women have been inducted on jobs which were changed to accommodate the physical strength of women.

3. Situations where women alone have been employed and a negotiated rate agreed upon.

We have no contention to offer with respect to Mr. Davis' reasoning on situations 1 and 2. It is only in connection to the third category that we desire to offer comment.

Mr. Davis' letter states in part: "The rates for such jobs (referring to classifications to which only women have been assigned in the past) especially when developed by collective bargaining, are presumed to be correct in relation to other jobs in the plant."

That is unwarranted presumption in so far as such rates in General Motors are concerned. Historically, a differential in women's rates was established on the basis of sex alone and it was almost solely because of this differential that management employed women. Because it was possible to secure women at lower rates than those paid to males, their use resulted in a saving in wage costs and none of the factors which would tend to equalize rates were given consideration by management.

However, inasmuch as we have been proceeding on the basis that "concrete and specific evidence" must be adduced in support of a claim for women's rate equalization to each specific instance, and have agreed with the Corporation on the use and forms to facilitate the submission of such evidence and for the purpose of making comparisons between job content between men's and women's jobs, we can see little point in offering protest.

The question seems to be one of name rather than principle. In the case of rates for women employees how can an intra-plant inequality be said to exist, unless reliance and support be gained from application of the equal pay for equal work principle?

We note that when certain phases of the application of the equal pay for equal work principle are termed intra-plan inequalities, they become subject to War Labor Board approval while if related to the equal pay principle they would not. This device simply entails a further delay and gives management an added opportunity to indulge in legalistic argument. It may and probably will have some bearing on retroactive adjustments resulting in a saving to the Corporation.

The language of Mr. Davis' letter would appear to be at variance with that in your Opinion in cases 125 and 128. Mr. Davis' letter state: "The rates for such jobs, especially when developed by collective bargaining are presumed to be correct in relation to other jobs in the plant."

Your Opinion states: "the Board believes . . . that rates for women already established should be presumed to be correct in the absence of concrete and specific evidence that the rate has been established in violation of an equal pay for equal work principle."

Strictly stated, Mr. Davis' letter is restrictive and unqualified, almost absolute when comparison is made with the Opinion.

With best personal regards, I am

Sincerely yours,
GM Department, UAW-CIO
T. A. Johnstone, Int'l. Representative

DOCUMENT 13
Photograph, *Mrs. Phipps Just Convinced Me of the Need for Better Child-Care Facilities*, 1943

Courtesy of the Library of Congress, LCUSZC4-5599.

This cartoon from 1943 depicts a mother changing her baby's diaper on the nose of an airplane. Finding affordable and reliable child care was one of war workers' major challenges.

Document 13

DOCUMENT 14

Film Script Excerpt, from *Problems in Supervision: Supervising Women Workers*, 1944, Herbert Kerkow Productions, US Office of Education

Courtesy of the Prelinger Archives, Library of Congress, Washington, D.C.

This short film focuses on training women in the factories during the war and presents Joe Haley, a foreman, talking with factory manager Frank Brooks about how "women scare me." The rest of the film, created by the US Office of Education, details strategies for training women and reflects common gender stereotypes at the time.

Supervising Women Workers
Number One in a Series
of
Supervisory Training Films
for the
Office of Education
Produced by Herbert Kerkow
480 Lexington Avenue
New York, NY

1. TITLE

UNITED STATES OFFICE OF EDUCATION
TRAINING FILM
(Over Federal Security Agency Seal)

DISSOLVE TO
2. TITLE

Produced by
DIVISION OF VISUAL ARTS
U.S. OFFICE OF EDUCATION
J. W. STUDENBACKER, COMMISSIONER
Federal Security Agency
Paul. V. McNutt, Administrator

3. TITLE

PROBLEMS IN SUPERVISION
SUPERVISING WOMEN WORKERS
Copyright MCMXLIV
By Herbert Kerkow

FADE OUT

FADE IN

4. STOCK SHOT   FACTORY   DAY

Pan down smoke stacks to factory building.

DISSOLVE TO

5. MEDIUM SHOT   FACTORY INTERIOR

Joe Haley, foreman, his hand on the back of his head, and Frank Brooks, plant manager, gray-haired, wise in the ways of men and machines. On the wall are production charts and personnel records, but the most prominent are the distinctive graphs of industrial plants.

CUT TO

6. TWO SHOT   BROOKS OVER HALEY'S SHOULDER

BROOKS

You know how to handle men and you know to keep the line moving.

JOE

Thanks, Mr. Brooks.

BROOKS

You work hard, Joe. You're a good foreman.

Brooks looks out window.

CUT TO.

7. FULL HIGH ANGLE FACTORY YARD

Women workers are jostling their way to the factory entrance.

BROOKS

Yes, women workers do present problems, Joe. It's tough, I know, but there's thousands of others just like you all over the country facing the same problem. Pretty generally.

CUT TO

8. TWO SHOT   HALEY OVER BROOKS' SHOULDER

BROOKS

You'll all find about the same answer.

JOE

I know most of the answers—as far as men are concerned.

CUT TO

9. TWO SHOT   BROOKS OVER HALEY'S SHOULDER

BROOKS

I think we can say that the broad principles involved in supervising
<u>men</u> apply equally well in the case of <u>women</u>.

CUT TO

10. MEDIUM SHOT   HALEY AND BROOKS

JOE

That ain't what I learned about <u>women</u>.

Brooks smiles at Joe's depression.

CUT TO

11. MEDIUM TWO SHOT   BROOKS OVER HALEY'S SHOULDER

BROOKS

There are some new and different problems, Joe, I'll admit that.

JOE

<u>Women scare me</u>—at least they do in the factory.

BROOKS

Well, maybe the <u>women</u> are <u>scared</u>, too, Joe. Let's see.

DISSOLVE TO

12. MEDIUM C.U.   SHOP

Women workers are inspecting various machines.

BROOKS' VOICE

Most of them are working on their first

CUT TO

13. MEDIUM SHOT   BENCH

A girl is examining a collection of tools.

BROOKS' VOICE

industrial job, Joe. It's

CUT TO

14. MEDIUM SHOT   BLUE PRINT

Two girls are standing before a blue print.

BROOKS' VOICE

a totally unfamiliar world.

CUT TO

15. MEDIUM SHOT   BENCH

Girl places piece of work in magnetic chuck and starts surfaces grinder,
forgetting to turn on chuck and securing work.

CUT TO

16. CLOSE UP

Piece flys [*sic*] from chuck, startling girl.

DISSOLVE TO

17. OFFICE INTERIOR   BROOKS AND HALEY AT DESK
BROOKS

You see, they are not naturally familiar with mechanical principles—
or machines. Why even the language applying to common processes
and tools is new to them.

JOE

It must sound like double talk to them.

CUT TO

18. LONG SHOT   GROUP AND INSTRUCTOR
INSTRUCTOR

Now, if anybody wants a flamsoan, give with the double left-handed
jerry wrench, on account of it might sosbobulate the orange crate
with a toroid. On the other hand, if the span flam is wanted, that's
singe right-handed, provided

CUT TO

19. MEDIUM SHOT

Girls in overalls listening to overshoulder instructor.

INSTRUCTOR

the pressing puncture is adjusted to the conkront of thirty-two
seven-eighths. Is that clear?

CUT TO

20. MEDIUM SHOT   THREE GIRLS

Looking puzzled.

CUT TO

21. MEDIUM SHOT

Brooks at desk seen over Haley's shoulder

BROOKS

I know, Joe. It takes time to make them feel at home,
but it can be done.

JOE

You talk like a man who knows women.

BROOKS

We'll see, Joe, we'll see. You know, women workers can be surpris-
ingly good producers and it helps a lot to them off to a good start.

DISSOLVE TO

22. MEDIUM SHOT   INSTRUCTOR AND TWO GIRLS

They are watching their instructor as he explains the tools on the bench before them.

BROOKS' VOICE

When breaking in any new worker and, of course, especially women, you've got to explain every angle of the process down to the last detail.

CUT TO

23. TWO SHOT   INSTRUCTOR AND WORKER

Instructor is explaining the drill press to a woman worker.

BROOKS' VOICE

And since most of them lack mechanical background, you've got to study every job and subdivide

CUT TO

24. C.U. SAME AS 23

BROOKS' VOICE

it into simple operating steps.

CUT TO

25. GROUP SHOT   AT ANOTHER BENCH

The instructor is carefully pointing out each object.

BROOKS' VOICE

It's a good idea not to use trade terms except, of course, where we must, and then to explain plain language exactly what such terms mean.

CUT TO

26. CLOSE UP   INSTRUCTOR

We see him adjust the pliers and put it in the hand of the woman worker.

BROOKS' VOICE

And no matter what the job, he fits the tools and the work arrangements to suit the worker.

CUT TO

27. MEDIUM C.U.   WOMAN'S HANDS

putting small parts together with tweezers.

CUT TO

28. CLOSE UP   WOMAN'S HANDS

BROOKS' VOICE
Women workers

CUT TO

29. C.U.   HANDS

Working on assembling a small motor.

BROOKS' VOICE
don't mind the routing

CUT TO

30. C.U.   HANDS

different angle, working on assembling a small motor.

BROOKS' VOICE

repetitive work and they're particular good on work that requires high

CUT TO

31. MEDIUM SHOT   GIRL

Inspecting small parts.

BROOKS' VOICE
dexterity or an unusual sense of accuracy.

CUT TO

32. MEDIUM SHOT   WOMEN INSPECTING MACHINE

BROOKS' VOICE

The inspection foreman did a good job of breaking in those girls.

DISSOLVE TO

33. MEDIUM TWO SHOT   ON JOE OVER BROOKS' SHOULDER

BROOKS

He remembered that what's old stuff to you and me
is brand new to them.

JOE

I was just thinking what a dub I'll be doing something that's old stuff
to my wife but new to me—like baking a pie.

LAP DISSOLVE TO

34. C.U. HANDS

Woman's hands are cutting apples.

36. MEDIUM C.U.   MOLLY   NIGHT

CUT TO

36. LONG SHOT   KITCHEN

Joe putting on his tie.

MOLLY
How did it go today, Joe?

JOE

Oh, all right.

MOLLY

You're troubled about something?

JOE

Everything went all right, Molly, but you know I had

CUT TO

37. MEDIUM SHOT   MOLLY

Cutting apples.

JOE

seven requests for time off. I guess women don't realize
what it means to stick on the job.

MOLLY

Maybe they don't.

JOE'S VOICE

How was your day?

MOLLY

Oh, pretty quiet. I did the washing this morning and cleaned the
house. Took junior to the dentist's and did the shopping.

She glances at Joe with a quizzical look in her eye.

MOLLY

Put up sixteen jars of jam this afternoon, and then went
to work on Junior's clothes.

CUT TO

38. MEDIUM LONG SHOT   JOE OVER MOLLY'S SHOULDER

He listens to his wife and his troubles fall away. Molly isn't complaining,
she's telling Joe something important and he's getting it.

MOLLY

Joe, I'm sorry supper's late.

Joe grins and nods his head.

JOE

Nice going, old lady.

39. CLOSE UP   JOE AND MOLLY

He moves in to his wife and puts his arms around her.

JOE

You know, Molly, I've been thinking—

MOLLY

Yes, Joe

JOE

Maybe some of these women and girls coming into the plant—
maybe they have home responsibilities, too.

MOLLY

Could be.

JOE

Maybe they need time off perhaps. I could rearrange
their work schedule.

MOLLY

They'd like that. So many of them have two jobs, Joe—
one in the home, and one in the plant.

JOE

Gee, I'm glad I thought of that.

MOLLY (dutifully)

Yes, dear.

FADE OUT

FADE IN

40. MEDIUM SHOT   BROOKS OFFICE   DAY

Joe is busily writing across the desk from where Brooks sits when
Brooks enters.

BROOKS

Morning, Joe.

JOE

Morning, Mr. Brooks

BROOKS

How go the ladies?

JOE

As a matter of fact, I was just jotting down a few points on that
subject from this manual of yours. Why?

41. TWO SHOT BROOKS AND JOE

He picks up the manual and thumbs through it.

BROOKS

Women are individualistic by nature and are not apt to make a
personal application of any action, rule or regulation.

JOE

You're telling me.

BROOKS (reading on)

The supervisor should scrupulously avoid spending too much time with any individual woman worker—holding everyone to the standard of performance and avoiding

CUT TO

42. TWO SHOT JOE OVER BROOKS' SHOULDER

BROOKS

any appearance of favoritism.

Joe

That's a neat trick if you can do it.

43. MEDIUM TWO SHOT   BROOKS AND JOE

Brooks puts the manual aside.

BROOKS

Joe, this all boils down to four things to remember; one, don't mix pleasure with business; two, women can be awfully jealous of

CUT TO

44. TWO SHOT   JOE AND BROOKS

BROOKS

each other; three, avoid undue familiarity, and finally, women are more sensitive than men.

JOE

I'll say they're sensitive. Why, only yesterday, after I was talking with you, I saw a foreman take it right on the chin when he caught a girl working on her drill press without her safety cap on.

CUT TO

45. MEDIUM SHOT   DRILL PRESS

Mary is busy at work drilling castings. She is not wearing a cap and as she leans over watching the drills biting into the castings, her hair comes dangerously close to the pulleys driving the drill head. Foreman comes into the scene and we pan up to include both in frame.

FOREMAN

Mary, you're supposed to wear a cap when you're working near a drill press.

MARY

Why pick on me? The other girls aren't wearing their caps.

FOREMAN

(A little belligerently) Look, the rule book says wear a safety cap.

CUT TO

46. C.U.   MARY

Very angry—putting on the cap.

> FOREMAN'S VOICE
>
> So, put the cap on.

CUT TO

47. BROOKS' OFFICE   BROOKS OVER JOE'S SHOULDER

> JOE
>
> There, you see what I mean? They give you an argument
> and a crazy one at that.

> BROOKS
>
> (Smiling) Yes. A man probably would have kept the argument about
> himself and not trapped the foreman the way she did.

CUT TO

48. MEDIUM SHOT   HALEY OVER BROOKS' SHOULDER

> JOE
>
> What do you mean, trapped him?

> BROOKS
>
> Bless their souls, but it's an old stunt, Joe. You go after a woman
> worker on one point and she switches the issue.

> JOE
>
> Why limit it to women workers?

> BROOKS
>
> Now, the issue was—

CUT TO

49. TWO SHOT   BROOKS AND JOE

> BROOKS
>
> why wasn't she wearing a cap—she switched him over the fact
> that the other girls didn't wear them and all he did was to stand on
> his dignity—a bit stuffily I might say. Now, if she'd been a man, he
> would not have laid down a safety rule so arbitrarily. You know, Joe,
> you've got to tell them the why of any rule and particularly
> women. Now supposed he handled it this way.

CUT TO

50. MEDIUM SHOT   DRILL PRESS

Mary is at work at her press, drilling castings as before.

FOREMAN

(As he demonstrates) Mary, your hair is just about two inches from
this drill press. That's why we ask you to wear this cap—so that
your hair doesn't get caught. Safety rules are here to help protect
you and the girls working around you.

MARY

Well, gee. I saw all the other girls not wearing any caps.

FOREMAN

That's right, but they are not working with machines. They sit
at a bench and just assemble things. Nothing dangerous to them
or people nearby.

MARY

You know I never thought of it that way before.

FOREMAN

You have your cap with you, haven't you?

MARY

Yes, O.K., I get it (as she reaches in the pocket of her jumpers
and puts it on).

CUT TO

51. TWO SHOT   BROOKS OFFICE

BROOKS

A foreman'll always have the eternal feminine to contend with, Joe.

DISSOLVE TO

52. TWO SHOTS   FOREMAN OVER GIRL'S SHOULDER

BROOKS' VOICE

You know, jealously can cause you no end of trouble.

CUT TO

53. C.U.   FOREMAN

BROOKS' VOICE

Avoid spending any more time than one has to with another—

54. MEDIUM SHOT   GIRLS LOOK JEALOUS

BROOKS' VOICE

treat them all the same—pleasantly and friendly, but with no
favoritism and avoid undue familiarity.

DISSOLVE TO

55. TWO SHOT   BROOKS AND JOE

BROOKS

Watch the little things, Joe. The eternal feminine is very
conscious of them.

CUT TO

56. MEDIUM C.U.   JOE AND BROOKS

BROOKS

And finally, I don't have to tell you not to mix pleasure with business.

57. C.U.   BROOKS

BROOKS

To all the rules in handling women, one more—act quickly so a situation never gets under way. Remember, Joe, we couldn't have won this

CUT TO

58. CLOSE UP   LAPEL

In the buttonhole of this lapel is an Army-Navy "E" insignia.

BROOKS' VOICE

(points to his lapel) without the help of the women in this plant.

FADE OUT

59. TITLE

THE END

U.S. OFFICE OF EDUCATION AND TRAINING FILM

A Herbert Kerkow Production

DISSOLVE TO

60. TITLE

U.S. OFFICE OF EDUCATION

COMMITTEE

C. F. KLINEFELTER, CHAIRMAN

W. P. Beard	W. P. Loomis
W. H. Coope	C. R. Rakestraw
J. H. Hawke	S. M. Ransopher
L. S. Hawkins	W. A. Ross
S. J. Hoexter	W. T. Spanton

Division of Visual Arts

C. F. Klinefelter	Paul Reed
Technical Specialist	Visual Aid Specialist

DOCUMENT 15
Poster, "Good Work Sister," 1944

Courtesy of the Library of Congress, LC-USZC4-55973.

This poster was published by Bressler Editorial Cartoons, Inc., on May 5, 1944. The focus of many of these poster campaigns was to make women appear both feminine and capable of heavy industrial labor, but this poster is unique in that it seeks to present men and women on equal footing.

DOCUMENT 16

Appeal Hearing, Case File #728, April 5, 1944

*Courtesy of the National Archives Record Administration–
Northeast Region (Boston), Records of the War Manpower
Commission, RG 211.*

In this appeal, shoe manufacturing worker Dorothy L. Dugan
appeals to the Management-Labor Appeals Committee of
the Dover US Employment Service to change her job to the
Washington Navy Yard to make more money. She is denied the
appeal, but the process shows how war labor was regulated and
the degree to which women were willing to fight for better wages
even during wartime.

Appeal Hearing
Mrs. Dorothy L. Dugan
R.F.D.#3 Central Park
Dover, New Hampshire

Employer: Prosper Shevenell and Sons Company, Dover, New
Hampshire

Appeal heard by the Management-Labor Appeals Committee,
Wednesday, April 45, 1944. Present were: Mr. Whittemore represent-
ing Management, Mr. Cate representing Labor and Mr. John L. Barry,
Area Director.

Taken from USES form 536

On March 24 Mrs. Dugan requested a Statement of Availability from
the Dover United States Employment Service. Her reason was as follows: "I wish to change jobs in order to make more money. I get $15
after deductions. I have no previous experience in Sheet Metal Work but
have the offer of a job as helper at the Navy Yard."

Mrs. Dugan has been working as a Skiving Machine Operator in the
Leather Department of the Prosper Shevenell Sons Company, Dover,
from December 1943 to the present time. Her hourly rate of pay was 40¢

and weekly average hours were 48. She wished to go to the Portsmouth Navy Yard as a Sheet Metal worker's helper at a daily rate of $6.16 on an average weekly workweek of 48 hours.

Present Employers' Statement: Has received form from the Navy Yard. Is returning form and objecting to releasing the applicant.

On March 27 the Dover United States Employment Service denied Mrs. Dugan a Statement of Availability because the facts did not meet requirements of the Area Stabilization Plan.

On March 29 the following Notice of Appeal was received from Mrs. Dugan by the Area Director:

"I have a chance to better myself from present job and also have a chance to learn a trade and to work for 100% defense which my present job is not. My husband is working at the Navy Yard and I would like to work there with him. My pay at the Navy Yard would be much more than where I am at the present employed."

Minutes of the Hearing

Mr. Barry: She was denied a Statement of Availability by the Dover USES because the facts did not meet the requirements of the Stabilization Plan. In other words, the young lady asked for a release because of money and that is not a cause for a change of jobs unless there is something else to go with it.

Mrs. Dugan: I have nothing left after I get through paying my board and I want to make more money.

Mr. Whittemore: What does the Shevenell Company Manufacture?

Mrs. Dugan: Counters for shoes.

Mr. Whittemore: Mr. Barry, what is the essentiality of the Company?

Mr. Barry: They are on civilian essential and Army production.

Mr. Shevenell: We have been on Army and Navy lend-lease I should say for the last two years. We specialize in juvenile shoes. Today we have 75 to 80 employees.

Mr. Whittemore: What is your job at the Shevenell Company?

Mrs. Dugan: I have been skiving about two weeks. I have been working there since December. I earn $20.80 for 48 hours.

Mr. Shevenell: Her rate is 40¢ an hour.

Mr. Whittemore: Is that what most girls on their job are making?

Mr. Shevenell: That is their starting rate. They advance as they learn their job.

Mr. Whittemore: How much would experienced girls be getting on the type of work this girl started on?

Mr. Shevenell: She could earn 50¢ an hour day work.

Mr. Barry: She took an appeal against the Dover USES and she indicated she had a chance to better herself and also a chance to learn a trade and work for a 100% defense job which she said her present job is not.

Mr. Whittemore: You are married—how many in family?

Mrs. Dugan: Just myself and husband—no dependents.

Mr. Cate: What does your husband do at the Yard?

Mrs. Dugan: He is a craneman.

(Mr. Whitttemore asked about sub-standard wages)

Mr. Barry: Anything below 40¢ an hour.

Mr. Whittemore: I think the young lady should be given to understand that the idea of the government is that there are other things just as important to winning the war as building submarines etc. Shoes are needed. Many people get the idea that their job is not so dramatic as guns and submarines but the government ruled that other things also must be produced. If many people changed around things which are necessary would not be made.

Mr. Shevenell: The young lady has protested in several operations she is doing. We have tried to find something that she would be adapted to. She has been skiving two weeks and we would have to put her on Army shoes.

Mr. Cate: Are you working now?

Mrs. Dugan: No, I left a week and a half ago.

Discussion

Mr. Barry: There is just one thing I wish to call your attention to and that is this week, Monday, we had a conference at the Navy Yard—Mrs. Wilder, State Manpower Director, a representative of the U.S. Civil Service and Navy Yard officials. They told us what they believed was their needed labor requirements. As far as men are concerned we have not objected to their going outside of the Area because we could not furnish the men. Talked of possible needs for training in the immediate future. They need 50 sheetmetal workers' helpers and they only had 33 on the Register, four in the Area and one would not accept work unless it was at Somersworth and that left them going outside of the Area for 36. We objected to 36. We said there might be related trades over there from which they could draw. We allowed them to go outside of the Area for 28. That situation arose because of some particular job that had started and they asked permission to go outside of the Area. This girl had her name on the Register and undoubtedly that is why they called her.

Mr. Whittemore: Nevertheless we must interpret the rules as they are written down here.

Mr. Barry: That is right. They have exhausted the Register on sheetmetal workers, female. She is asking for more money.

Mr. Whittemore: There is no personal hardship. Her husband is working in the Navy Yard and there are no dependents.

Mr. Cate: As a craneman her husband must be making good wages and, therefore, there is no personal hardship at all as far as I can see.

DECISION: Unanimous to uphold the decision of the Dover USES whereby she is denied a Statement of Availability.

J. L. Barry, Area Director

DOCUMENT 17

Brochure, "Women Want to Get It Over!," Radio Corporation of America, Camden, New Jersey, c. 1940s

Courtesy of the National Archives.

This brochure, produced by Radio Corporation of America (RCA), was intended to provide advice to employers that were considering hiring women. The brochure is peppered with positive slogans such as these: "Women are Careful," "Women are Teachable," "Women are Cooperative," and "Women are Patient."

"Women Want to Get It Over"
Whenever You Employ a Woman

Limit her hours to 8 hours a day, and 48 a week if possible.

Arrange brief rest periods in the middle of each shift.

Try to make nourishing foods available for lunch periods.

Try to provide a clean place to eat lunch, away from her workplace. Make pure and cool drinking water accessible.

See that toilet and rest-rooms are clean and adequate.

Watch work hazards—moving machinery; dust and fumes; improper lifting; careless housekeeping.

Provide properly adjusted work seats; good ventilation and lighting.

Recommend proper clothing for each job; safe, comfortable shoes; try to provide lockers and a place to change to work clothes.

Relieve a monotonous job with rest periods. If possible, use music during fatigue periods.

When You Supervise a Woman

Make clear her part in the process or product on which she works.

Allow for her lack of familiarity with machine processes.

See that her working set-up is comfortable, safe and convenient.

Start her right by kindly and careful supervision.

Avoid horseplay or "kidding"; she may resent it.

Suggest rather than reprimand.

When she does a good job, tell her so.

Listen to and aid her in her work problems.

Finally—Call on a Trained Woman Counselor
in Your Personnel Department

To find out what women workers think and want.

To discover personal causes of poor work, absenteeism, turnover.

To assist women workers in solving personal difficulties.

To interpret women's attitudes and actions.

To assist in adjusting women to their jobs.

When You Put a Woman to Work

Have a job breakdown for her job.

Consider her education, work experience and temperament in assigning her to that job.

Have the necessary equipment, tools and supplies ready for her.

Try out her capacity for and familiarity with the work.

Assign her to a shift in accordance with health, home obligations and transportation arrangements.

Place her in a group of workers with similar backgrounds and interests.

Inform her fully on health and safety rules, company policies, company objectives.

Be sure she knows the location of rest-rooms, lunch facilities, dispensaries.

Don't change her shift too often and never without notice.

DOCUMENT 18
Poster, "Their Real Pin Up Girl," 1944

Courtesy of the Library of Congress, LC-USZC4-5601.

This colorful poster created by Cy Hungerford (1889–1983) shows a sailor, soldier, and airman giving a "thumbs-up" to a female factory worker. Like most propaganda posters, it focused on a simple message that appealed to the viewer's emotions. Women are presented as fellow partners in the war effort, but a nod is given to pin-up posters widely used in the war.

Document 18

DOCUMENT 19
Excerpt, Oral History, Ernestine J. Slade, April 28, 1992

Courtesy of Kennesaw State University Archives, Cobb County Oral History Series, no. 28.

In this excerpt from an oral history conducted by Kathryn A. Kelley, Ernestine Slade describes her experience working at the Bell Bomber plant in Marietta, Georgia, with specific attention to the experiences of African Americans.

KK So what a big change, then, from you doing laundry and being more or less self-employed, to going to work at a big company like Bell Aircraft. Tell me about—how did that come about?

ES Well, I tell you, I had been working for this family of people helping them. And I was always one who wanted to make as much money as I could possibly make to help carry on the family. And I worked for this family of people I'm going to tell you about off and on for eight years. It was a little difficult when Bell first came here for a person who had a regular job, a domestic worker, to get on. Because, see, like they had an understanding or had discussed or didn't want to take nobody's help away from them, especially a person who was working for, you know, a well-to-do family.

KK So you mean the rich, white people had an agreement with Bell that—

ES If you went there, and you were working for one of these well-to-do families, you could not get on at Bell easily. And you made so much money at Bell—much more money at Bell than you could make working for a permanent family. So me and my friends, we didn't go to the employment office here in Marietta. We went into Atlanta to the employment office. And that's how I got hired. Then I came back, and I told this lady that I had been working for, they hired me that day, told me when I could start to work. So that weekend, I told her. I said, "Now I'm going to start working at the Bomber Club"—that's what we called it. Well, naturally, she didn't like it, but she didn't fuss too much about. And I said, "I'll be leaving you." And so I went on that Monday morning to work out at Bell.

KK So she wasn't very happy about that?

ES She wasn't pleased about it at all, huh-uh. She asked me what was I going to do when the war was over and the plant would be closed down. "Had you thought about you're going to need somewhere to work?" I said, "Well, I'm sure I'll find something."

KK So you were confident you had enough skills you could find a job?

ES Well, I had always been able to find work.

KK Now was your husband already working at Bell when you went to interview?

ES Yes, he was still working there.

KK What was his job?

ES He was in the janitorial department.

KK I see. What was his name?

ES Horace Slade.

KK Horace Slade?

ES Uh-huh.

KK And did he enjoy working there?

ES Yes, he did enjoy working there, but as time went on, he quit for some reason or other.

KK Now when you went to Bell, what kinds of job openings were there and what led you to the job that you took?

ES I can tell you what I did. It was something like the finishing department where they sent all parts that went into the airplane, regardless of how small they were, through some kind of treatment process. We would clean those parts, and they would put it in a machine and then some kind of solution and what-have-you. I don't know whether it was strengthening or just to be sure it was clean or what. And then sometimes, after they had got a part of the plane completed, we'd go inside of that plane and clean it all in the inside. Those long parts to the plane, sometimes we'd have to take something like steel wool and rub them; and then they would put them through this process I'm telling you about. And the little, bitty pieces like that, we had in the buckets, we'd drop them in. They'd put them through this process.

KK Did you work Monday through Friday?

ES Yes, yes, I did.

KK From like nine to five?

ES No, I went on the evening shift.

KK Because your husband—that's right, your husband was working days.

ES Yes. We would go in around 11:00 or 11:45 and work until—now my older children had started to school. And see, I'd get here early enough to see that all was well with them and that their clothes and everything were on properly and so forth, and they could get to school without being late.

KK Uh-huh. So you went to work at what time, then?

ES I think it was around 12:00, 12:45.

KK Was that noon or at midnight?

ES At night—midnight.

KK Midnight?

ES Uh-huh.

KK And then you worked until about 8:00 in the morning?

ES That's right.

KK So when you came home then, some of your children were just getting up and getting ready to go to school?

ES Yes. I'd come in from work, do my cleaning, do my wash and my laundry work, wash the children's clothes, iron whatever needed to be done, then I would lay down and go to sleep. And when they would come in the afternoon, I'd get up and do their dinner, fix their meals for them, and have that ready for them so they could eat. Then I'd lay down again and take another little nap before going to work at night. I'd comb the girls' hair at home for the next day, and I put stocking caps over their heads so their hair would stay nice, and give them their bath and get them ready for bed and get them in the bed before I'd leave.

KK I see. Did they leave for school before you got home in the morning, then?

ES No, no.

KK But you didn't have time to do all of that?

ES I lived right over there just above the school. They could get to school in three or four minutes, you know.

KK I see. Was your husband a big help at home?

ES Yes, he was very helpful.

KK So he helped you with the chores around the house? It wasn't as divided as some people talk now, where the woman does all the housework and the man works outside of the home. Did you all work together?

ES Well, see, he couldn't do much toward helping me in the mornings because he went to work on the morning shift. But we managed, you know. We had an understanding and we managed.

KK How much money did you make at Bell, do you remember?

ES Oh, Lord. It was like a million dollars, my first paycheck—it was about 33 or 34 dollars. I can't tell you the exact amount.

KK For one week?

ES For one week.

KK And what had you been used to being paid?

KK Ten—seven and ten dollars a week.

KK Now it sounds like a very small amount, but at the time, was that enough money for you?

ES It wasn't enough, but we had to manage, you know. No black woman made a whole lot of money. I remember some of our neighbors and friends used to work for five dollars a week.

KK What would a white woman make at that time compared to that?

ES You know, I don't rightly know.

KK But a lot more?

ES But it would be some more, it was a difference.

KK When you went to Bell, do you think black people and white people were paid the same for the same jobs?

ES Well, you know, I'm not sure about that. But I did hear them say that there was a difference—it was a difference in the salaries, but more than what they had been used to making.

KK So as a black woman, you made more than you had made before, but you didn't necessarily make as much money as a white woman at Bell?

ES That's right, that's right. Uh-huh.

KK Well, that was about three times what you were used to making.

ES Yes.

KK I can see that that was a lot of money.

ES Big money, big money—I tell you. And I was proud of it.

DOCUMENT 20
Photograph, *Woman in Kitchen*, 1946, Federal Public Housing Authority

Courtesy of the Library of Congress, LC-USZ62-112356.

After the war, women were expected to give up their jobs in factories to the returning soldiers and resume their roles as wives and mothers. This image reflects the domestic ideal that white, middle-class women were expected to fulfill when their husbands returned from the war.

DOCUMENT 21

Faye Goolrick, "Rosie the Riveter/World War II Home Front National Historical Park Long-Range Interpretive Plan," 2010

Courtesy of the National Park Service.

This historic site was established by the National Park Service in Richmond, California, and seeks to interpret the "stories and places of our nation's home front response to World War II." Excerpts from this interpretive plan explain the goals for the park and its role in interpreting women's history to future generations. This publication was prepared by the National Park Service's Harpers Ferry Interpretive Planning Center.

Introduction

Rosie the Riveter/World War II Home Front National Historical Park, established in 2000, encompasses the nation's largest concentration of intact civilian World War II historic structures and sites. Located within the 1940s historic setting of Richmond, California, in the northeastern section of the San Francisco Bay Area, the park was established to preserve the stories and sites associated with the wide-ranging citizen, industrial, and governmental efforts that supported the nation's war effort during World War II.

World War II home front activities brought about unprecedented changes in American life. With nearly 16 million of the nation's male workforce deployed to military service overseas, millions of other potential workers were encouraged to relocate to centers of industry around the country. Women's roles changed significantly, women and people of color were offered job opportunities formerly denied to them, momentum increased in the continuing struggle for equal rights, and innovations such as employer-sponsored health and child care services began to evolve.

The name "Rosie the Riveter" was made famous by a popular song from 1943, and it quickly became a catchphrase that represented all the women war workers in shipyards, airplane factories, ammunition plants, railroads and other defense plants. As an emblem of the times, "Rosie" symbolized the "We can do it" spirit of the war effort.

A Partnership Park

Rosie the Riveter/World War II Home Front National Historical Park was conceived from the outset as a "partnership park," with the National Park Service functioning as a partner—but significantly, not a landowner—among a loose consortium of other interested parties. These other stakeholders include public agencies (primarily the City of Richmond and Contra Costa County), several not-for-profit organizations, and private owners. While innovative and flexible, this newer approach to preserving and protecting historic sites depends heavily on the financial health, managerial capabilities, and vision of the partners, as well as the resources of the National Park Service.

The Long-Range Interpretive Plan

Within the planning hierarchy of the National Park Service, an individualized 20-year General Management Plan provides broad-based management guidance for each national park unit. The first General Management Plan for Rosie the Riveter/World War II Home Front National Historical Park was finalized in January 2009.

A Comprehensive Interpretive Plan is a critical component of a park's 20-year planning cycle. Unlike the broader scope of the General Management Plan, interpretive planning focuses on identifying and delivering the park's essential stories and messages to visitors. A Long-Range Interpretive Plan provides guidance for a park's interpretive programming for the next seven to ten years. Together with an Annual Implementation Plan and an Interpretive Database, the Long-Range Interpretive Plan completes the park's Comprehensive Interpretive Plan. Accordingly, this Long-Range Interpretive Plan identifies park themes, describes visitor experience goals, and recommends a variety of personal and non-personal interpretive services and outreach activities that will best communicate this park's purpose, significance and themes.

Work on this plan began in February, 2006, when an interpretive planner from the Harpers Ferry Center met with park staff and facilitated initial public workshops and staff meetings in Richmond, California. Subsequently, the park and Harpers Ferry Center sought additional services from a contracted consultant team to complete the plan. The consultant team conducted a second stakeholder open house and workshop on November 18–19, 2008, followed by a recommendations workshop on August 4 and 6, 2009.

Barring legislative changes or major new revelations, the foundational elements expressed in this plan, including purpose, significance, themes, and visitor experience goals, are expected to remain constant over the life of the plan. Specific recommendations about media and programs may need to be updated as staffing, funding, technology, or resource conditions change. Further design documents must be produced to implement some of the goals and recommendations in this plan.

Executive Summary

In the nine years since its establishment on October 24, 2000, Rosie the Riveter/World War II Home Front National Historical Park has built upon existing resources in Richmond, California, to create engaging interpretation for visitors and community residents regarding the nation's home front efforts, and their far reaching consequences, during World War II.

Created as a partnership park with numerous public and private owners dispersed across multiple locations, the park is one of a handful of national parks in which the National Park Service is an administrator and cooperative partner, but not the owner of the physical landscapes and facilities available for visitor exploration. The park's partners include city and county government, arts and cultural heritage organizations, historic preservation groups, private-sector businesses, individual property owners, and not-for-profit community groups.

This Long-Range Interpretive Plan offers a blueprint for developing the park's interpretive program over the next ten years.

Primary Interpretive Themes

To help the National Park Service and its partners provide a cohesive and exciting visitor experience for the park's diverse future audience, the planning team reviewed the primary themes and subthemes proposed in the park's recent General Management Plan and, with minor amendments, adopted them as guidance for interpretive planning for the park over the next ten years.

These four primary interpretive themes can be summed up as follows:

- Mobilizing America

  As millions of soldiers left home to fight in World War II, millions of other Americans mobilized on the home front to support the war effort in ways that resulted in profound changes to American life.

- Common Purpose / Disparate Experience

  Although many Americans working and living on the home front were united in a common purpose to support the war effort, they often had quite disparate experiences due to prejudice and discrimination.

- Shedding Light on America's Promise

  Social upheavals and social role changes on the home front exposed America's unfulfilled promise of equality and "liberty and justice for all."

- America Today—The Home Front Legacy

  Many technological innovations, institutional changes and social developments that took place on the World War II home front have had lasting influence and continue to be relevant today.

Recommendations for Interpretation

This Long-Range Interpretive Plan presents a strategic, sequential interpretive framework to help the park and its partners prioritize their interpretive efforts over the short, mid- and long term. Much will depend on the successful rehabilitation and adaptive reuse of various sites and facilities that are not owned by the National Park Service. However, community stakeholders and the planning team envision a compelling, inspirational interpretive program using these key elements:

- enthusiastic, well-trained interpreters (both National Park Service and partners) offering accessible programs at various locations throughout the park;

- a new visitor education center with engaging, hands-on interactive exhibits appealing to many different learning styles and with numerous artifacts on display;

- outreach to the community, the region, and the nation through innovative approaches such as the "Rosie's Girls" youth program, a "Roving Rosie" interpretive bus/van, and a virtual network connecting home front sites and resources throughout the nation; and

- a strategic mix of tools and techniques enabling self-guided exploration of the park, including

  - prominent wayfinding/identity signs

  - printed tour maps/brochures

  - interpretive signs at numerous sites

  - library holdings with some level of visitor access (perhaps in cooperation with county/city public libraries)

  - visitor-accessible displays inside various historic buildings

  - state-of-the-art electronic resources (interpretive programming, mapping, tour information) for pre-visit or on-site/on-demand download via personal media devices.

Wherever possible, these interpretive programming steps should be taken with the following priorities in mind:

First, a local focus: Over the short term (1 to 3 years), interpretive programming will focus on the four primary themes and also seek to build up the park's local, community-based identity and involvement, including youth outreach, training volunteers, and helping strengthen partnership organizations.

Next, outreach to the region: Mid-range goals (4 to 6 years) address the four primary interpretive themes while also increasing the park's interpretive outreach and presence throughout the Bay Area.

Then, a national presence: Long-term goals (7 to 10 years) will focus on activities that address the four primary interpretive themes while also expanding the park's national presence through a national web presence (including interactive mapping of relevant sites), traveling exhibits, liaisons with other parks/sites that tell parts of the home front story, and similar activities.

CHAPTER 2

New Opportunities, New Challenges

Although many women moved into industrial labor during the war, opportunities in white-collar jobs also expanded for women. Far and away the largest employer of women was the federal government. "Government girls," as they were popularly known, stood one million strong (over one-third of all civil service workers) by the end of the war. For the first time, the government opened professionally classified jobs that had been the domain of men. Women also moved into other kinds of professional work, despite male assumptions about women's lack of ability in these fields. Women seeking medical and law degrees doubled, for example, and they moved into the fields of engineering, banking, insurance, and business administration. Though clerical work, widely considered a female occupation, also expanded, women broke through traditionally male professions in numbers previously unseen. The documents in this section examine the growth of women in professional work and illustrate the struggle women faced in their new positions.

DOCUMENT 22

Table, "Women as Proportion of All Workers, by Occupational Status, 1940–1947"

Courtesy of the US Department of Labor.

The Department of Labor studied and charted women's labor under the auspices of the Women's Bureau, which still exists today. Frances Perkins, who served as secretary of labor from 1933 to 1945, was the first woman to be to be appointed to the US Cabinet. This 1953 table compares changes in women's work in professional and industrial labor from 1940 to 1947.

TABLE. Women as proportion of all workers,
by occupational status, 1940–1947

OCCUPATION	1940 (%)	1945(%)	1947 (%)
Professional	45.5	46.5	39.9
Managerial	11.7	17.4	13.5
Clerical	52.6	70.3	58.6
Sales	27.9	54.1	39.9
All white collar	35.8	49.6	38.9
Craftsman, foreman, Skilled	2.1	4.4	2.1
Factory operative	25.7	38.3	28.1
Domestic service	93.8	93.8	92.3
Other service	40.1	47.8	43.6
All blue collar	26.2	31.7	24.6
Agriculture	8.0	22.4	11.8
All occupations	25.9	36.0	27.9

Source: Women's Bureau, Women as Workers, A Statistical Guide (Washington, D.C., 1953), pp. 15–17.

DOCUMENT 23

Table, "Black Women's Employment Status, 1940–1947," *Monthly Labor Review*, 1947

Courtesy of the US Department of Labor.

World War II brought new opportunities for African American women, but racial prejudice in hiring practices remained staunchly in place. In part because of President Franklin D. Roosevelt's initiatives to implement safeguards with the Fair Employment Practices Commission (see chapter 1, document 3), black women made gains in industrial work, but their numbers in professional work remained static.

TABLE. Black women's employment patterns, 1940–1947

	1940 (PERCENT OF	1944 (PERCENT OF	1947 (PERCENT OF
Occupation	1,656,000[a])	2,345,000[a])	2,086,000[a])
Professional	4.1	4.2	4.8
Other white collar	1.7	4.6	5.7
Industry	5.8	17.6	17.3
Domestic service	57.0	43.7	44.5
Other service	10.4	18.9	20.5
Agriculture	20.9	10.9	7.2

Source: Seymour L. Wolfbein, "Postwar Trends in Negro Employment," Monthly Labor Review 65 (December 1947), 664.

[a]*Total number of black women workers.*

DOCUMENT 24

Excerpt from "Women's Employment in Aircraft Assembly Plants in 1942," by Ethel Erickson, US Department of Labor, *Bulletin of the Women's Bureau*, No. 192-1, 1942

Courtesy of the National Archives, Atlanta.

The Women's Bureau released narrative reports on women's work in a range of industries. In coverage of women in aircraft plants, author Ethel Erickson took account of professional work in wartime industries. Classified as "nonproductive," this work included clerical jobs and there were a small number of engineers.

FACTORY CLERICAL AND NONPRODUCTIVE JOBS

Factory clerks in aircraft plants in normal times were almost all men, and at the time of this study men still were the preponderant group. As would be expected, women are steadily coming into the factory clerical jobs as substitutes for men in larger numbers, but the influx seemed to be chiefly in the typing, stenographic, and general factory clerk activities. A small number of women were employed as production clerks in planning and control divisions but preference still was for men. Few women were timekeepers. Experience has demonstrated that women can serve as stock- and tool-room clerks, as has been noted, and more may be employed as the labor market is further depleted of men. With the increase of women on the force, it seems a natural sequence that the number of women in personnel administration should increase.

Training courses have been established to train women as scientific and engineering aides. A few women engineers—an average of less than one to a plant—were pointed out, and an occasional woman was making architectural or prospective drawings of new plane models and parts. Drafting aides—tracers and letterers—had a few women representatives. Women with some engineering training or mechanical-drawing ability and a mathematical background were reported as possibilities for engineering aides to draw diagrams for parts. In the weight-control and stress-analysis divisions of engineering, many mathematical computations are made and a few women have been admitted to the ranks, but many more women who have a background in mathematics and short courses of special training in aerodynamics should find opportunities for war-production jobs. Girls who in their schooldays had a flair for descriptive geometry, trigonometry, and graphic production methods should be useful in lofting.

SUPERVISORS

Supervision of women by women in the aircraft plants is still a moot question. Management often tended to shy off when questioned about the policy toward and possibilities of women supervisors with a statement that women prefer to be directed by, and work better with, men bosses. A few women supervisors were found in fabric divisions and as leadwomen in electrical, small assembly, and inspection, and these were reported as satisfactory. Most women have as yet not had enough experience in the industry to be in a position to take supervisory jobs that require a proficiency in the work of their department and an all-round knowledge of the processes involved.

DOCUMENT 25
Photograph, *Santa Anita (California), a Young Evacuee (Japanese American Woman) Serves as Secretary of the Center Manager's Office*, ca. 1942

Courtesy of the Library of Congress, LC-USZ62-91982.

Japanese American internment, covered in depth in chapter 5, affected 120,000 people of Japanese descent, the majority of them US citizens. Within the assembly centers and "relocation" camps, some women internees could find work, including clerical work for the Wartime Civilian Control Agency and the War Relocation Authority (the government agencies that supervised the assembly centers and camps, respectively).

DOCUMENT 26
Eleanor Roosevelt, "My Day," February 23, 1945

Courtesy of the Estate of Eleanor Roosevelt, Eleanor Roosevelt Papers Project.

First Lady Eleanor Roosevelt (1884–1962) was known as an outspoken advocate for equal treatment of women (among her many causes in the realm of human rights). Like her husband, President Franklin D. Roosevelt, she was savvy in her use of media to communicate these views to the American public. Her daily column, "My Day," started in 1936, charted her public service work in the 1930s and 1940s and allowed her to champion women's rights in a popular format.

WASHINGTON, Thursday—Yesterday afternoon about thirty men from the naval hospital in Bethesda, Md., came to visit the White House. Afterwards I had some people interested in veterans' education, and a gentleman who is shortly going back to Paris, in for tea.

Early this morning I left for New York City where I am going to speak at the children's unity festival at the Horace Mann School.

• • •

Last night and tonight I have been free—that is to say, I have been able to do my mail and catch up on personal letters and even do a little reading, so that I hope, in the course of the next few days, to be able to tell you about two books which I have enjoyed in my leisure time.

• • •

Every now and then I am reminded that even though the need for being a feminist is gradually disappearing in this country, we haven't quite reached the millenium.

A woman who went down to testify before one of the Congressional committees, the other day, wrote me an interesting fact on the man-power situation. It appears that the Civil Service Commission has a number of women who could be filling higher positions in the government if the requisitions from government agencies did not usually specify "men only." Perhaps this is another hurdle which we must jump in this period when women are really needed to replace men. We must accept qualified women for positions which in the past have been offered to men, even through civil service.

It looks to me also as though some special consideration should be given to women with husbands in military service, particularly to those whose husbands are missing. It is, of course, not necessary to give them any special preference—they should be capable of doing the jobs which they hold. But they need the jobs very badly, and where they could be appointed without lowering the standards of the Civil Service for those jobs, it seems they might be given some extra consideration.

• • •

It is interesting to find so often the little ways in which women are discriminated against, but with the passage of the years one does find a great improvement. One must not let this improvement, however, lull one to complete oblivion, for when the war is over there will be new situations to meet and they must be met with open minds and with fairness to both men and women.

Even the children will have to come in for consideration, so we will have to keep a broad and tolerant attitude and be willing to discuss new situations and reach conclusions which will be beneficial to all those involved.

E. R.

DOCUMENT 27
Photograph, Washington, D.C., *Telephone Operators at Telegraph Office*, 1943

Courtesy of the Library of Congress, LCUSW3-032335-E.

The women in this photograph were part of the force of women workers known as "government girls." World War II opened up to women clerical jobs in the government previously only held by men. Though they received less pay than their male counterparts, government work provided women a pay scale and benefits (such as pensions) that other types of work did not offer. This image was taken by Esther Bubley (1921–1988), who, in 1943, was a new documentary photographer at the Office of War Information. Bubley went on to become an award-winning photojournalist.

DOCUMENT 28
Letter Excerpts, Patricia Murphy to James B. Taylor Jr., 1942

Courtesy of Patricia Taylor Mosier.

Patricia Murphy (1918–2006) was a young woman living in New York City during the war. She wrote often to her future husband, James B. Taylor Jr., who worked as an engineer building Quonset huts in Newfoundland, Canada, before he enlisted in the US Army.

Murphy's letters to Taylor are illustrative of everyday life during the war but also of the opportunities open to middle-class women. At the beginning of the war she worked for a sports-advertising firm on Madison Avenue, but as jobs opened elsewhere she moved to stenographic work for the Federal Bureau of Investigation. She flirted with joining the navy auxiliary unit, the WAVES, until her mother's disapproval stopped her.

April 11, 1942

My dear Jim,

You will have to excuse the school notepaper but I have been out of all of my "deckle edge" and in rummaging through the drawers this was all I could find. However maybe the lines will make the writing more legible.

I left my nice easy job last Tuesday night and took Wednesday off. Now I'm sorry that I didn't take a vacation until Monday. That probably sounds "give in-ish" but honestly I feel as if I'll never catch up on sleep.

I started down at the U.S. Court House where the F.B.I. is located on Thursday morning. The hours are 9–5:30—6 days a week—almost as bad as your Newfoundland schedule. The work is quite different from what I've been doing—not difficult but everything seems quite involved. I suppose that I really haven't given myself time to catch on yet. . . .

I felt much better today though and I think I'll get used to it gradually. Helen Henning . . . who is down in the same office with me said— "You'll be alright, you're just working for a change"—and I think she's right.

All those jokes about "the working girl" have come true. . . .

August 8, 1942

My dear Jim,

I'm quite disgusted with myself because a letter that I wrote to you Wednesday came back today for additional postage. I don't know, but I don't seem to have the Postal regulations down yet and I've been writing you for over a year. . . .

It's something like the "rating" basis that you were talking about when you were home. Down at work, you do a stenographer's work but you only have a typist's rating and that means $1620 a year. Then when you pass the stenographic test like I did about 3 weeks ago you get a stenographic rating and your salary becomes $1800. So that's has happened to me. Isn't that good? I'm kind of happy about it. . . .

August 22, 1942

My dear Jim,

. . . Things are getting pretty tight regarding the Draft. I suppose you've seen the papers and know that they're going to reclassify all married men. Rita Weber expects Jay to be going soon and is contemplating joining the WAVES. Gee, college graduates can get commissions that pay the same salaries that men get and I think you train at Smith College. How would you like to see me in an Ensign's uniform? Or maybe I'd be smart and get to be a Lieutenant. There's a lot to it and there's a stipulation that the WAVES do not leave the country! Maybe I'd be sent to Newfoundland or would that be leaving the country??!!!

August 30, 1942

My dear Jim,

. . . Frank [Murphy's brother] came up this evening and we began to discuss me and the WAVE situation. My mother became quite violent because she thought I was more serious than I really was. The set-up does seem pretty nice though—a three month training period at Smith College and then a Commission as an Ensign with the guarantee that you won't be sent across. And WAVES are allowed to get married, too. However, my mother didn't take very kindly to the idea and in fact, let off quite some steam over it, so it's practically a dead issue.

DOCUMENT 29
Poem, "Civil Service," by Constance C. Nichols, Printed in *The Crisis*, April 1945

Courtesy of the NAACP.

Though some African American women found employment in civil service and clerical work, they often encountered hostility on the job from white coworkers and managers. In her poem,

Constance Nichols captures the irony of working in civil defense, ostensibly for a common goal, and encountering the kind of race prejudice that underlined some of the most undemocratic practices, such as segregation laws, that existed in the United States.

My desk sits facing yours across the floor,

Yet your fair head is stiffly held aloof

From my own darker one, though 'neath our roof

With one accord we do a job. For war

Has linked us as no pleading could before.

Yet, seemingly, you wait for further proof

That we are spun the same . . . the warp and woof

Of new, strong fabric, draped at Freedom's door . . .

For you are still reluctant to obey

The impulse that would bring you to my side;

You send your memos on a metal tray,

And coldly killed each overture I've tried.

Why hope to rid charred continents of gloom

'Till we have learned to smile across a room?

DOCUMENT 30

Beulah V. McDowell, Complaint to the President's Committee on Fair Employment Practice, March 18, 1944

Courtesy of the National Archives, Atlanta.

In 1941, President Franklin D. Roosevelt established the Fair Employment Practices Commission (FEPC) as part of his effort to end discriminatory hiring practices in US industries with government contracts. Part of that agency's role was to accept and monitor complaints from workers who experienced discrimination in hiring, work assignment, or firing practices. Beulah V. McDowell issued such a complaint in Atlanta, Georgia, in 1944, noting a failure in the Civil Service Commission, Atlanta, to refer her to jobs in that city. She was told that Atlanta had no open jobs—in reality, civil service jobs were often reserved for whites in the segregated South—and was referred to Washington, D.C.

Question 8. *Detailed statement of the facts supporting your complaint. (Why do you believe you have been discriminated against? Give name and title of person you dealt with and dates of conferences. State your qualifications briefly. Are there other members of your minority group employed? If so, in what capacities?)*

Passed examination for clerical position in December 1943. She was directed to note on her application that she wished to work in Washington. Person giving examination said "You understand this will be for work in Washington. There is nothing available for you in Atlanta." Complainant was only Negro taking examination.

Complainant has been called in to Civil Service and offered work in Washington, but she is unable to go—so she wishes to work in Atlanta. Receptionist in Civil Service office in Ten Forsyth St. Bldg. directed her to this office.

Complainant worked for six months in Washington in Civil Service position in War Department. She started in CAF 2 and finished in CAF 4. She had to stop work in Washington because of illness, but she is completely well now.

Complainant is graduate of Atlanta University, having done work on Master's degree at New York University, so she feels she is well qualified for government clerical position.

DOCUMENT 31
Oral History, Ada Glasser Bloom, November 18, 1996

Courtesy of the Rutgers University Oral History Archives.

Ada Glasser Bloom was born in New Jersey and educated at Douglass College in library science. In 1941 she took a job in New York City as a film librarian in Pathe Films' newsreel division and was later film librarian for the Office of War Information (OWI), an agency created by Franklin D. Roosevelt in 1942 to manage wartime information. Here she reflects on the OWI's need for professionals, her work there during the war, and life in New York with a roommate who was a professional writer and also married to a soldier.

Interviewer: You worked for the Office of War Information. How did you go from Pathe News to . . .

Bloom: Well, they were, people in my field were really sought after, at that time, because there were very few of us who were professional librarians who also trained as film librarians. There were a lot of clerks, but there were very few professionals. And one of the divisions of the Office of War Information was their overseas motion picture division. It was not stationed overseas, but they handled the overseas distribution and production of films for overseas. And they were looking for someone to establish their film library. And I don't know how I heard about it. Possibly somebody who came into the library mentioned it. And I was looking for a more responsible position, 'cause I had gone as far as I could. My supervisor, my boss had left and her job was open, but I looked very young. I looked like a baby and I was rather offended, because they gave that position to someone else who I didn't feel was as well qualified. And I wasn't just gonna leave. But I felt that if there was a good opening, I would leave for it. And sure enough, I heard about this position and I applied. And they were very anxious to have me, and it took a long time, because the agency wasn't even totally established yet, and then, of course, I had to be cleared and everything. Not that the work was that confidential, but during the war, I guess, anybody who worked for the government had to have a good, clean record.

Interviewer: Did the FBI investigate you?

Bloom: No, no, that they . . . Not that I'm aware of.

Interviewer: You didn't have that kind of clearance?

Bloom: No, I didn't have that kind of clearance. Because it wasn't, I wasn't doing anything that was that confidential. And, I guess, I left Pathe News in the spring of 1943. When I took the job, I said, "You know, I'm gonna have to have time off this summer, because I'm getting married." And they said, "Well, don't worry about it. Do whatever you have to do." And I worked there until 1946, until Lew returned. And I set up their library for them and managed it and it was a very busy job, because they used to receive a lot of the foreign overseas footage of the war activity. And also a lot of the captured film. And that's what we would catalog. And we would service the same type of people that we served at Pathe News. In fact, our library, you wouldn't call it competition, but actually, we were doing a lot of the services that Pathe News had done before. Pathe News would come to us, actually, for a lot of footage.

Interviewer: Which must have made you feel good.

Bloom: It did. It made me feel good, because a lot of the people I worked with, came to me now, and I had to help them.

Interviewer: Yeah, and there's such a direct . . .

Bloom: Well, there were very few people, really, who were qualified to do it.

Interviewer: How many people did you supervise? It sounds like you had a lot.

Bloom: No, at OWI really not. I had, I worked with a lot of people. But I had only one person under me who did a lot of my clerical work for me.

Interviewer: So you were responsible for watching most of these films.

Bloom: I had, I watched them and wrote up the descriptions and cataloged them. And then, one person [who] was directly responsible to me was sort of my, I guess, secretary. But then, there were other people who did the actual storage of the film for me. But I didn't have any direct supervision over them. They were supervised. It was, if you know anything about government agencies, there's a lot of supervisors, I should say. But I had no problems. You know, we were all very cooperative. We all knew we were working for the war effort.

Interviewer: In your previous job, you would watch one film a week of the newsreel and you would catalog them.

Bloom: That was it, yeah.

Interviewer: Whereas here, it seemed like you got a lot more.

Bloom: Oh, we were always behind here, because there was a lot more coming in than we could possibly handle. We didn't have a bigger staff because there just wasn't the money for it.

Interviewer: So how many films could you catalog in one week?

Bloom: You mean how many feet?

Interviewer: Yeah.

Bloom: Probably, whatever the same amount of footage a newsreel would have, so we were often behind, and what would happen is, many times, other directors and producers who were working there, and film editors, would see a lot of the material that came in that wasn't cataloged yet and they would say, "Well, they'd like to get their hands on something that they knew they had seen." And I would try and dig it out. You know, I would, by knowing what period the film covered or what area it covered, I was often able to pick out for them what they were looking for.

Interviewer: But you were also watching these films in different languages.

Bloom: Yes, true. Yeah.

Interviewer: How did you catalog those?

Bloom: Well, I just had to do it by describing what I saw, not so much [by] what I heard. Actually, you're more interested in the image, because a lot of the foreign film that was captured, was propaganda film.

Interviewer: It's curious that you were looking at all these different films.

Bloom: Well, I tried to identify things as best I could I guess. If I couldn't identify them, you know, I just describe what I saw. Three motored plane.

Interviewer: What did you think of all these propaganda films you were watching?

Bloom: By following the war reports in our own media, I recognized the enemy's attempts to make it appear that we were losing the war. Well, actually most of what I saw, I saw some propaganda film, but not that much. Most of what we got in, was the war footage, that war film footage that was taken by Army photographers.

I don't think the OWI had their own photographers, but other government agencies did.

Interviewer: Where were you located?

Bloom: We were in the old Pathe News building, which I had been so glad to get away from. We were at 35 West 45th Street. And that's where my first office was, with Pathe News, before they moved to Madison Avenue. Well, they moved there because all the facilities were there for them. The film vaults were already there, the projection room was there. All their editorial, editor rooms were there.

Interviewer: What did the Office of War Information actually do?

Bloom: The office I was with produced propaganda films and documentaries for overseas and, of course, very often they would use some of the stock shots that we had cataloged. There was also the Domestic Bureau of the OWI, which was located on West 57th Street in New York City. I believe that that office handled much of the printed materials that were distributed to other areas of communication.

·   ·   ·

Interviewer: So who did you report to?

Bloom: I reported to a person by the name of (Irving Lerner?), who really hired me. Now, of course, he had people over him that he reported to, who, I think, were probably stationed in Washington. Our unit in West 45thStreet was strictly the overseas motion picture division. But we answered to somebody in Washington.

Interviewer: Now did your unit make . . .

Bloom: Yes, they produced newsreels, and, I think, some training films, not too many, and, of course, films for propaganda.

Interviewer: Were you aware of what was going on or were you just simply so busy with your cataloging that you really didn't know how the rest of your division was working?

Bloom: I didn't know too much. I, how should I put it? There were no secrets or anything, but it's true [that] I was very busy. I knew what each editor was working on at the time. And I didn't always know who else was working on it with them, who was doing the commentating and the commentaries and who was doing the final, making the final decisions on what remains in the film and what ends up on the cutting room floor. So I didn't get too involved, really, I guess, because I was so absorbed in what I was doing.

Interviewer: Did you ever watch some of the products that they produced?

Bloom: Yes.

Interviewer: Would you catalog those, too?

Bloom: No, those wouldn't be cataloged. No, no. It would be impossible to get all that done. Sometimes, I would see the finished product, but not always. I mean, I could, anytime I wanted to, I didn't have to wait for an invitation. But most of the time, I just didn't have time.

Interviewer: It sounds like you had a lot of work on your hands.

Bloom: We had very little time, and that's why I worked nights for, very often, I would work at night to do the viewing. Because if somebody else was using the projection room during the day, I couldn't get into it, so I would have to do it at night. And I didn't mind.

Interviewer: And you worked a full day.

Bloom: Oh, yeah, and it was six days a week, too.

Interviewer: Oh, very interesting.

Bloom: It was Monday through Saturday, And holidays, we never had a holiday off.

Interviewer: Did your pay go up?

Bloom: At Pathe News, we used to get our dinner paid for. We never got overtime, we got our dinner paid for. I think they would give us three and a half dollars for dinner. And at OWI, I didn't know until many years later, that I could have put in for overtime and I never did. My bosses never told me. Yes, yeah.

Interviewer: And you didn't get dinner?

Bloom: No, no, it was on my own.

Interviewer: But you also knew that this was helping with the war.

Bloom: Oh, yeah, I was very dedicated to what I was doing. I wouldn't have wanted to do anything else.

Interviewer: You mentioned that you had a roommate in New York. Where did she work?

Bloom: She worked for one of the magazines that, in the apparel trade. I can't remember the name of it, but she was a writer. And we got along beautifully because her husband was also overseas. And we didn't know one another before.

Interviewer: How did you meet her?

Bloom: We had a mutual friend. My mutual friend Madeline had gone to Michigan with Rhoda. And Madeline was supposed to move in with Rhoda, but I needed an apartment, I didn't have any place to go. So, Madeline said, "Well, look, you need it more than I do," because Madeline was still living at home with her parents, I grew up with Madeline. She said, "Why don't you move in with Rhoda, and then when you find an apartment, you know, I'll take over." Well, Rhoda and I got along so well. Madeline wasn't married, and Rhoda decided that she and I had a lot more in common and it was a very friendly decision. Madeline took it very, very graciously. She agreed, she thought it was a good idea. And we are very close friends to this day.

Interviewer: And you really did have a lot in common, because you were both married.

Bloom: That's right. Both married, and our husbands were both overseas. We had no children. She had a very responsible job. We were both very, very involved professionally and it worked out beautifully.

DOCUMENT 32

Photograph, *All-American Girls Professional Baseball League Members Performing Calisthenics, Opa-locka, Florida,* 1948

Courtesy of the State Archives of Florida.

During the war, a new professional opportunity opened for women who had athletic skill—that of baseball. Professional baseball teams lost many of their players to the front lines, and sports managers turned to women to continue American's favorite pastime. In 1943 they began recruiting women from many backgrounds to the All-American Girls Softball League, which soon after was called the All-American Girls Professional Baseball League. Teams such as the Racine Belles and the Rockford Peaches won crowds of baseball fans across the country. The league continued until 1953. This 1948 photograph depicts the same kinds of uniforms women wore during the war and demonstrates that the league outlasted wartime necessity.

DOCUMENT 33

Oral History Excerpt, Ann Petrovic, Grand Valley State University Veterans History Project, All-American Girls Professional Baseball League Collection

Courtesy of Grand Valley State University.

Though the All-American Girls Professional Baseball League fulfilled the dreams of some women athletes to play ball, they did not have the freedom of male professional players. Their actions when traveling for games were monitored (for example, they were accompanied by chaperones when visiting cities away from home) and they were pressured to attend charm school. In this interview, Ann Petrovic reflects on this insistence on femininity within the league. This aspect of women's professional ball was dramatized in a popular 1992 Hollywood film, *A League of Their Own.*

Interviewer: "When you joined the league, did they give you a list of all the rules and regulations and how you were supposed to behave and the way you were supposed to dress?"

Petrovic: Oh yes, you had to be in at ten o'clock and when you're in your own home town, of course, you're always with a family and there's always two of you. They never go in with one person, so they did put me with a roommate and get me a place to stay in the town where we stayed, like in Minneapolis or Kenosha.

Interviewer: "Did they have a dress code that you had to follow?"

Petrovic: Oh yes and you've heard this a hundred times, you had to wear a skirt. You could wear shorts inside when nobody saw you, but you had to wear that skirt and dress up when you would go outside. Both of us never smoked, but you couldn't smoke or anything like that and you had to dress up when you went out into public, and they had the charm school. When they had the charm school they looked at me and they picked me out of that whole bunch and used me as an example. I just came up and I wasn't the type to—I was a tomboy anyway—dress up anyway, and they would say "Ann you come up here, we're going to use you," so they fixed my hair and fixed me all up and I was a little embarrassed. I was only fifteen you know, and never been—anyway, they used me as an example when they had the charm school. They would teach you how to walk and how to sit and when you go to someone's home they wanted you to be ladies—to be ladies and play like men, that's what they wanted me to do, so that's what I did.

DOCUMENT 34
Photograph, *Joan Crawford as Mildred Pierce*, 1945

Courtesy of the Wisconsin Historical Society.

Hollywood deserves credit for depicting the challenges of professional women in the 1940s. The film *Mildred Pierce* (starring Joan
Crawford) dramatized the life of a woman who, to support her
two daughters as a single mother, became a successful proprietor
of a Southern California restaurant. Her success, however, comes
with a price: the death of one daughter and the loss of the other
to greed and social climbing. Though the movie is notable for
creating a central role for a professional woman, it also suggests
that danger would befall women who tried to succeed without
the help of a man.

DOCUMENT 35

Letter, Lt. Colonel Harold Rorke to Toni Frissell, May 1, 1945

Courtesy of the Library of Congress.

The war opened new opportunities for women journalists and photographers, many of whom had been relegated to covering women's fashion and society columns in mainstream newspapers. By 1945, in fact, 127 women reporters and photographers were officially covering the war overseas for the US military. Toni Frissell (1907–1988) was one such woman photojournalist, and this letter from Lt. Colonel Harold Rorke of the Army Air Corps highlights the roles that women played in capturing scenes from the front lines.

Miss Toni Frissell,
480 Lexington Avenue,
New York, New York

Dear Miss Frissell,

It is indeed good news that you have returned from your tour of the European combat area. The photographs which preceded your return have all been reviewed and cleared for publication by the War Department. They represent as fine a set of pictures as has been our pleasure to inspect for a long time. It looks as though you will be among the most valuable collaborators the AAF can number from all the "guests" we have taken overseas to help us get our story not only told, but understood.

It is hoped that you will be able to make prints appropriate for publication purpose as soon as possible, because it is my opinion it would be greatly to the advantage of the military service and the war effort as a whole to have your work presented promptly to the Nation. The edge will go off the story if there is much delay and the value of our joint effort will be lost. That would be a sad end for an enterprise in which the AAF has so much invested—all those special planes we arranged to fly you here and there and all that collateral extra effort expended to get the material each of the several AF generals in Europe considered so vital.

You may rely upon this office for whatever special services you require to expedite our part of the process of getting your European photographs published.

Congratulations for a fine job.

Sincerely,

[signed]
Harold B. Rorke
Lt. Col., Air Corps
Acting Assistant to Director for Army Air Forces.

DOCUMENT 36
Officer's Identification Card, Antoinette Frissell Bacon, 1942

Courtesy of the Library of Congress, LC-USZ62-128566.

Photojournalists working for the armed forces were commissioned as officers in the branch they were serving so that, in the event of their capture, they would not be identified as a spy. Toni Frissell began her career as a fashion photographer for *Bazaar* and *Vogue* and became a photojournalist during the war. This officer card presents her picture and fingerprints.

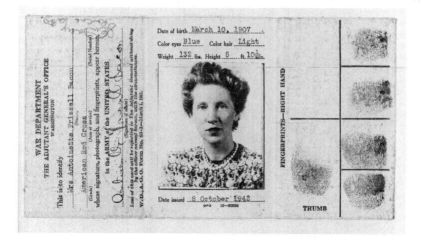

DOCUMENT 37

Photograph, *War Correspondent May Craig with a Flight Crew in England*, 1944

Courtesy of the Library of Congress, LC-USZ62-125636.

May Craig (1889–1975) had a distinguished career as a news correspondent and, when she died in 1975, she was heralded by President Gerald Ford as a "pioneer in American journalism." She was the president of the Women's National Press Club during most of the war and served during those years as a war and overseas correspondent for several Maine-based newspapers. In the photo, she surveys maps with a US flight crew in England.

DOCUMENT 38
Comic Book, *Photo Fighter*, 1944

*Courtesy of the Library of Congress, LC-USZC4-9007,
LC-USZC4-9008, LC-USZC4-9009.*

Women photojournalists became heroines in their own day. Their popularity is captured in the comic book *Photo Fighter*, which tells the story of Thérèse Bonney (1894–1978). Bonney, an American who moved to France in 1919, began covering the European war in 1940, deciding it was her mission to "get the truth and then bring it back and try to make others face it and do something about it."

Document 38

She published photo essays in popular magazines and launched exhibitions of her work at the Library of Congress and Museum of Modern Art.

Document 38

DOCUMENT 39
Photograph, *Flight Nurse with Wounded*, by Dickey Chapelle, 1945

Courtesy of the Wisconsin Historical Society.

Dickey Chapelle (1918–1965) began her photojournalism career during the war. Born Georgette Louise Meyer, she graduated from high school with a full scholarship to Massachusetts Institute of

Technology. While there, she developed a love for photography and journalism and soon left school to pursue a career in New York. During the war, she traveled to Panama and Iwo Jima to photograph naval operations as well as the work of flight nurses. After World War II, her career continued into the 1970s. She was fatally wounded by a Vietcong mine in Vietnam in 1965, making her the first woman photojournalist to be killed in action.

DOCUMENT 40

Excerpt, Testimony of Dr. Emily Barringer, Hearings before the Committee on Military Affairs, House of Representatives, on H.R. 824 and H.R. 1857 (the Sparkman Act), 1943

Courtesy of Drexel University College of Medicine, Archives and Special Collections.

H.R. 824 and H.R. 1857, named for sponsoring senator John Sparkman, provided for the commission of women physicians in the US military. In the hearings, women doctors played a crucial role in advocating for the passage of the act—none more so than Dr. Emily Dunning Barringer (1876–1961). Barringer was a well-known surgeon from New York who had earned her medical degree in 1901. Here she related examples of the discrimination women doctors faced in serving the military.

Dr. Barringer: The next case must remain anonymous for various reasons. But the physician involved is a woman of similar splendid education and special training . . . and [she] has done anesthesia for 15 years. In one of the military camps there was a shortage of anesthetists and this physician was asked to give anesthesia. She was employed on a non civil service basis, and was not even offered a contact surgeon appointment, but was classified as a special technician.

The further details of her job are as follows: A 48-hour week with a salary of $150 a month, out of which she must pay her own living expenses. She was allowed to buy her own gasoline at Army prices and pay for her own lunches in the officers' mess hall at 22 cents a day. In addition to giving anesthesia to the military patients, she was instructor of groups of corpsmen, who take a 3 months course in anesthesia. As to insurance, she received only compensation insurance while on the grounds. She wears no uniform and has no rank. Again, if this woman physician were a member of the Medical Corps, she would undoubtedly be a major. And right here I would like to ask one question. Supposing your son or mine were out in some emergency hospital with some terrible war injury, where his chance for life might be only one in a thousand, would you not prefer having the skill and experience and cool nerves of either of these trained women giving him anesthesia rather than a well-intentioned, clumsy, inexperienced, recent graduate who might otherwise do it?

Mr. Harness. You do not use that as a reflection up on the present Medical Corps, do you?

Dr. Barringer. May I finish what I am saying about education, because it has its repercussions, and answer that later?

Mr. Harness. Yes.

Dr. Barringer. No one who has not faced the possibilities of life and death in major surgery can possibly realize what a difference a trained and experienced anesthetist makes to the operating surgeon. My last case deals with a repercussion of the other three cases and has to do with the incoming medical students. Because women physicians are not eligible to the Medical Reserve Corps of the United States Army, certain of the medical schools are cutting down or refusing their usual quota of positions to women physicians. The University of Arkansas attempted this last fall and the dean frankly admitted this was the reason. Such a mighty protest from the alumni followed that this order was rescinded and women are now taken again. But my case No. 4 assures me that she is having greatest difficulty in getting into any medical school in her vicinity, which is Midwest, and that she has been informed that three of well known coeducational universities in that section have been asked to bar women students for the duration. This young woman and a number of others writing me stress the fact that the Government is allowing a subsidy to its male medical students to complete their medical education while this is not allowed its women students. It is not necessary for me to draw your attention to the fact that if this state of affairs continues, it will not be long before the women medical students will begin to deteriorate and the position of the woman physician will slip backward from the high plane of accomplishment which she enjoys today after a hundred-year struggle for her right to exist.

Mr. Durham. Has the question you have mentioned been taken up with the educational committee, which at the present time is giving these allotments to colleges throughout the country?

Dr. Barringer. This matter has just come to my attention very recently. You see, as chairman of this committee, I have been receiving letters from all over the United States, and this is a situation that has just recently been brought to my attention.

Mr. Durham. If I understand your statement correctly, you are entirely barred from the colleges of the country?

Dr. Barringer. No; there is a struggle, a tendency toward that.

Mr. Johnson. Has any one college barred you women?

Dr. Barringer. Arkansas State tried to. They did it for a while, because no women were admitted in the fall to the University of Arkansas, and there was such a fuss made that the order had to be rescinded.

Mr. Merritt. Has the Manpower Commission at any time made reference to women?

Dr. Barringer. May I make the final statement? Then I shall be glad to answer your questions.

Mr. Merritt. Certainly.

Dr. Barringer. In concluding, I wish to stress two facts: The women physicians of American know their womanpower and what ability and talents they have ready to give their beloved country in this time of terrible urgency. They have made a coast-to-coast registration of all women physicians available. When Mr. McNutt called for 5,000 doctors for July 1 of last year, the women physicians were ready to furnish their quota and would immediately have volunteered if they had been allowed to do so. In the hard struggle ahead every physician, man or woman, will be needed. We ask you to remove all sex discrimination and to let us go forward as free women, able to respond to any duty that calls us, and have our individual qualifications for our work the only criteria. In order to be able to do this, we must have equal opportunities, privileges, and protection that the state accords its men physicians. We, therefore, earnestly request full membership in the Medical Corps of the United States Army.

DOCUMENT 41
Correspondence, Barbara Stimson, MD, to American Women's Hospitals, January 27, 1942

Courtesy of Drexel University College of Medicine, Archives and Special Collections.

Barbara Stimson (1898–1986) was a noted orthopedic surgeon and the first woman admitted to the New York Surgical Society. When she was denied the chance to serve in the US military as a surgeon, Stimson successfully joined the Royal Army Medical

Corps in Great Britain, where she stayed for the duration of the war. She eventually traveled to North Africa and Italy with the Medical Corps and rejected an offer to return to the United States to serve in the Women's Army Corps as a gynecologist. In a letter to American Women's Hospitals organization, Stimson described her duties with the Royal Army Medical Corps.

Excerpt of Letter from Barbara B. Stimson
Dated Tuesday, Jan. 27, received Feb. 10,
1942—the rest of letter is business.

By the time this reaches you you'll have heard that Achsa and I have gone into the Royal Army Medical Corps for I'm going to cable as soon as I know my address. However mail coming here will be forwarded all right. We've been terribly busy for several weeks interviewing people and getting things straightened out and now we are rushing around getting uniforms made etc. before going on duty Feb. 1st. You see, as this winter has been very different from last, the civilian hospitals haven't been over worked and there really hasn't been much to do. We waited quite patiently until we got into the war and then we began to find out if there really was any work for us over here or not. And we learned that we could be of use in the Army. We both had quite a talk with our Ambassador and he thoroughly approved and the head of the Emergency Medical Services said he would do the same thing if he were in our shoes and finally the War Office said they'd take us. They've been as nice as possible for we are not having to sign up for the duration but only for the remainder of our year. We are going in under the same terms that we signed in New York so that's perfect. Achsa is going to work with the Women's Units and have a wonderful opportunity to see how their organization functions and do the health education that she knows so well. She is starting out as a 1st Lieutenant but will go up rapidly, I'm sure. I'm being assigned to a military hospital as an Orthopedic Specialist and consequently am going right in as a Major. We're pretty excited as you can imagine. I'm to be at Shanley, about 16 miles north of London and Achsa is starting in London proper. It's a grand chance and we are amazingly lucky. People have been terribly nice and I think the Ambassador's influence with the War Office here has had a lot to do with it. He's a charming man.

DOCUMENT 42
Photograph, *First Class of Women Admitted to Harvard Medical School*, 1945

Courtesy of Harvard University Medical School.

In 1944, due to a wartime shortage of male students, the faculty of Harvard Medical School voted to open its doors to women. The absence of male students opened up doors for women across the professions, and women's numbers in graduate schools and higher education increased dramatically.

CHAPTER 3

Women's Auxiliary Services

With courage and determination, more than 350,000 women joined the United States military auxiliary services during World War II in the male-dominated armed forces. These American women made up part of the more than 1.5 million women who assisted the Allies during the war. As radio operators, mechanics, and ordnance specialists, women often served with distinction. Although commanding officers and soldiers doubted the effectiveness of their new recruits, by the end of the war their performance and skill was celebrated in popular culture and by military leaders, including Dwight D. Eisenhower. By joining organizations such as the Women's Auxiliary Army Corps (WAAC, later the WAC) and the Women's Air Force Service Pilots (WASPS), American women served the war effort in myriad ways. To honor their contributions, in 1948 President Harry Truman signed the Women's Armed Service Integration Act, opening the door for women to serve full-time in the armed forces, though not in active combat roles.

DOCUMENT 43

Photograph, *Captain Mary Converse Instructing Candidates for US Navy Ensign Commissions in the Use of Navigational Instruments in Classroom–Dining Room, Denver, Colorado*, ca. 1940s

Courtesy of the Library of Congress, LC-USZ62-115742.

Although women were often assigned low-level positions within the auxiliary services in support of the US armed forces, some achieved significant success. This photograph, distributed by the

Office of War Information, shows Captain Mary Converse (1872–1961) instructing young male recruits on the use of navigational tools in 1941. Converse attended the American Merchant Marine Academy at King's Point, New York, and was the first woman to be commissioned in the Merchant Marine prior to the outbreak of World War II.

DOCUMENT 44
Executive Order 9163, Establishing the Women's Army Auxiliary Corps, May 15, 1942

This executive order by President Franklin D. Roosevelt founded the Women's Army Auxiliary Corps and concluded a yearlong attempt by lawmakers to create a women's army auxiliary service. In May 1941, Massachusetts congresswoman Edith Rogers first introduced a bill in Congress to create such a reserve. However, it was only after the Japanese attack on Pearl Harbor in December 1941 that the president took steps to utilize the "knowledge, skill, and special training of the women of this Nation."

By Virtue of and pursuant to the authority vested in me by the Act entitled "An Act to establish a Women's Army Auxiliary Corps for service with the Army of the United States," approved May 14, 1942 (Public Law 554, Chapter 312, 77th Congress), and in order to accomplish the purpose of said Act, I do hereby establish a Women's Army Auxiliary Corps for non-combatant service in the Army of the United States for the purpose of further making available to the national defense the knowledge, skill, and special training of the women of this Nation; and do hereby authorize and direct the Secretary of War, as a first step in the organization of such a Corps, to establish units thereof, of such character as he may determine to be necessary to meet the requirements of the Army, with the number of such units not to exceed 100 and the total enrollment not to exceed 25,000.

DOCUMENT 45
Public Law 689, H.R. 6807, Establishment of a Women's Reserve, July 30, 1942

The establishment of a Women's Reserve Act amended the Naval Reserve Act of 1938 and allowed women to be recruited into the US Navy seven months after the attack on Pearl Harbor. The passage of this bill allowed women to join the navy in many supporting roles, and it was designed to free men from clerical and administrative jobs. These women would become popularly known as the WAVES. This law was passed when the navy and the US military, more broadly, were drafting a large number of male recruits.

Establishment of Women's Reserve, Public Law 689, H.R. 6807, July 30, 1942 [Chapter 538]

AN ACT

To expedite the war effort by releasing officers and men for duty at sea and their replacement by women in the shore establishment of the Navy, and for other purposes.

Be it enacted by the Senate and House of Representatives of the United States of America in Congress assembled, That the Naval Reserve Act of 1938, as amended, is further amended by adding after section 401 thereof an additional title as follows:

TITLE V—WOMEN'S RESERVE

"SEC. 501. A Women's Reserve is hereby established which shall be a branch of the Naval Reserve and shall be administered under the same provisions in all respects (except as may be necessary to adapt said provisions to the Women's Reserve, or as specifically provided herein) as those contained in this Act or which may hereafter be enacted with respect to the Volunteer Reserve.

"SEC. 502. Members of the Women's Reserve may be commissioned or enlisted in such appropriate ranks and ratings, corresponding to those of the Regular Navy, as may be prescribed by the Secretary of the Navy: *Provided*, That there shall not be more than one officer in the grade of lieutenant commander; nor more than thirty-five officers in the grade of lieutenant; and that the number of officers in the grade of lieutenant (junior grade) shall not exceed 35 per centum of the total number of commissioned officers: *And provided further*, That military authority of officers commissioned under the provisions of this Act may be exercised over women of the Reserve only and is limited to the administration of the Women's Reserve.

"SEC. 503. The Reserve established by this title shall be composed of members who have attained the age of twenty years.

"SEC. 504. Members of the Women's Reserve shall be restricted to the performance of shore duty within the continental United States only and shall not be assigned to duty on board vessels of the Navy or in combat aircraft.

"SEC. 505. Members of the Women's Reserve shall not be used to replace civil-service personnel employed in the Naval Establishment, but shall be composed of women trained and qualified for duty in the shore establishment of the Navy to release male officers and enlisted men of the naval service for duty at sea.

"SEC. 506. The benefits provided by section 4 of the Act approved August 27, 1940 (Public, Numbered 775, Seventy-sixth Congress), and by the Act approved March 17, 1941 (Public Law Numbered 16, Seventy-seventh Congress), shall not be applicable to members of the Women's Reserve who suffer disability or death in line of duty from disease or injury while employed on active duty: *Provided*, That if any member of the Women's Reserve suffers disability or death from disease or injury incurred in line of duty while employed on active duty, she or her beneficiaries shall be entitled to all the benefits prescribed by law for civil employees of the United States who are physically injured or who die as a result thereof.

"SEC. 507. The Secretary of the Navy shall fix the money value of the articles of uniform and equipment which enlisted members of the Women's Reserve are required to have upon their first reporting for active duty: *Provided*, That he may authorize such articles of uniform and equipment, or parts thereof, to be issued in kind, or, in lieu thereof, that payment in cash of the money value fixed in accordance with the foregoing, not to exceed $200, be made to such members so ordered to active duty, for the purchase of such articles of uniform and equipment.

"SEC. 508. The authority conferred by this Act for appointments and enlistments in the Women's Reserve shall be effective during the present war and for six months thereafter, or until such earlier time as the Congress by concurrent resolution or the President by proclamation may designate."

Approved, July 30, 1942.

DOCUMENT 46
Excerpt, Oral History with Anna Marie Hulick, Conducted by Judith Rosenkotter, May 7, 2003

Courtesy of the Veterans History Project, Library of Congress.

Anna Marie Hulick, who was from a small town in Nebraska, described her experience of joining the Women's Army Auxiliary Corps (WAACs), her motivations for enlisting, and her desire to travel abroad. The Women's Army Auxiliary Corps, created in 1942, enlisted women into the military; this released men soldiers to fight on the front lines and increased the operating capacity of the US Army. These women performed men's jobs behind the lines; however, they were legally treated as auxiliaries, which impacted their pay, pensions, and other labor conditions. In this excerpt, Hulick describes life in the WAACs and the types of work that she did while enlisted.

Anna Marie Hulick [AMH]: Well, I started out in the Woman's *[sic]*
Auxiliary Army Corp *[sic]*, and, later on, about several months
later, it was—became the Women's Army Corps. And I served
at—everywhere from Pfc right up to tech three and I was in—
had my training at Fort DeMoine, started out in what they called
stable role.

Judith Rosenkotter [JR]: Okay. What prompted you to enlist?

AMH: Well, I was working in a small town, Rushville, Nebraska, and
all the fellows in town—the population was about 1,100 people.
All the boys were either being drafted or signing up. And I was
23, 22 years old and I thought I can't do this. And I was working
for the government and I found out that the only thing I could do
to save my job was to go into the service. They guaranteed that I
would return to that position if I wanted it. Or I could be sent to
Colorado to the main office.

• • •

JR: Into the Army. And is there any particular reason you chose the
Army?

AMH: Well, I actually picked the Navy first because I liked the uniforms. And I wrote and asked them about it and they told me I
had to go to Kansas City, Missouri, take all the tests and everything else, and pay my own way. Well, from Rushville, Nebraska,
which is practically South Dakota, that was a long way. And I
wasn't that rich. So I went, asked the Army and they said come to
Omaha, we'll pay for everything. That took care of it.

JR: So, do you recall your first days in the service?

AMH: Yes, We worked hard, all the shots and everything else. I
remember we took all kinds of tests. And I was a secretary. And I
did not want to be a secretary in the Army. So when we took our
shorthand and typing test—I did take the shorthand because you
just copied it out in longhand. But I failed the typing test. I sat
there and I didn't really type. The typewriter wasn't any good anyway. So that was the way it worked out. And it turned out it didn't
do me any good. They sent me to a place called—well, no. First I
had to go to Arkansas. And I was working as a secretary there.

JR: What place in Arkansas?

AMH: Monticello. And it was a prisoner of war camp, for Japanese, had never been used, and they started it up as a sort of small, basic training camp for women. And of course I went down. I was in the transportation department down there.

• • •

JR: —and tell me something about your boot camp.

AMH: Oh, gosh, it's kind of hard to remember all that. We didn't have much in the way of clothes. This was so early. I can remember one of the first pictures, I was standing there with a man's army coat on, because this was January and it was cold, saddle shoes and some kind of cap on and that was our uniform. And underneath it I had one of these seersucker dresses. But it was a while before we had uniforms. And we just sort of took it in our stride.

• • •

JR: Then after that, you were starting to tell me where you went.

AMH: I went to Fort Leonard Wood.

JR: Okay.

AMH: And there's where I took tests and failed. And they called us all in and were gonna give us our assignments. I think there were about 20 of us. And she read off all the assignments for everybody but me. And I looked at her and I says what am I supposed to do? She says you report for KP tomorrow morning. Oh, what a disappointment. So I went to KP the next morning and the woman, the colonel in charge, came in and she told me, she said we have ambitions for you. We want you to eventually start working for the colonels or the general. I said I didn't pass my test. She said it doesn't matter. She said report to officer's personnel at noon time. So I went up to officer's personnel and I'm sitting there and I'm typing these cards and I thought I'll go out of my mind. I can't stand it. But, eventually, a couple of young fellows come by and said officer, do you take shorthand? And I said yes. Oh. So I started doing letters and stuff. . . . But I worked for the general. He was, I would say close—in his 70s. And he was wonderful to me. We just got along beautifully. But he knew my one ambition was to go overseas.

DOCUMENT 47
Photograph, *Uncle Sam's Nieces*, Office of War Information, December 1942

Courtesy of the Library of Congress, LC-USE6-D-007496.

This publicity photograph, taken in Washington, D.C., shows women in each branch of the armed services: Second Lieutenant Doris Hyde of the US Army Nurses Corps; Ensign Mary E. Hill of the US Navy Nurse Corps; Lieutenant Marion R. Enright of the WAVES (Women Accepted to Voluntary Emergency Services), and Lieutenant Alberta M. Holdsworth of the Women's Army Auxiliary Corps (WAAC). Depicting the women in uniform helped introduce the public to these new service branches and made them comfortable with the idea of women serving in the military.

DOCUMENT 48

Oral History Excerpt, Mary Meigs, "Saying 'No' Was the Only Way You Could Become a WAVE," in *Beyond the Home Front: Women's Autobiographical Writings of the Two World Wars*, edited by Yvonne M. Klein (New York: New York University Press, 1997), 158–60

Courtesy of New York University Press.

This excerpt from Mary Meigs highlights the difficulty that lesbian women had serving in the auxiliary services during World War II. They faced significant discrimination and were often compelled to deny their sexual orientation. In this extract, Meigs describes how sexuality was hidden and her constant fear that discovery would end her work with the auxiliary services.

With our eyes reverently fixed on Old Glory hanging beside the interrogating officer, each of us said, "No," to his perfunctory question, "Are you a homosexual?" Don't tell is still the law in the USA, and it takes a very courageous woman like Gretta Cammermeyer to risk her career by saying, "I'm a lesbian." For me in 1943, "No" was not quite an outright lie. I had not yet engaged in the sexual activity classified as "homosexual" and I did not yet think of myself as a lesbian, yet I knew perfectly well that saying "No" was the only way you could become a WAVE.

My sister-trainees, many of whom could have said yes, had evidently made the same prudent decision. We were billeted in the wonderful old Northampton Inn where the peacetime staff still ran the kitchen and dining-room (we were served lobster thermidor for our farewell dinner). I was keenly aware of the vibrations of suppressed sexuality between officers and trainees and among the trainees themselves. We were assigned eight to a room which was crowded with four double-decker bunks. Above me was a woman ambiguously named Preston; she had a caressing Mississippi accent and curly hair that sprouted defiantly in every direction from under the confines of her WAVE hat. After lights-out I heard a stealthy sound as some of my roommates climbed into upper bunks, or occupants of upper banks climbed down. The sound of giggles and cautious movements was accompanied by the whispered confidences of straight WAVES who had changed bunks in order to talk. It surprises me still that the straight WAVES didn't squeal on us. I, too, climbed up to Preston's welcoming arms one night, was surprised by the ardour with which she wrapped them around me, and wriggled out and down. I had conjured up the spectre of an officer-on-watch bursting in, and of subsequent dishonorable discharge.

When I graduated as an Ensign, I was assigned to the Bureau of Communications (BuComm) in Washington, DC, where I was aware only of WAVES who took themselves and their patriotic duty with appropriate seriousness. I was transferred after a period of incompetence to the Bureau of Personnel (BuPers) across the Potomac, to the Artists' Unit. The Post Office Department where I worked in BuComm was run by a crusty sergeant who shouted at us in the time-honored male way; now I was with compatible artists and writers, with civilian hearts unchanged by their uniforms. I fell in love with a russet-haired lesbian WAVE who gave me my first lesson in sex. I also fell in love with a WAVE lieutenant whom I passed sitting at her desk every time I walked up the corridor. When a round-eyed, round-faced sailor gave me an envelope with, inside, a big studio photograph of my WAVE lieutenant, of her twinkling eyes and smiling mouth, I felt discomfited and uneasy. Was this a way of saying, "I know, and can denounce you at any time?" or (but this only occurred to me recently) was he telling me that he was gay and understood why I stopped so often in front of the WAVE lieutenant's desk? The necessity for secrecy made us suspicious of everybody. I shunned the sailor with the round eyes, and would look away when we passed each other, for I read a kind of sly suggestiveness in his face. "We're buddies, you and I," it said. I was glad when I fell in love with men, too, even if these loves were never consummated. The russet-haired WAVE fell in love with a succession of sailors and was briefly married to one of them. It was standard practice for lesbians to hint at male lovers in their lives and claim to be mourning a lover who had been killed in the war.

The spy system in the services got underway when the mother of an enlisted WAAC surprised her daughter in bed with her lesbian love and sounded the alarm. Enlisted lesbians who took the risk of sleeping together in barracks were likely to be denounced by informers, whereas officers, who lived in houses and apartments, were neither identified as lesbians nor denounced. In this time before the feminist revolution, I was politically ignorant and had never thought about injustices to women based on class differences. When one of the WAVE typists in my BuComm unit suddenly lashed out at me with, "You treat me like the ground under your feet!" I thought she was angry because I seemed to ignore her existence. It didn't occur to me until years later that she probably thought I'd ignored her existence because I was an upper-class snob.

DOCUMENT 49

Oral History Excerpt with Violet Cowden, conducted by Owen Chappel, August 15, 2003

Courtesy of the Veterans History Project, Library of Congress.

This oral history excerpt details Violet Cowden's experience as a WASP during World War II. Cowden discussed joining the military in 1943, her work during the war, how she was replaced by returning soldiers, and the war's impact on her life.

Owen Chappel: Ms. Cowden, why did you decide to become a WASP?

Violet Cowden: I already had my private pilot's license before war was declared so when war was declared, everyone at that time wanted to do their part, and I thought, "Well, what better way to serve my country than to fly and do the thing that I love the most, and I didn't have to pay for the gas."

• • •

Owen Chappel: What happened to the WASP program?

Violet Cowden: The WASP program, being it was an experimental program, we were paid by civil service and we had—we were under the jurisdiction of the—of the Air Force so we did—I mean, we took our—the training that we took in Sweetwater, Texas, was exactly the same training that the men had. It was— we went through primary with the PT-19, in basic the BT-17, and then to advance, the AT-6. And it's the same program that the men went through. But we weren't paid by the military so when the men started coming back from overseas, they wanted their job back. And really our job was to release men when we did all the missions in the U.S. which was—I mean, we did—we flew all the missions. I mean, we did everything that the men did, and I was in the Air Transport Command so I—I delivered airplanes. But when the men came back, they wanted their jobs back. So they deactivated us. And we didn't have our veterans benefits until 1977.

Owen Chappel: When did you join the military?

Violet Cowden: I joined the military March 1943. I think it was—I think it was—the day I soloed was on March the 5th. And the reason I remember that was because I was out here staying with my sister because she was going to have her first baby. And I got my call to go into—go to Sweetwater. So I had to leave, and I felt so bad because I wanted to be with my sister. And on the day that I soloed with the Air Force, somebody came out with a telegram that said that my nephew was born. So he was—that was on March the 5th. So last year on his 60th birthday I flew up to Washington to be with his—to be with him. So, I mean, to think that 60 years have passed, it's—it's unbelievable.

• • •

Owen Chappel: What kind of work would you do on the planes?

Violet Cowden: Well, I would—my mission really was to go to the factory and pick up the planes and take them to the point of debarkation either the east coast or the west coast. Sometimes I'd pick up the plane in Buffalo, New York, and fly it to Great Falls, Montana. And I flew all over the United States, but the trainers that we—when they needed the trainers. So it—it was—really it was like a taxi. I mean, I'd pick up the plane and take it where—where they needed—where they needed it. And every plane that I was supposed to pick up had been—should have been flown an hour. And this one time I jumped in the plane, it was a P-51, and I looked at the ship's papers, and it hadn't been tested. So I went back into operations and I said, "This plane hasn't been tested." And so the mechanic went out, he wrote down one hour in the ship's papers, so I knew that it had been flown. I probably flew others, you know, that hadn't been flown, but this one I knew hadn't been flown. So I wouldn't have had to flown it.

• • •

Owen Chappel: While pioneering in aviation what do you think is your greatest contribution?

Violet Cowden: When I was going through the program, I certainly didn't think I was a pioneer. I was doing a job. It was a job that was strictly in the male field. It was opening the doors for young women of today through what we did then that they can now fly combat, they can almost do—do anything they want. But they still—there's still a ways to go. But I'm glad that I was a pioneer that opened the door for Eileen Collins the first woman to fly the shuttle and Trish Beckman who is working for Boeing. She's a test engineer. She flies on all the flights now to test out the airplanes for—for Boeing. And I'm glad that I'm their mentor. I feel that at the time I didn't think I was contributing anything, but now, I—I realize that through my experiences I now can experience what the women of today are doing in aviation as well as other fields, I mean, doctors and lawyers. It's—I mean, I'm glad that I had that opportunity at that time of—in history.

DOCUMENT 50
Poster, "US Cadet Nurse Corps," 1945

Courtesy of the Library of Congress, LC-USZ62-100305.

The Cadet Nurse Corps, a civilian organization created in 1943, grew rapidly to meet the increasing demand for trained nurses to help wounded service men. Propaganda posters, like this, appealed to patriotic emotions and also offered financial support, such as free education, to encourage women to join the Nurse Corps.

A LIFETIME EDUCATION *FREE*
FOR HIGH SCHOOL GRADUATES WHO QUALIFY
U.S. CADET NURSE CORPS
GO TO YOUR LOCAL HOSPITAL OR WRITE TO U. S. PUBLIC HEALTH SERVICE, BOX 88, NEW YORK 8, N. Y.

Document 50

DOCUMENT 51

Poster, "It's a Woman's War Too! Join the WAVES," 1942

Courtesy of the Library of Congress, LC-USZC4-1856.

The vast scale of World War II necessitated that women serve in the US military to supplement the millions of men fighting across the globe and the non-combat roles that they left behind. Posters such as this one, created by John Philip Falter (1910–1982), an American artist well known for his cover paintings for the *Saturday Evening Post*, encouraged women to join the Women Accepted to Voluntary Emergency Services, or WAVES, as the women in the US Naval Reserve were known.

NAVY RECRUITING STATION OR OFFICE OF NAVAL OFFICER PROCUREMENT

DOCUMENT 52

Letter, Dorothy C. Stratton, Director of the SPARS, in the *Spar Cutter* 1, no. 9 (November 23, 1943)

Courtesy of the Manuscript, Archives, and Rare Book Library, Emory University, MSS121, box 1, folder: SPAR Newsletter.

The US Coast Guard Women's Reserve (SPARS) was created in November 1942. The nickname SPARS originated from the coast guard's motto, "Semper Paratus," and its translation, "Always Ready." On the one-year anniversary of the creation of SPARS, director Dorothy C. Stratton wrote this letter for the *Spar Cutter*, a newsletter for enlisted SPARS; she reflected on the challenges of that first year as well as the commitment of the women for the future.

On this, our first birthday, may I send my personal greetings to each one of you and my congratulations on a job well done.

Our most important assignment during the past year has been to prove our value to the regular personnel of the Coast Guard. We knew we could do many of the short jobs; we knew we could work long hours without extra pay and keep smiling and cheerful; we knew we could "take it," but we had to prove ourselves on the job. To those of you who were the first in the field, who by your high standards both on and off the job changed the quizzical smiles of the old salts to friendly grins of comradeship and made the way easier for those who have followed you, go the laurels for establishing the value of the SPARS.

The excitement of being something new is over. Now we are in for the long pull. The Coast Guard can count on us to perform our jobs ashore with the same devotion to duty that marks the performance of the officers and men at sea. November 23 will alway [*sic*] be an important date in each of our lives. May it soon be a date on which to remember with pride a task well done, rather than one on which to respond to the call of active duty.

Dorothy C. Stratton

DOCUMENT 53

Letter, Lloyd T. Chalker, Assistant Commandant of the US Coast Guard, in the *Spar Cutter* 1, no. 9 (November 23, 1943)

Courtesy of the Manuscript, Archives, and Rare Book Library, Emory University, MSS121, box 1, folder: SPAR Newsletter.

Accompanying Dorothy C. Stratton's letter, which marked the one-year anniversary of the creation of the SPARS, the US Coast Guard Women's Reserve, was a letter from the assistant commandant of the US Coast Guard, Lloyd T. Chalker. He extolled the work of the SPARS, proclaiming, "You are an integral part of the service, an important member of the Coast Guard family."

On November 23, 1943, the U.S. Coast Guard Women's Reserve will complete one year of service. Under the popular name of "SPARS," you have won national recognition as an efficient and alert organization devoted to the performance of duties essential to a successful prosecution of the war. During this year you have made your place within the Coast Guard. You are an integral part of the service, an important member of the Coast Guard family. You have done this not by chance but by your loyalty, your cooperation, and your devotion to the service.

It gives me great pleasure to congratulate you on this the first birthday of the "SPARS" and to wish you continued and increasing success in the years ahead.

Signed: L. T. Chalker, Assistant Commandant

DOCUMENT 54

Letter, from Dorothy C. Stratton, Director of the SPARS, in the *Spar Cutter* 1, no. 10 (December 20, 1943)

Courtesy of the Manuscript, Archives, and Rare Book Library, Emory University, MSS121, box 1, folder: SPAR Newsletter.

One month after the anniversary of the SPARS, Dorothy C. Stratton wrote this Christmas message to the women who served under her. She encouraged the SPARS to give to others during the Christmas holiday and to continue doing the important work of the SPARS despite the inevitable feelings of homesickness.

Merry Christmas

This will be a Christmas of "firsts" for many of us—our first Christmas in the Service, our first Christmas away from home, our first Christmas with those we love far from home and in danger.

This will be a Christmas of realities with less tinsel, fewer presents, and less gaiety, but with more understanding of the courage and caliber of our fellows and more appreciation of the everyday things in life.

This will be a "doing" Christmas. Rather than sitting in our rooms feeling sorry for ourselves, we shall be visiting the wounded in hospitals, entertaining new arrivals who have not yet had time to make friends, helping to plan entertainment for others in the Service and writing letters to friends whom we have neglected. It will be a Christmas in which we think of others first.

To you all I send my congratulations on having the opportunity to share, as John Mason Brown puts it, "emotionally and experimentally in the major challenge of our time." Please consider this a personal greeting expressing my deep sense of pride, not only in your accomplishments but in the kind of people you are.

Dorothy C. Stratton

DOCUMENTS 55 AND 56
Photographs, *Making Flags for Military Use in the Quartermaster Corps Depot, Philadelphia, Penn.*

Courtesy of the Library of Congress, LC-USZ62-95525 and LC-USZ62-95526.

Women were admitted to work in branches of the military other than the auxiliary services during World War II. The US Quartermaster Corps, responsible for supplying troops with supplies, munitions, and all materials needed for service, employed women throughout the war. These photos show African American women sewing US flags for military use.

DOCUMENT 57

Survey of Ethel Carlson Cerasale, of the Army Nurses Corps, for the National Women Veterans Foundation, Inc., Conducted by Evelyn Monahan, PhD, No Date

Courtesy of the Manuscript, Archives, and Rare Book Library, Emory University MSS1201, box 3, folder: Loose Item.

This questionnaire, completed by Ethel Carlson Cerasale, a member of the Army Nurse Corps from April 1943 to February 1948, explores the wartime experience of a member of the Army Nurses Corps (ANC). The ANC was the only branch of the military that permitted women to serve in peacetime prior to World War II. During the war the number of women in the service expanded from roughly one thousand in 1941 to over fifty thousand in 1945. Cerasale's responses speak to her experience in the ANC as well as her reflections on the war and the roles of women in the military since.

Name: Ethel Carlson Cerasale
Date of Birth: 23 August 1921
Address: [Redacted]
Phone: [Redacted]
Branch/Dates of Service: U.S. Army Nurse Corps.
Marital Status: Married
Children: Steven Anthony Cerasale, Patricia Cerasale Loll, Scott Alan Cerasale
Grandchildren: Krista Noelle Cerasale

What honors or awards have children/grandchildren won?
Steven won honors in High School, was semi finalist for Calif. Scholarship, graduated from UCAA with BS. Patricia has AA at Brevard Comm College, working toward BS in [unreadable]. Scott has AA Brevard Comm College.

Which decorations, if any, were awarded to you? Which, if any, of those awarded, have you not received as yet?
No decorations, lacked 2 flights with patients for air medal while in

ETO. Made more flights, but as assistant with material, patients had been transferred.

Why did you enlist?
It was the patriotic thing to do. Men our age were drafted, and the war was an all-out effort.

What was the reaction of your family/friends when you enlisted?
My parents were sad, because my brother was in the Navy, and they felt it wasn't necessary for me to go. They thought I should at least not go into flight nursing, as in that position, I was sure to be sent overseas. My friends were all enlisting, if not drafted.

What do you remember most about your first days and weeks in military?
I was frightened at the type of life I had gotten into. I was "on my own" for the first time—away from home. Duty at my first station, Jefferson Barracks, Missouri, was similar to what I'd done—I was working on a maternity ward!

Where were you stationed? What were your assignments?
After Jefferson Barracks in 6 months I went to Air Evacuation School at Bowman Field, KY. About 8 weeks later to Camp Kilmer, NJ, to go to England. There I flew with Troop Carrier C47's, taking material, gasoline for Patton's tanks to France, returning with patients. Had kidney infection while in Southern France TDY, was sent to general hospital, and returned to US on hospital ship in Feb 1945.

Did you serve overseas? If yes, where?
Yes—as above.

Were you ever stationed in or near combat zones?
Yes—we flew into air strips just behind action

Were you ever under fire, strafing, or bombing?
Yes. We were fired upon near Nancy, France, not hit. Pilot took evasive action.

If yes, what were you feelings & thoughts?
I was upset because of the sudden turn and change in altitude.

Did you lose any close friends as a direct or indirect result of the war?
Yes. Betty Harven, a flight nurse who was killed in Italy while I was still at Air Evac school. She had been stationed with me at Jefferson Barrack, went to school in class ahead of me, was sent as a replacement for nurses lost in Albania in 807 MAES.

What is your strongest memory of WWII?
The camaraderie we shared, the feeling of doing something important.

What was the most surprising thing you learned about yourself as a result of your service during WWII?
?

If you did, when & why did you decide to make the military a career?
I didn't want it be a career—only something that needed to be done in war time.

What would you like the world to know about women who served in the military during WWII?
We worked under unusually severe conditions, but no one resented it. It was a job we where qualified to do, and we were doing what we could do for our country in a difficult time.

What would you like to tell the women in the military now? The women who are considering joining the military?
I think the military service is a great career, especially today. Training is available as in no other type of work, and benefits are many. Working conditions for women in the military have improved as in other occupations, and it's a good way to organize one's life.
[Redacted]
[Redacted]

What would you most like to be remembered for?
?

What do you see for women in the military in the future?
Better opportunities for advancement, but problems if a war should occur since they now stay in service while raising a family.

Are there any other comments you would like to make? Questions you would like to pose?
[Left blank]

DOCUMENT 58

Survey of Effie Mocas Tolis, of the WAVES, for the National Women Veterans Foundation, Inc., Conducted by Evelyn Monahan, PhD, No Date

Courtesy of the Manuscript, Archives, and Rare Book Library, Emory University MSS1201, box 3, folder: Loose Item.

This survey conducted after the war highlights the wartime experience of Mocas Tolis, a member of the WAVES from December 1942 to December 1945. The feelings of patriotism and sacrifice and her increased self-esteem and feelings of self-worth are particularly notable in Tolis's answers.

Name: Effie Mocas Tolis
Date of Birth: 11 September 1921
Address: [Redacted]
Phone: [Redacted]
Branch/Dates of Service: WAVES Dec 1942–Dec 1945
Marital Status: Married
Children: 2 Elizabeth Jean, Victor John
Grandchildren: 4
What honors or awards have children/grandchildren won?
Son—Phi Beta Kappa—Bates College 1974
Daughter—Rivier College 1978

Which decorations, if any, were awarded to you? Which, if any, of those awarded, have you not received as yet?

[Left blank]

Why did you enlist?
Pure and simple—PATRIOTISM!!!

What was the reaction of your family/friends when you enlisted?
Originally family had mixed feelings—then extremely proud. Nothing amazed my friends about me.

What do you remember most about your first days/weeks in military?
I felt the regimentation was a bit too much, but being young and very

energetic, I really enjoyed it. Loved meeting girls from different parts of the country and seeing sights I had only read about.

Where were you stationed? What were your assignments?
Boot training at Iowa State College for Women and Yeoman training at Georgia College for Women. Then was stationed at Hunter College in the Personnel Office. Last assignment—separation Center—NYC. Favorite duties at Hunter were meeting and greeting recruits at Grand Central Station and also taking trained recruits to duty stations all over the USA.

Did you serve overseas? If yes, where?
No

Were you ever stationed in or near combat zones?
No

Were you ever under fire, strafing, or bombing?
No

If yes, what were you feelings & thoughts?

Did you lose any close friends as a direct or indirect result of the war?
Yes—several high school classmates.

What is your strongest memory of WW II?
My strongest memory is of the willingness and cooperation of all our neighbors to make sacrifice in order to win the war. We were all so proud to be Americans.
Second strongest memory is of the adventure—the horrors of what was really happening did not hit home until much later.

What was the most surprising thing you learned about yourself as a result of your service during WW II?
I learned that I could stand on my own two feet and that I could deal with all kinds of people and situations and it gave me much confidence.

If you did, when & why did you decide to make the military a career?
[Left blank]

What would you like the world to know about women who served in the military during WW II?
How capable they were and how patriotic and proud their felt to serve their country.

What would you like to tell the women in the military now? The women who are considering joining the military?
Do your best as you would in any career and wear your uniform proudly.

What were your feelings & thoughts about the military's segregation policies during WW II?
Wasn't really aware of it. At the time, I accepted segregation as a fact of life.

Did you associate with or have friends of another race?
No

What would you most like to be remembered for?
Becoming one of the first Chief Petty Officers in the WAVES.

What do you see for women in the military in the future?
Very fine opportunities in any field.

Are there any other comments you would like to make? Questions you would like to pose?
Please God—no more wars!!!

DOCUMENT 59

The Women's Army Auxiliary Corps Oath, from *Women's Army Auxiliary Corps Regulations (Tentative)*, 1942, 7, Produced by Publications Office WAAC, Fort Des Moines, Iowa

Courtesy of the Manuscript, Archives, and Rare Book Library, Emory University, MSS1201, box 6, folder: WAC Regs 1942.

This oath was taken by every member of the Women's Army Auxiliary Corps, an auxiliary organization created on May 15, 1942, upon enlistment. The oath was similar to that taken by men who enlisted in the armed forces in World War II.

"I,_____(First Name)_____(Middle Name)_____(Last Name), a citizen of the United States, on this _____ day of _____, 19___, do hereby voluntarily enroll as a member of the Women's Army Auxiliary Corps under the following conditions: That I will serve in said Corps for the period of (word and figure) _____ year prescribed by law which in time of war, or of national emergency declared by the Congress or the President, the Secretary of War may, by order, extend to include the period of war or national emergency plus not to exceed 6 months, unless I am sooner discharged by proper authority; and I do also agree to accept from the United States by such bounty, pay, rations, and clothing as are, or may be, established by law. And I do solemnly swear (or affirm) that I will bear true faith and allegiance to the United States of America; that I will serve them honestly and faithfully against all their enemies whomsoever; and that I will obey the orders of the President of the United States, and the orders of the officers appointed over me, according to the regulations of the Women's Army Auxiliary Corps and the Rules and Articles of War, when applicable.

"I further solemnly swear (or affirm) that I have read and understand the provisions of the law * printed in Instruction "B"; that I am not a member of a political party organization that advocated the overthrow of the Government of the United States by force or violence and that, during such time as I am a member of the Women's Army Auxiliary Corps, I will not advocate nor become a member of any political party or organization that advocates the overthrow of the Government of the United States by force or violence.

Signature _____(First Name)_____(Middle Name)_____ (Last Name)"

The Hatch Act (Bul. 26, W. D., 1940).

DOCUMENT 60
Letter to the Editor of *Our Army*, from Richard E. Daley, Lt. Col., Air Corps, April 11, 1944

Courtesy of the Manuscript, Archives, and Rare Book Library, Emory University, MSS 1201, box 6, folder: WAC Rumors.

On April 11, 1944, the public relations officer of the Army Air Force wrote to the editor of *Our Army*, a World War II magazine published for the civilian population, disputing recent depictions of the Women's Army Corps (WAC) in the magazine. In this letter, the difficulties in recruiting WACs and some of the problems facing the organization are highlighted. The tension between the press and the armed forces is also evident.

Headquarters
Army Air Forces Training Command
Fort Worth, 2, Texas
11 April 1944

The Editor, Our Army
11 Park Place
New York 7, New York

Dear Sir:
The War Department Bureau of Public relations has called our attention to the cover of OUR ARMY for March, 1944, since this Command is responsible for Women's Army Corps recruiting for the Army Air Forces.

As you know, the Army is urgently in need of Wacs [*sic*] and faces a number of problems in the recruiting of these women soldiers. One such problem is that there is at times not enough appreciation of the seriousness and dignity of the work Wacs [*sic*] do. In attempting to publicize their ability and the importance of their work, especially among other Army enlisted personnel, illustrations such as the cover referred to above prove a major setback.

Unhappily enough, the artist is himself a soldier in this Command, although the illustration was not cleared through this Headquarters for review prior to being forwarded to your magazine.

Paragraph 1, page 4 of the March issue also refers to "acs [*sic*] in a manner which is not consonant with the high purpose of these women who are doing such a magnificent job in the service of their country.

Please believe me to be not ungrateful for the many fine stories you have published about the Women's Army Corps, and I call your attention to the above facts only to tell you how we need all the help we can get from service publications in selling the Wacs [*sic*].

This letter is not for publication, but I did want to tell you about these things because you can be, and have been, so valuable in bringing to army personnel a proper appreciation of the Women's Army Corps.

Yours sincerely,
Richard E. Daley
Lt. Col., Air Corps
Public Relations Officer

DOCUMENT 61

Letter from Burton R. Morley, Area Director of the War Manpower Commission, to Dr. B. F. Ashe, Regional Director of the War Manpower Commission, June 16, 1943

Courtesy of the National Archives, Atlanta.

This letter from Burton R. Morley to the regional director of the War Manpower Commission offers insight into the way that some men viewed the recruitment of women into the auxiliary services and their opinion that there was a "type of woman" who would be willing to join them.

---

616 First National Annex
Mobile, Alabama
June 16, 1943

TO: Dr. B. F. Ashe   ATT'N: Mr. Frank Gonstanga
Regional Director   Deputy Regional Director

FROM: Burton R. Morley
Area Director

SUBJECT: WAAC Advertising Campaign in Mobile

As you know, the WAAC organization has been doing a very intensive campaign of recruiting throughout the country. Thus far, no advertising in support of this campaign has appeared here in Mobile. Recruiting is, however, going on. Representatives of the Mobile Press Register have raised the question to this office as to why they may not accept and run the standard WAAC advertising. Thus far, I understand the War Department has been unwilling to allow this advertising to appear in No. 1 Critical Areas. The paper, however, raises the point that the type of woman who would be interested in joining such organizations as the WAACS, WAVES, or SPARS is not the type who would be interested in going into shipyard employment here in Mobile. With this position I am inclined to agree, and may cite as evidence the fact that although we put on an intensive week's campaign to register women for shipyard work, the results were not particularly encouraging. It appears to me also that insofar as stenographic and clerical help is concerned, most of the organizations here in Mobile are pretty well staffed. I would suggest, therefore, that you consider the matter and see what steps should be taken to permit the local papers to have the advantage of running this very profitable advertising. I would like to see it tried with the idea in mind, of course, that if the situation should develop to the point where local industries were suffering a drain in their feminine clerical force, we could always halt the procedure.

Please let me know what your reaction is, and what steps must be taken if the advertising is to be released here in Mobile.

[Signed]
Burton R. Morely
Area Director
War Manpower Commission

DOCUMENT 62
Letter from Lucy Lovett Domby, May 7, 1945

Courtesy of the Manuscript, Archives, and Rare Book Library, Emory University, MSS816, box 4, folder: 8.

Lucy Lovett, a member of the WACs, recalled, in this letter to her parents how she, other WACS, and some soldiers greeted the news that the war was over in Europe in May 1945. In 1943, the WAACs were designated by Congress as the Women's Army Corps (WAC) ensuring that women were part of the army rather than just supporting it. This letter is part of a collection sent between Lucy and her family during her service in the WACs, and it reflects the often anti-climactic end to the war for many service personnel.

May 7, 1945

Dear Folks,

For that soon to be famous book "the Clines View the War or How to appear wise though dumb" here is my contribution of the very quiet way the news was received in an army hospital.

When the news came over the radio in the adjoining office I was calmly working away in the library. As I happened by the door someone inside said casually "Hey, did you hear that the war is over". Hardened by now to such statements I merely replied "Is that so?", and proceeded back in the library to say to everyone there "Hey, did you hear the war is over", to which they in inanimately answered "is that so?" This somewhat dampened my spirits, as I expected more of a reaction. So I suggested that if they wanted to listen the radio was in the front of the library. So we gathered there—about fifteen soldiers and WACs to hear of the peace in the little red school house. Everyone was quiets [sic] and seemed a little tired—they could have been tired of war, of peace rumors, or from a hard weekend.

The general comments were "we've waited so long that now its hard to know what to do", "some of the boys will be coming home now", "I've got a quart of rye in my foot locker—want to get together for a celebration", "Personally, this is a time for church rather than for drinking",

"I wonder if it will affect my furlough", "The Russians won't know a thing about this until tomorrow. It isn't fair for a few to keep such facts away from a people."

After about ten minutes most people drifted away from the radio back to work or to reading. I took a cart of books out and as I was half thought [*sic*] the first ward it dawned on me that there were no radio's on. To the boy in bed I said "Say, did you know the war is over?" "When did this happen?" he asked. I told him, and he appeared satisfied, but laid down without calling the news over to his buddies. At the next bed I tried again, and on through several wards, but received no responses worth mentioning. It is obvious that there is excitement in the air, everyone is a little on edge, but life goes exactly as usual.

Today the army surprised me—not so much by the act itself, but by the purpose which I'm sure is behind the act. All military personnel is restricted to the camp until further notice, no soldiers can be seen on the streets of Augusta [Georgia]—which is aimed at preventing wild celebrations and drunken brawls. Often the army almost seems to encourage these, so an order like this is amazing. This war has dragged on a long time. Many soldiers have developed a hardness, an apathy and a lack of emotion that made V.E. day here almost like another day. Probably half of Oxford [Georgia] was crying, but few tears were shed here. It's "Two down and one to go."

Love,
Lucy

DOCUMENT 63
Public Law, Women's Armed Services Integration Act, 1948

The Women's Armed Services Integration Act of 1948, signed by President Harry S. Truman, granted women permanent status in the regular and reserve forces of the US Army, Navy, and Marine Corps, as well as in the newly created US Air Force, and allowed women to service in the military in peace time. This marked a significant shift from the government's previous policy toward women in the military and came as a result of significant pressure being placed on the government after women were forced to leave the auxiliary services after the war's end in 1945.

(Public Law 625-80th Congress)
(Chapter 449-2d Session)
(S. 1641)

AN ACT

To establish the Women's Army Corps in the Regular Army, to authorize the enlistment and appointment of women in the Regular Air Force, Regular Navy and Marine Corps, and in the Reserve components of the Army, Navy, Air Force, and Marine Corps, and for other purposes.
Be it enacted by the Senate and House of Representatives of the United States of America in Congress assembled, That this Act may be cited as the "Women's Armed Services Integration Act of 1948".

TITLE II

Navy and Marine Corps

Sec. 213. (a) Women may be enlisted or appointed in the Regular Marine Corps under the provisions of this title, and the provisions of this title (except as may be necessary to adapt said provisions to the Marine Corps) are hereby made applicable to women enlisted or appointed in the Regular Marine Corps in the same manner as such provisions apply to women enlisted or appointed in the Regular Navy.

(b) The number of enlisted women on the active list of the Regular Marine Corps at any one time shall not exceed 2 per centum of the enlisted strength now or hereafter authorized for the active list of the Regular Marine Corps: Provided, that for a period of two years immediately following the date of this Act, the actual number of enlisted women in the Regular Marine Corps shall at no time exceed one thousand.

(c) The number of commissioned and warrant women officers on the active list of the Regular Marine Corps at any one time shall not exceed 10 per centum of the authorized number of enlisted women of the Regular Marine Corps: Provided, that for a period of two years immediately following the date of this Act, the actual number of women officers in the Regular Marine Corps shall at no time exceed one hundred commissioned women officers and ten warrant women officers, and such number of commissioned women officers shall be appointed in increments of not to exceed 40 per centum, 20 per centum, 20 per centum, and 20 per centum at approximately equally spaced intervals of time during the said period of two years.

(d) From the women officers serving in the grade of major or above in the Marine Corps, one officer may be detailed to duty in the office of the Commandant of the Marine Corps to assist the Commandant in the administration of women's affairs. She shall have the rank of colonel while so serving, and shall be entitled to the pay and allowances as are now or may be hereafter prescribed by law for a colonel of the Regular Marine Corps, and her regular status as a commissioned officer in the Marine Corps shall not be disturbed by reason of such detail. The provisions of section 207 of this title relative to the retirement of women officers detailed as assistant to the Chief of Naval Personnel shall apply in the same manner and under the same relative conditions to women officers of the Marine Corps detailed to duty in the office of the Commandant of the Marine Corps as provided in this subsection.

Sec. 214. (a) The Secretary of the Navy, under the circumstances and in accordance with regulations prescribed by the President, may terminate the commission or warrant of any woman officer in the Regular Navy or Marine Corps.

(b) The Secretary of the Navy, under such regulations as he may prescribe, may terminate the enlistment of any enlisted woman in the Regular Navy or Marine Corps, and each such person whose enlistment is so terminated shall be discharged from the service.

Sec. 215. The provisions of title III of the Officer Personnel Act of 1947 shall not be applicable to women officers of the Regular Navy and Naval Reserve and those provisions of titles I and II of the said Act which are not inconsistent with the provisions of this Act shall be operative with regard to women officers of the Regular Navy from the effective date of this Act.

Sec. 216. Women officers of the Naval Reserve who on the date of approval of this Act are serving under temporary appointments in grades above commissioned warrant officer may continue to serve under such temporary appointments until such appointments are terminated by the President, or until such officers are appointed in the regular Navy, but no such temporary appointment may continue in effect later than six months after June 30 of the fiscal year following that in which the present war shall end or the first day of the twelfth month following the effective date of this Act, whichever may be earlier: Provided, That, notwithstanding any other provisions of law, women officers of the Naval Reserve who at the time of appointment in the Regular Navy are serving under temporary appointments which by their terms are for a period of limited duration, may on appointment in the Regular Navy, be given temporary appointments pursuant to the provisions of the Act of July 24, 1941 (55 Stat. 603), as amended, which shall be under the same conditions, in the same grade, and with the same precedence as those temporary appointments held by such officers in the Naval Reserve at the time of their appointment in the Regular Navy.

CHAPTER 4

"Make Do and Mend": Women and the Home Front

In addition to filling labor shortages created when millions of men joined the armed forces, many women helped maintain stable conditions at home in the face of the social and economic turmoil created by World War II. When the government introduced rationing in response to shortages of sugar, meat, rubber, and gasoline, women had to do more with less. In order to ensure that military personnel were adequately supplied on the front lines, a spirit of "make do and mend" swept the nation. These documents, focused on the home front, show that although wartime life was challenging, women as the heads of households embraced frugality and conservation and reinvented the way that they fed, clothed, and cared for their families and homes. Many women felt liberated and enjoyed their new roles as providers and innovators at home, others welcomed the end of the war and the return to more traditional gender roles.

DOCUMENT 64

Poster, "Service on the Home Front," January 21, 1943

Courtesy of the Library of Congress, LC-USZC2-1107.

Mobilization for war was a family affair, and men, women, and children were encouraged to do their part. The Work Projects Administration (WPA) mounted a campaign to encourage civilians of all ages to participate in civil defense efforts, such as the Citizens Defense Corps, in salvage efforts, and in planting victory gardens. The Works Progress Administration (renamed the Works Projects Administration in 1939), which was begun in 1935 in an effort to put unemployed citizens back to work during the Great Depression, provided employment for over 8.5 million Americans between 1935 and 1943. It was disbanded after the nation reached full employment because of the expansion of war industries.

DOCUMENT 65

Photograph, *Farm Security Administration Trailer Camp for Negroes*, April 1942, Arlington, Virginia

Courtesy of the Library of Congress, LC-USF34-100017-E.

Photographer Marjory Collins worked as a freelance photojournalist before joining the Office of War Information in 1941. She was assigned to document home front activities and focused on women war workers, small towns, and ethnic communities, such as this Farm Security Administration (FSA) trailer camp for African Americans that was set up in Arlington, Virginia, to house the families of war workers. Although President Franklin D. Roosevelt

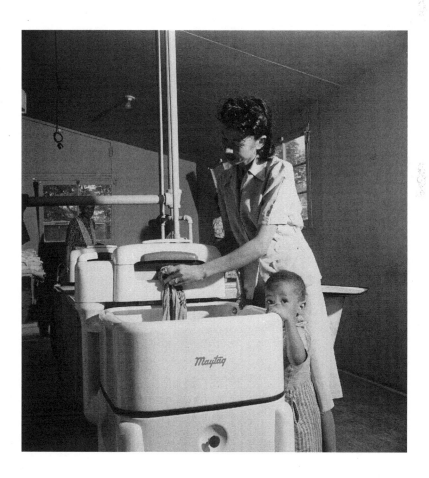

had issued Executive Order 8802 in June 1941, declaring that there would be "no discrimination in the employment of workers in defense industries or Government because of race, creed, color, or national origin," segregation by race remained embedded in US society, with separate "white" and "colored" housing and other facilities. The caption reads, "FSA (Farm Security Administration) trailer camp project for Negroes. Well-equipped laundry in the community building."

DOCUMENT 66

Lithograph, *War Gardens for Victory*, by the Stecher-Traung Lithograph Corporation, Rochester, New York

Courtesy of the Library of Congress, LC-USZ62-128566.

During World War II, through posters, radio broadcasts, and advertisements, the US government encouraged families to plant victory gardens to alleviate food shortages. Because canned food was rationed, vegetable gardens became a practical way to stretch ration coupons and save money. An estimated two million gardens were planted, producing 40 percent of the vegetables needed during the war. This poster helped promote these efforts.

DOCUMENT 67

Photograph, *The Sheriger Family Planning Their Victory Garden by Reading Up on the Subject—They Had Not Had a Garden for Some Time—Washington (Vicinity), D.C., February 1943*

Courtesy of the Library of Congress, LC-USZ62-115986.

The US government encouraged individuals to grow produce in their own back yards to stabilize the output of goods going overseas. Victory gardens provided produce that was not otherwise

Document 66

available, as shown in this photograph. Urban dwellers without yards often created gardens in window boxes or on apartment rooftops. Schools often set aside land to plant gardens that were tended by students.

DOCUMENT 68
Poster, "We'll Have Lots to Eat This Winter, Won't We Mother?," Office of War Information, 1943

Courtesy of the University of North Texas Digital Library, Posters WW2, Parker 1.

In addition to growing their own food in victory gardens, women were encouraged to can their excess produce so that they would have fruit and vegetables throughout the year. The Office of War Information distributed posters, such as this one designed by Alfred Parker, which showed a mother and her daughter canning vegetables from their victory garden in glass canning jars.

DOCUMENTS 69–71

Article, "Berry Farmerettes," *Southern Highlander,* Winter 1943–44, and Photographs, *Berry Farmerettes,* ca. 1940s

Courtesy of Berry College Archives, Rome, Georgia.

A small, coeducational college located near the northwestern Georgia city of Rome, Berry College was well known for its emphasis on agriculture, its student work program, and its vast campus of almost thirty thousand acres. Since the school's founding in 1902, students had raised crops and livestock to feed themselves as well as to sell in the local community. Traditionally, male students were responsible for crop cultivation and operation of the dairy, while female students tended smaller garden plots. The decline in male enrollment during the war years precipitated a call for volunteers to assist with farm operations at the school. This document and related images illustrate the role women played on Berry's campus.

Berry has always been justly proud of her splendid, sturdy farm boys. Through the years these young men have enjoyed driving the tractors, working with all the farm machinery, and learning the up-to-date methods of farming, under the direction of our able farm Superintendent, Clifton Russell—one of Berry's own graduates.

Alas! Berry men are good soldiers in battle as well as soldiers of the soil. All the older boys have answered the call to arms. Producing food is as essential as fighting the battles, Mr. Russell insists, and the emergency must be met. For more than forty-two years Berry has faced, and solved, problems. She must not fail in this crisis!

We still have girls—more girls than ever before—and no one is more anxious than our girls to contribute to winning the war. The Dean of Women, recently, asked for girls to volunteer to drive the tractors—to work now, and all summer, on Berry's farm and in the orchards to produce food for our large family and for the war needs. The volunteers were asked to meet in a certain class room. Ninety-seven girls crowded in, while others clamored out-side the door to volunteer their services.

Documents 69–71

The Dean had expected quite a large group, but was astounded to find that there was barely room for her to slide in at the door.

Mr. Russell is hopeful of some much needed help, however, he also hopes that all the girls will not report for training at once, as he fears his soil would be too much trampled for his seeds to come through.

DOCUMENT 72

"Answers Given to Child's Questions about War," *Science News Letter*, June 20, 1942

Courtesy of Science News Letter.

The *Science News Letter* was published from 1924 to 1955 by the Society for Science and the Public, an organization that was founded in 1921 to advance public understanding and appreciation of science through publications and educational programs. Science Service, a nonprofit organization in Washington, D.C., encouraged students, parents, teachers, and communities to explore the world of science through publications and programs, science fairs, and scholarship competitions. This article provided practical advice for parents about how to discuss the war and the impact on the family.

Frank, honest answers to his questions is one way of keeping the child from worry and fear about the war. Real answers that helped dispel the fears of a group of American children are given by Mrs. Mary Shattuck Fisher, chairman of the child study department at Vassar College and director of its nursery schools, in the *Journal of Home Economics*.

To the question, will New York be bombed, the answer was in part:

"Yes, New York may be bombed and it is important for us to be ready. We will build up defense just as we have fire departments to project us in case of fire."

The child's fear about air raids might be relieved by an answer such as the following:

"Yes, air raids are dangerous, but so is city traffic. We will all learn how to obey the new rules, how to watch for the right signals, how to project each other."

If the child is frightened at the possibility of being evacuated to a safer but far away place, the answer is to explain that it is better for families to stay together, even in war, but that if he does go away for a while it will be like going to camp. Other children and probably his teacher will go along. It will not be too far for his parents to visit him occasionally.

Hardest to answer are the questions about Daddy who has gone away to war. Suggested answers are:

"No, we don't know how long Daddy will be gone. We are all trying to help win the war as soon as possible so he will come back soon."

"Yes, of course we hope Daddy will come back safe and we believe he will. Yes, some men will be killed on our side too, but that is what war means. When our country is attacked, men are proud to fight for their country."

Especially important is the reassurance in the following:

"No, you will not be alone. If Daddy doesn't come back I will still take care of you."

DOCUMENT 73

Photograph, *Public Nurseries for U.S. War Workers' Children*, ca. 1940s

Courtesy of the Library of Congress, LC-DIG-ds-03563.

In 1942 the War Manpower Commission stated, "The first responsibility of women with young children, in war as in peace, is to give suitable care in their own homes to their children." However, the federal government recognized that in order to meet the production demands of the war, women, some of them with young children, would be needed in industry. Consequently, the government designated some funds to support child-care centers for women working in the defense and defense-related industries. The caption for this photograph reads, "Public nurseries for U.S. war workers' children. After a warm meal at noontime, these American children take off their shoes for their nap in their public nursery, one of forty-one servicing an industrial area of thirty miles on the western U.S. coast. Their parents are working in a shipyard and their nursery school was established through funds appropriated by the U.S. Congress for the benefit of war workers' children. The nursery is open from six a.m. to six p.m."

Document 73

DOCUMENT 74

Ann Ross, "What Seven Mothers Did," *Parents' Magazine,* May 1943

Courtesy of Meredith Corporation.

Popular magazines such as *Parents' Magazine* regularly presented articles focused on helpful tips or inspirational stories about women's commitment to the war effort. First published in October 1926, *Parents'* features information about child development and is geared toward women ages eighteen to thirty-five. This article, from 1943, details how a group of mothers in New York worked to solve their day care needs in a cooperative fashion, creating a unique solution to a growing problem.

Mothers have time for war work while their children keep happy in this nursery. Seven New York mothers who wanted to do their share of war work, but who had children between two and six years of age, are responsible for the first cooperative nursery school to receive official rating from the Office of Civilian Defense as a war project. Mothers who wish to enroll their children in this school must pledge themselves to devote a certain number of hours each week to some form of war work.

What this group did others can do. This is the way the New York group went about it. The first step was to find out whether or not the community wanted or needed a nursery. The Committee for the Care of Young Children in Wartime supplied this group with survey cards and leaflets. The survey questions were set up by an expert questionnaire man and had been thoroughly tested. These questionnaire cards, incidentally, are available to any community or individual who requests them.

Some 400 individuals were interviewed and it was discovered that, almost without exception, mothers with nursery-age children wanted such a nursery. So enthusiastic were they that the membership mushroomed from 12 mothers to 60 in three weeks.

A money-raising committee was elected and authorized to go ahead with plans to raise funds. A treasurer was added to the officers and a committee was set up to get in touch with community leaders in order to secure sponsors for the project. These sponsors, it was hoped, would give not only advice, but financial aid as well. Another source of income was derived from membership dues. Each mother who joined the Inwood Nursery Group paid 50 cents a month.

In the meantime, it was thought advisable to start a temporary play group for the children of members so that mothers could devote more time to the business of actually getting the organization worked out and financed. A competent, professional nursery-school teacher was persuaded to take charge for a nominal fee. She donated much of her time and also became a project member, giving her experience and knowledge to the group.

A dinner and other money-raising projects brought in enough to pay rent for the nursery-school headquarters for one month, and to buy some essential equipment as well. Four light, airy, spacious rooms formed a splendid set-up, large enough for upwards of 70 children. A play yard, belonging to the apartment located on the ground floor, was an unexpected and welcome bonanza. The building owner, who became a project member, offered the apartment at a reduced rental.

A carpenter was called in to build shelves. One mother donated some small tables and chairs. Another contributed a radio. A clock, curtains, pictures, books, paints and colored papers and a host of other items poured in. Local tradespeople contributed equipment. The hardware shop gave a mop, broom and scrubbing paraphernalia. The druggist gave cotton, iodine, bandages. Toys of all kinds found their way to nursery headquarters.

The play yard was cleaned up and since sand is a never-failing source of interest, especially to the two and three-year-olds, a sand pit deep enough to permit real digging and large enough for free play was constructed. Buckets, pails, pans, shovels, scoops, and containers of various sizes and shapes were provided.

A large sign, patriotically painted red, white and blue and bearing the legend, Inwood Community Day Nursery, affiliated with the Office of Civilian Defense, was placed where passers-by could see it. The school opened. It was not completely equipped, the carpenter was still working, there was only one trained supervisor. But still there it was—the first cooperative school in the city to receive recognition as a war project.

Sixteen children came to school that first Monday morning. Each child carried a doctor's certificate of health. This is required of any child entering the nursery. Regular check-ups will be made so that there will be no health hazard. These physical examinations are to be made by a local physician who donates his services.

By the end of the week, there were 35 children who were discovering the value of one another as playmates. They soon learned to share, to lead and follow, to assert or accept as the group demanded, and were having all the other character-building experiences that nursery school provides.

The school day is divided into two sessions. The younger children attend from 9 to 12 in the morning, the older ones come to school from 2:30 to 5:30 in the afternoon. The informality of the school routine appeals to the children. There are opportunities for exercise of both mind and body. The youngsters spend most of their time playing freely, with pauses for refreshments—milk and crackers or cookies—and certain minimum rest periods. A definite plan, however, is maintained, though the children aren't aware of it, so that there is balance between rest and activity. Music, stories and organized games and handicrafts all have their place in the schedule.

Most important during this emergency period, these children are becoming accustomed to being way from their mothers and with their teachers and playmates each day. This is a very vital experience for children, particularly today. If evacuation should come, the child who has never been away from his mother's side for half a day is the child whom it may be difficult to manage. The nursery school experience is also excellent preparation for the child's later school experience since it teaches them to get along with other children and develop self-reliance.

DOCUMENT 75

Excerpt, Florence Hollis, "The Impact of the War on Marriage Relationships," *Proceedings of the National Conference of Social Work* 70 (1943)

Courtesy of the William Allan Neilson Library, Smith College.

With women assuming many male-dominated jobs and roles, gender relationships were often altered in the 1940s. This article was presented at the National Conference of Social Work by Florence Hollis in 1943. Hollis was an esteemed professional in the field of social work, working at family agencies in Philadelphia and Cleveland in the 1930s and early 1940s, as well as teaching at Western Reserve University in Cleveland. Hollis used a case-study approach to explore how the war affected the dynamics of marital relationships.

In spite of the fact that we have now been at war for over a year we are still just beginning to understand some of the effects of our industrial and military mobilization on human lives.

• • •

We know that the war effort has two main phases—the industrial and the military. Each has its own effects on civilian life and each must be considered separately in its impact on marriage. Though we are sometimes loath to admit it, there is no denying the fact that industrially the war has brought some definite advantages. Certainly today there is a job for almost everyone who wants one. There is no question but that this in itself has had a favorable effect on many marriages. While we may doubt whether financial distress alone causes serious marital conflict, it can scarcely be denied that it frequently increases existing conflicts. During the depression we learned what money and a job mean to a man and a woman. To both, the ability to earn money is a symbol of adequacy, and money given by a husband to his wife usually represents an expression of his love and his wish to care for her. Furthermore, the absence of money causes a series of physical and social privations which, in turn, make it more difficult for people to tolerate each other if they already have reason for mutual irritation. Conversely, under present conditions of employment, possession of an adequate income may increase the tolerance of a husband and wife for each other's foibles.

The Foley family provides an interesting illustration. Mr. Foley is a good-natured alcoholic. Typically, he married a rather motherly, dominant, capable woman who has alternately loved and nagged, while he has alternately deserted and returned to his ever growing family. Mr. Foley was a skilled workman, but he had long been unemployed. Although he had been drinking less during the last few years, he had little initiative in looking for work. Shortly after Pearl Harbor he secured work in a shipyard. After a brief period of employment he became ill and was absent for about a week. The illness may have well been psychological reaction to his new responsibilities, and in ordinary times his faint effort toward self-support would thus have ended in failure. However, his work was really needed, and he was welcomed back. Mrs. Foley, meanwhile, had gained considerable understanding of her husband. She took every opportunity to show her appreciation of the usefulness of his work and pointed out to him his importance to the war effort. As she commented to the case worker, "To hear me talk you'd think he was winning the war by himself."

It has been interesting to watch Mr. Foley's use of his money. At first he wanted it all for himself, for he had not had a new suit for years and had had no spending money. Gradually, however, he reached the point where he was willing to contribute a fair proportion of his wages to the upkeep of the home.

This is a familiar pattern. Before the depression case workers had considerable success in helping the motherly but dominant woman to use her warmth and strength to support her husband rather than to weaken him. In depression years we lost some of our skill and confidence in this approach because so often industry could not absorb the borderline worker, and eventually the wife's unrewarded patience wore thin as the husband's half-hearted efforts to get work met continual rebuff. We need to pick up these skills again. The current of events is with us now, and many borderline workers may be recruited for useful war work and kept on the job if supportive help can be given to their family relationships.

The Foley case also demonstrates the increased prestige value of manual work. Most marriages run more smoothly if a man and his wife feel that he is doing something worth while. A marriage is not made or broken on that score alone, but it is one of the valuable props of successful family life.

Another generally beneficial effect of the war has been the increase in wage rates. This, of course, has been very uneven in its effects. Many workers have not had substantial wage increases and find themselves at a greater disadvantage than ever with rising living costs. It cannot be concluded, however, that this generally healthy and desirable trend has in all instances favorably affected married life.

Mr. Martens, for example, was employed in a useful and necessary job by a utility company. He was adequately paid and had opportunities for advancement and security for the future. However, his friends were making more money in war industries. His contribution to the war effort would be no greater in the job to which he wanted to shift; he would merely be exchanging postwar security for more immediate benefits. The case worker encouraged him to stick to his work. Nevertheless, the pull of high wages was too strong, and he made the shift. While he was learning the new job his pay was low, and the financial burden became so heavy that he threatened to desert his family. First the public agency and then the private family agency supplemented his wages. Finally his wife took a job in a hospital, in spite of the fact that she had eight young children. From our point of view, it was a foolish choice, but for him it was a necessary one. It then became the job of the case worker to help make the situation a workable one and to keep it from disrupting a marriage that in many respects was satisfying.

A counterpart of this situation arises when the wife rather than the husband presses for higher wages. When she sees that other women's husbands earn more money, a wife's latent dissatisfaction with her husband's position may flare up. If the husband is not willing or able to make a change, his wife's pressure may cause him to lose satisfaction in his job. His pleasure in taking care of her and the children may disappear, and bickering and quarreling result.

· · ·

One of the dominant trends of the war is the increasing employment of women. What the general effect of this will be on marriage is hard to say. If Pearl Buck is right in stressing the consciousness of boredom and uselessness in the average middle- and upper-class woman we might expect her entrance into industry would increase a woman's sense of well-being and, in turn, her ability to contribute to a healthy marriage. There seems little reason to doubt that this is often true.

We know, however, that in our complicated society, with its traditional concept of employment as a masculine prerogative, a woman's working may have symbolic meaning for her husband and may be a threat to him if he is not altogether secure in his masculinity. There is certainly a real question as to whether a mother can carry a double load without becoming so fatigued that she is unable to carry her share of mutual living, either physically or emotionally. This depends, of course, on a variety of factors, including health, natural energy, and the extent of home responsibilities.

There were several illustrations among the records of increased marital conflict resulting from the entrance of a wife into industry. This was particularly true where the woman's earnings were higher than her husband's or where her general work adjustment was more successful. The records also demonstrated some of the effects of work opportunities for women in marriages where there was already considerable conflict. In each instance greater employment opportunities meant the practical possibility of separation without too severe financial privation.

· · ·

Many married men enlisted in the armed forces when enlistment was a possibility, others have already been drafted and many more will soon be called. What is the impact of this on marital relationships?

No one would deny that many married men did enlist for strongly felt patriotic motives and entered the Army or Navy despite the fact that their affectional ties at home were strong. It is equally true, however, that there is a group of men for whom enlistment provided a welcome escape from wives with whom they found it difficult to get along. Sometimes the enlistment was impulsive, as in the case of Mr. Muncy, who took his first steps toward enlistment after a quarrel with his wife. He actually hoped and expected that she would stop the proceedings by claiming dependency, but she was angry, too. Now both are sorry. Both made desperate attempts to have him released, for she was pregnant and in a highly emotional state, but it proved impossible. It is hard to know what the ultimate effect on this marriage will be. The fact that both people were involved in the step may make it somewhat easier to bear. There had been ups and downs in the marriage before, and it may be that a period of separation will not be without its advantages.

• • •

Another type of behavior appears in these records. Frequently there are cases in which a wife reports her husband to the selective service board for nonsupport, thus causing him to be drafted. Case workers have long been familiar with the angry, punishing wife who wants the judge to "teach her man a lesson" by sending him to jail. Now she possesses a weapon of no mean power. Sometimes she uses it as a threat; sometimes she actually does cause her husband to be drafted. She usually does not face the possibility of his being injured or killed, but rather thinks of the "wonderful discipline," and hopes "it will make a man of him."

• • •

The most common situation of all remains to be discussed—that of the married man who is drafted in the natural course of events. Since the material from which this discussion was gathered [came] entirely from agencies dealing with civilians it will be impossible to discuss only the woman who is left at home. Here we have a wide range of reactions depending partly on the personality patterns of the wife and partly on the type of relationship that existed in the marriage. Since most marriages are a mixture of satisfaction and dissatisfaction, almost every wife whose husband enters the service has a sense of severe loss, a sense of deprivation and of frustration.

. . . If a woman is grieving we need to give her a chance to act out and live out these feelings, not try to smother them in admonitions to be "brave."

There is, however, a second step in this process of adjustment—

the reorganization of energy, turning it out again, away from the self into new channels that give a goodly measure of substitute satisfaction. Some women will already have well-developed channels for their energies; others will need help in finding new ones. For many, entrance into industry may be part of the solution; and a very useful part, for through this they will advance the war effort as well as contribute to their own peace of mind.

• • •

It is exceedingly important that we learn how to help women to adjust to the drafting of their husbands. We are now moving into that phase of the war in which married men will be drawn into the services on a larger scale. They cannot put their best into their new jobs if their relationships with their wives are strained, if letters from home are full of troubles and complaints. Neither can the wives carry their extra burdens if they have not found a way of working out their feelings concerning the separation.

DOCUMENT 76
Excerpt, Oral History, Clare Marie Morrison Crane

Courtesy of the Veterans History Project, American Folklife Center, Library of Congress.

Clare Marie Morrison Crane, a native of Cleveland, Ohio, married Second Lieutenant Herbert G. Johns on May 29, 1943. Crane was interviewed by Elizabeth Henderson as part of the Veterans History Project in 2002, and her experience highlighted the life of soldiers' wives during the war, from frequent relocations to supporting the local USO. For the complete transcript, visit http://lcweb2.loc.gov/diglib/vhp/story/loc.natlib.afc2001001.01754/#vhp:other.

Elizabeth Henderson: When the war first started, how did you first begin to help on the Home Front?

Clare Marie Crane: I was in my junior year of college and our Dean of Women asked me to participate in the USO program.

Elizabeth Henderson: Was this soon after America joined in World War II?

Clare Marie Crane: Yes, it was early '42, after Pearl Harbor December 7,1941.

Elizabeth Henderson: Were you with anybody during the war years?

Clare Marie Crane: Actually I married in '43 and traveled as an army wife for 5 months.

Elizabeth Henderson: What was your spouse's name?

Clare Marie Crane: I was married to Second Lieutenant Herbert G. Johns.

Elizabeth Henderson: What was his wartime occupation?

Clare Marie Crane: He was a graduate of Case School of Applied Sciences and Western Reserve University. And he went into the army Air Forces as a communications officer, doing mostly radio work.

Elizabeth Henderson: When were you married?

Clare Marie Crane: I graduated on May 23, 1943, and the following Saturday, May 29, I was married. It was completely unplanned. There were alot of girls who were engaged and getting married. The time was right for them.

Elizabeth Henderson: Where did you travel with your husband?

Clare Marie Crane: We left from Cleveland Terminal and went to Chicago. If was beastly hot that Decoration Day Weekend. Then we started to travel west on an old steam train called The Challenger. It took us four days to travel west and finally ended up at Salt Lake City, Utah.

Elizabeth Henderson: Where did you live during your travels?

Clare Marie Crane: During our travels in Salt Lake City and then on to Tucson, I was the person who had to go out and find the quarters for us to live in. My husband, all he had to do was go to base and check into the bachelor officers' quarters so he had shelter and food, but I had to make the arrangements to find a room.

Elizabeth Henderson: Where [sic] there any humorous stories involved?

Clare Marie Crane: Oh, yes indeed, (laughs). When I was in Salt Lake City, most of the people there—the townspeople—were

Mormons and they'd ask me, "Are you a Mormon?" and I'd say
"No." Then they dismissed me right away. I caught on to it, and
when they'd ask me if I was a saint, I would say "No, I'm not a
saint but my husband is" (laughs).

Elizabeth Henderson: Did you have a hard time finding housing in
Salt Lake City?

Clare Marie Crane: Salt Lake City was a very beautiful, clean city
with alot of Victorian type large houses where they had second
floors and third floors. While I was in Salt Lake City, I lived with
a woman named Mrs. Whitehead. She actually was a 60-year-old
lady with white hair. At first the rules of the house were: You
couldn't wash, you couldn't hang anything outside, you couldn't
iron, you couldn't have food in your room and you couldn't have
visitors. But I was there probably about a week, and they'd say
"Oh, if you want to wash, go ahead and wash. If you want to put
something in the refrigerator, go ahead and put something in the
refrigerator." So I got along very good with the landlady. I tried to
be very neat.

Elizabeth Henderson: I remember you telling me about the passes
you had to carry around with you.

Clare Marie Crane: Yes. When we traveled down in Tucson, Arizona,
we were to be stationed at Davis Monthan Air Base. There was
a big influx of people into Tucson. There was a big Navy contin-
gent at the University of Arizona and load of airmen at the Davis
Monthan Airfield. They had only three constables in the town,
so the whole police force was just Military Police—the town was
under martial law. I know I probably pulled a big boner, but [I
was] trying to get near the air base. So I got on this bus, and I was
going towards the airbase and I imagined that I would see a sign
"Welcome to Tucson, we have a room for you" but this did not
happen. And we were pulling onto the airbase, the MP's were
coming on the bus to check passes. But I didn't have a pass! So
the provost Marshall came in a jeep and hauled me away to some
type of military establishment. I told him that my husband was
here on the base and that he was going to bring me over to introduce me in a couple of days. So I told him his name and a few
minutes later, a Lieutenant came in and he said "I never saw this

woman before in my life!" and here it was a Lieutenant Johnson instead of a Lieutenant Johns. But I did get photographed and fingerprinted and did get my pass.

Elizabeth Henderson: While you were in Arizona, did you have any activities you were involved with over there?

Clare Marie Crane: Well actually, I had a little job. During my high school years and college years, I worked in a dress shop so I found employment in a dress shop where I lived. And I could even walk right up to the dress shop, which was at Broadway and Country Club Road. And it was interesting because we had a lot of starlets from Hollywood. They would make motion pictures right behind the little shopping area near the dress shop where I worked. The movies, which were Westerns, would be filmed out on the desert. And they would come in to buy their handbags and lingerie and jewelry. And of course, when the servicemen were paid, they'd come in to buy gifts for their mothers and friends.

Elizabeth Henderson: When did you move back to Cleveland?

Clare Marie Crane: We came back to Cleveland in October of '43. And we did this because my husband was being shipped from the Pacific area to the Atlantic area. We knew then that he would be going toward England.

Elizabeth Henderson: When you were in the Cleveland area, how did you serve in the War Front Effort?

Clare Marie Crane: Our Dean of Women asked me to go to the USO and look out for our girls who were going to serve as hostesses. They picked me because I was engaged. They did not want any of the girls falling for men in uniform; (laughs) It was called "khaki wacky."

Elizabeth Henderson: What type of activities were you involved in?

Clare Marie Crane: We did a lot of things. We served food, mostly doughnuts, coffee, sandwiches, and whatever pies and cakes people would bring in. We had an area where you could sing around the piano, or dance, or play records. There was an area where the servicemen could go to rest, wash up, and in the meantime we would press their blouses or middies. And we had a job also because of the Port of Cleveland. Whenever Navy personnel came in, they would have the name of their ship on their head-band, and it was thought that this was not a good idea that everyone know what ships were in port. So we would rip the headband off and just throw it into the wastebasket and put on a headband ribbon that said U.S. Navy. I wish now that I had kept some of the ribbons. What a momento [*sic*] those would be.

Elizabeth Henderson: What sections of Cleveland were you very active in?

Clare Marie Crane: Our USO was the main one located at East 6th and Prospect, about three blocks from the Public Square. And we did have a USO in the Terminal Tower Building, but that was mostly for servicemen who were waiting after hours for their trains to go out.

Elizabeth Henderson: What hours would you work at the USO?

Clare Marie Crane: We would go in around 7:30 in the evening and stay until 11:30 and then we would leave. There was to be no dating of service people. Sometimes we would come out, and they would be waiting for us. We would walk them to the square and show them where they could get shelter in the terminal USO and then my girlfriends' father would drive his car around the square to pick us up and take us home.

Elizabeth Henderson: Did you ever interact with prisoners of war?

Clare Marie Crane: Yes. There was a time when my younger brother was a patient at Crile Hospital in Parma, Ohio. For 16 weeks, I went out and visited with him and with the other people who were being treated. And sometimes I would even talk with the prisoners of war. When they had some free time, they could use the gym or use the swimming pool. And I would talk in German to these prisoners of war.

Elizabeth Henderson: What struck you the most about these prisoners of war?

Clare Marie Crane: Their youth. Just that they were nice young people so far from home and lonely.

Elizabeth Henderson: Why did you decide to go into the USO?

Clare Marie Crane: Well, I had two brothers that were going into the service and of course my fiance was in the service and I had a lot of friends who were going into the service. As a matter of fact, in our recreation room, I had a huge map of the United States, also the Pacific area and the European area, and I would put little pin points wherever I knew a serviceman.

Elizabeth Henderson: In your graduating class, were there any tragedies that occurred because of the war?

Clare Marie Crane: Yes, one of my friends, her name was Virginia Donahue and she was married—I believe it was in June—and her husband was stationed, a medical officer, in Hawaii. We thought, "How wonderful! What a grand place for a honeymoon!" She did not have any children at that time, but she was the kind of person that liked to do things, so she was driving a group of children either to or from Sunday school on Sunday December 7. The enemy planes flew over and strafed the open car she was driving. She and the children perished.

• • •

Elizabeth Henderson: Did you find that in your community everyone worked together?

Clare Marie Crane: Yes, the home front was very active. We had Victory Gardens, which supplied us some nice things because there was a rationing of food and gasoline and other things like leathers and metals. And the Victory Gardens—everyone pitched in from the schoolchildren to the really older citizens. Then a lot of the older men in the neighborhood became air-raid wardens and we would have practices—thank God (laughs)—alerts. But still they were scary. I mean, it was night and it was dark and there was no light showing and the sirens were going. It was a scary time. It was a serious time.

Elizabeth Henderson: What kind of civil defense and homeland defense was there?

Clare Marie Crane: Well I believe they had a number of air raid shelters but I don't think they were used because we were never attacked from the air.

Elizabeth Henderson: What was your reaction to December 7, 1941?

Clare Marie Crane: Well, we were overcome by the fact that our

Navy was practically destroyed and that it was what others called a sneak attack. It wasn't anticipated. Nobody was ready for it The men who were stationed in Hawaii were enjoying a Sunday! And then all of a sudden, this attack. The planes on the ground were destroyed and the battleships were destroyed and thousands of sailors were lost. We still commemorate the Arizona and the young men who were on that ship. They reported that they literally had to climb over bodies to get out. And when they did get out to a deck, they had to dive into a sea of burning oil. And then they could spend maybe 6–8 months having their burns repaired. So it was a devastating attack.

• • •

Elizabeth Henderson: Was it very difficult having your husband overseas? Did you write a lot of letters?

Clare Marie Crane: Oh, yes. (laughs) I tried to write about every other day. I can remember how we would watch the mailman go down the block and then turn around and come down our side of the block and we would just sit by the window and wait to see if his shoes would turn up our walk. And if they did, we would get so excited.

Elizabeth Henderson: You must have a lot of letters from him.

Clare Marie Crane: Oh yes. I must have around 500 letters, some v-mail and some airmail. You could send a regular letter for about $0.03 and an air letter was I believe $0.06.

Elizabeth Henderson: Can you tell me about V-mail?

Clare Marie Crane: V-mail was something to expedite your letters—to get them over to the service people quicker. They had two post offices—one was in New York and the other was I believe in San Francisco and you would purchase this sheet of paper and you would write your letter on one side, fold it up and write the address on the other side. The postal service would photograph it, reduce it to about Va [sic] of the size, and then send it off overseas.

Elizabeth Henderson: Was there a lot of censorship?

Clare Marie Crane: Oh, yes. My husband censored his own letters. He was very careful not to mention anything he shouldn't mention. Some young people tried to have a code to say where they were, but I don't think it really worked (laughs). Everybody was going to the "Salisbury Cathedral" and we were supposed to know exactly where that was in a foreign country, (laughs).

Elizabeth Henderson: Besides being active in the USO and helping out with the war effort, how would you entertain yourself?

Clare Marie Crane: Well, we always had the movies. We had a movie house in downtown Cleveland that hourly ran war news pictures and we could keep pretty much up to date with what was happening. They would show bits of a battle and then it would be made into a newsreel.

Elizabeth Henderson: Did you look forward to the newsreels or were they difficult to watch?

Clare Marie Crane: They were usually on an upbeat theme. And, of course, they had a lot of wartime movies. They had movies about Jimmy Doolittle and the boy next door and alot of different movies about the airplanes and about the ships and the submarines. You've probably seen some of them yourself.

Elizabeth Henderson: I have a question about your wedding. What was your wedding like? Because it took place in 1943, was it difficult to plan because of the rationing?

Clare Marie Crane: Well, since my mother had a dress shop, it was not a problem to get a dress—a wedding dress. Not the one that I would have probably picked (laughs) but it was there and I could use it. We serviced alot of weddings at that time. And I just called up my girlfriends and told them, and I said—we all had little semi-formal dresses—and I said "Just wear one of your pretty semi-formal dresses." And they had different colors. We had one girl in yellow, one in aqua, and one in peach and I was in white of course. And it was a beautiful wedding and in a brand new church. Our parish had built a brand new church and the first wedding was supposed to in June. But I sort of sneaked in and had the wedding in the end of May (laughs). So I was the first bride in the new church.

Elizabeth Henderson: Can you tell me about the signs you had in the window, with the "V" and the three stars?

Clare Marie Crane: Oh, yes. When servicemen went off to the war, their parents or spouses could purchase a little flag emblem that you would put in the window and it would have however many stars. First we had one star, then two stars, and then we had three stars, because my husband and two brothers were in. And then, if one of the soldiers perished, they had an embroidered gold star that you could affix over it. And they probably have something like that today, but the one I have is 60 years old. (see artifacts)

Elizabeth Henderson: I notice that there is a gold star on yours.

Clare Marie Crane: Yes, that's true. It was—my husband served all of '42, '43, '44, and half of '45. And they were processing him to go to Japan. The war in England had ended May 8th and they were processing them to go to Japan. There hadn't been any talk of any furloughs for them to come back home before going. I guess nobody knew of the plans for the atomic bomb. It was all secret stuff. But it was during this process when they were giving shots to go to Japan that they discovered my husband had leukemia. And it was a rapid illness—he died within ten days of the discovery. So I actually got the telegram that he died before I even knew that he was sick. So that was a very sad time for us. I had to tell his older parents—he was the youngest of the family. I had to tell his mother and father, who were in their late 60's. It was a sad time for them.

Elizabeth Henderson: I remember reading the chaplain's letter. That must have been comforting to receive that from him.

Clare Marie Crane: Yes, and I must comment on the Red Cross. When we got the telegram that he had died at Gander Field in New Foundland, the Red Cross let me have a phone call all the way to St John's Newfoundland to talk to the base there. And they assured me that it was a military funeral with all honors. From his dogtags, his religion was noted, so he was able to have the last rites of his faith. He was in repose there until '47 or '48 when they finally abandoned that cemetery and brought him to Arlington National Cemetery.

• • •

Elizabeth Henderson: What was it like on D-Day? On V-E Day?

Clare Marie Crane: Well, there was a lot of celebrating. People downtown were blowing horns and throwing papers out of the windows. They were generally just, you know, being happy. And everyone would say to me, "Aren't you happy that it is over?" I would answer, "Well, it won't be over til mine come back."

Elizabeth Henderson: Was it difficult because though there was a lot of celebrating, alot of young men did not return?

Clare Marie Crane: That's true. Though the war in Europe was over May 8, my brother didn't return home until December 8. It took him seven months to be processed and brought back to New York.

Elizabeth Henderson: Was there a lack of social opportunities because of the war?

Clare Marie Crane: When you would go into Cleveland, you just would not see any young men. There just weren't any—and if there were, they were in uniform. Even some of the big hotels in Cleveland did not want the women to congregate and come into the dining rooms or some of the cocktail lounges because they wanted to reserve that for the male military personnel. We had alot of Navy personnel in Cleveland. We had alot of army personnel. We had offices of price administration. It was embarrassing for these men to have to be in contact with so many women who were unescorted (laughs).

Elizabeth Henderson: What was your most memorable experience during the war?

Clare Marie Crane: Family get-togethers. We had every generation. We had a youngster 2 years old that was our pride and joy and happiness. And we had the young wives together and we had the mothers consoling one another and the fathers stepping up and doing some of the harder work—the yard work and the county work—and work that you couldn't get tradesmen to do. Everyone was doing his or her part.

Elizabeth Henderson: Didn't you say that your grandpa would have service men over?

Clare Marie Crane: Oh yes. Old Dutch. All the service members when they came back to Cleveland would want to visit Old Dutch. Because my grandfather came from a place in Germany that was on the Holland border and they had many cultural ways of the Dutch people. As a matter of fact, in my grandparents' garden, they wore their wooden shoes like rubbers. We would save up all our ration stamps for Sunday night and we would get cold cuts, spam, and different things to make sandwiches and we'd have coffee and pastries—whatever was available. And we always used canned condensed milk because that sweetened and colored the coffee. They had a regular open house on Sunday night for any service people.

Elizabeth Henderson: Did you learn how to improvise with meals and clothing during the wartime?

Clare Marie Crane: Well, actually I had a project while I was in my senior year at Notre Dame College. I was in a home economics tailoring class and just before my older brother went off to the war, he had bought himself a lovely Glenn plaid suit. I said, "It's just a shame that it is hanging there doing nothing." So we retailored the suit and out of the pants I was able to get a four-gore skirt and the jacket we just had to take out some of the padding and manipulate the back seams. We made a suit over for me. They photographed it and it was quite a to-do wearing my brother's suit.

Elizabeth Henderson: Did you find creative ways to make the meals stretch?

Clare Marie Crane: Yes, well if you had a Victory Garden and say you had as many as twelve vegetables in your Victory Garden with some of the vegetables and even a small amount of meat, you could make a pretty good soup or stew. We didn't have any supermarkets like we do today—we had a neighborhood butcher. Maybe you dealt with this butcher—your family—for 15 or 20 years and he would take care of you. You would go in, maybe on your regular shopping day and he would have three little parcels. You didn't even tell him what you wanted, but he'd have something for you. Maybe a little bit of chicken or a little bit of pork or sausages or bacon or something—he'd have three little packages for you. It used to be a riot, because my grandmother would go into the butcher and she would always want to cook a five-pound roast. And she (laughs) she would order this roast and then he'd ask for the ration points and she would hand the book to him and say "Here, take them out of here." Well there wouldn't be any in there, but we had a connection with a restaurant and my mother would always tell this restaurant when we were celebrating Fish Day. So they would give her the extra meat ration stamps. And she would give them to the butcher to make up for what grandma would order, (laughs).

Elizabeth Henderson: What do you think was one of your most humorous experiences during the war?

Clare Marie Crane: Well, do you remember how Winston Churchill used to give the "V" sign? Well, like I said, my grandfather had no accent at all but my grandmother had a little bit of an accent. And in Germany there are no "W's" Their name was "Walters" but it was pronounced "Volters". And if you remember the "Volksvagon", not "Volkswagon". So anyhow, "W's" were always pronounced as a "V". So we would say to her, "Grandma, do you know what that V-sign means?" She would say, "Sure. Yeah, sure." She'd say "Ve vant to vin." (laughs).

Elizabeth Henderson: Speaking of that, did you worry that our side would not win?

Clare Marie Crane: No. No. Never. We have the industry, we have the know-how, we have the talent. We had the raw materials. There was no way. We are a gifted country.

Elizabeth Henderson: Do you think that the rest of the nation had that morale?

Clare Marie Crane: Yes, mm-hmm. Pennsylvania could produce more coal and more steel then any place in the world. We could turn out automobiles and we could turn out tanks, planes, and shipping boats. It was just to get the effort going.

Elizabeth Henderson: Do you think that despite the difficult time, good came out of the war time period?

Clare Marie Crane: Well yes. I have had a good life since then. I had to reconstruct my home life. But I went on to marry again and have seven children, home, and retire and to have a reasonably good life.

Elizabeth Henderson: What happened after the war had ended?

Clare Marie Crane: Well, when the men came home, so much was needed because all of the efforts went to making war materials. People were living doubled up in housing for three or four years. Everybody wanted to go to the suburbs. Every fellow coming back from the service needed a new car. Many had an old car when they went in [the service] and it was used up. Everyone needed a car, people needed refrigerators—everything was booming. Everyone wanted to move to the suburbs. There was construction and that is where you get all the suburbs.

It was such a long time before the fellows came back. My brother that was released from Crile Hospital, we had him back right away. They had all types of programs to help these men. He went to John Carroll University and picked up his studies under the G.I Bill. We had very good legislation to help these men. They had Veteran's Villages where they would build housing. And they had college funding. So everyone was ready to get on with their lives.

Elizabeth Henderson: How do you look back on those times?

Clare Marie Crane: Well, if I could live my life over I would gladly, except I would not want to experience the 1940's again.

Elizabeth Henderson: What would you like to say to the next generation? Do you have any words of wisdom to impart?

Clare Marie Crane: It is true—we were the greatest generation. As we came after the roaring 20's and the gangster era. We grew up in the hard times of the depression years 1930 to 1937. We knew how to win and how to make do! Credit was no temptation—we had cash before the purchase. Prices seemed fairer. Products had more value and durability.

There should be more courtesy and hospitality and social grace. Everything seems too casual. So, be polite. Be refined. Be the best you can be.

DOCUMENT 77

Poster, "Be with Him at Every Mail Call," Recruiting Publicity Bureau of the US Army, 1945

Courtesy of the University of North Texas Digital Library, Posters WW2, Hiller 1.

V-mail (Victory mail), which originated in Great Britain, involved microfilming letters during World War II. To save cargo space, the microfilmed copies were sent overseas and then enlarged once they reached their destination. This process dramatically reduced the volume of mail that had to be transported—150,000 one-page

letters that would have required thirty-seven mailbags could be carried in one V-mail sack. Blue-striped cardboard containers held V-mail letter forms and became a symbol of the war. This poster, created and distributed by the Publicity Bureau of the US Army, encouraged women to write to provide emotional support to their husbands or boyfriends who were serving in the army through V-mail, which was described as "private, reliable, and patriotic."

DOCUMENT 78

Poster, "I Gave a Man!," US Department of the Treasury, 1942

Courtesy of the University of North Texas Digital Library, Posters WW2, Sarra 1.

One mechanism that the US government used to finance the war was the sale of war bonds. The first war bond was sold to President Franklin D. Roosevelt, who encouraged all Americans to support the cause. The US Department of the Treasury recruited celebrities to advocate for "patriotic Americans" to buy bonds, and they distributed posters to encourage workers to contribute 10 percent of their pay to the cause.

DOCUMENT 79

Photograph, *Margaret Mitchell at a War Bond Rally*, c. 1940

Courtesy of the Georgia Archives, Lamar Q. Ball Collection, lball0705.

Celebrities played an important role in encouraging the public to support the war effort through buying war bonds. In Atlanta, author Margaret Mitchell, who had become world famous following the 1936 publication of her bestselling novel, *Gone with the Wind*, worked tirelessly from 1940 until the end of the war, attend-

I GAVE A MAN !

SARRA

Will you give at least 10% of your pay in War Bonds?

Document 78

ing war bond rallies and promoting the purchase of war bonds to support the building of the USS *Atlanta*, a light cruiser designed to provide anti-aircraft protection for US Naval task groups. After the first USS *Atlanta* was sunk by the Japanese at Guadalcanal in November 1942, Mitchell led the campaign to replace the ship. On one day in mid-January of 1943, Mitchell and a group of marines spearheaded a rally in downtown Atlanta that raised over $500,000 for the new ship, which was launched in December 1944.

Document 79

DOCUMENT 80
Excerpt, Executive Order 8734, Establishing the Office of Price Administration and Civilian Supply, April 11, 1941

Courtesy of the American Presidency Project.

The Office of Price Administration (OPA) was a US government agency created in 1941 to help manage wartime inflation, which had spiraled out of control during World War I. In addition to setting ceiling prices for most commodities and rents, the OPA also rationed consumer goods. The agency was disbanded in 1947. The full text of the document is available at http://www.presidency.ucsb.edu/ws/?pid=16099#ixzz2gOXte31f.

By virtue of the authority vested in me by the Constitution and the statutes, and in order to define further the functions and duties of the Office for Emergency Management with respect to the national emergency as declared by the President on September 8, 1939, for the purpose of avoiding profiteering and unwarranted price rises, and of facilitating an adequate supply and the equitable distribution of materials and commodities for civilian use, and finding that the stabilization of prices is in the interest of national defense and that this Order is necessary to increase the efficiency of the defense program, it is hereby ordered:

1. There shall be in the Office for Emergency Management of the Executive Office of the President an Office of Price Administration and Civilian Supply, at the head of which shall be an Administrator appointed by the President. The Administrator shall receive compensation at such rate as the President shall determine and, in addition, shall be entitled to actual and necessary transportation, subsistence, and other expenses incidental to the performance of his duties.

2. Subject to such policies, regulations, and directions as the President may from time to time prescribe, and with such advice and assistance as may be necessary from the other departments and agencies of the Federal Government, and utilizing the services and facilities of such other departments and agencies to the fullest extent compatible with efficiency, the Administrator shall:

a. Take all lawful steps necessary or appropriate in order (1) to prevent price spiraling, rising costs of living, profiteering, and inflation resulting from market conditions caused by the diversion of large segments of the Nation's resources to the defense program, by interruptions to normal sources of supply, or by other influences growing out of the emergency; (2) to prevent speculative accumulation, withholding, and hoarding of materials and commodities; (3) to stimulate provision of the necessary supply of materials and commodities required for civilian use, in such manner as not to conflict with the requirements of the War, Navy, and other departments and agencies of the Government, and of foreign Governments, for materials, articles, and equipment needed for defense (such requirements are hereinafter referred to as "military defense needs"); and (4) after the satisfaction of military defense needs to provide, through the determination of policies and the formulation of plans and programs, for the equitable distribution of the residual supply of such materials and commodities among competing civilian demands.

b. Make studies of the Nation's civilian requirements for materials and commodities, the supply of goods and services, the status and trend of prices and factors thereof, and the impact of the defense program upon civilian living standards; exercise the powers of the President in requesting such studies pursuant to Section 336(a) of Title III of the Tariff Act of 1930 (Title 19, U.S.C., Sec. 1336(a)); and conduct such investigations, hold such hearings, and obtain such reports as may be necessary or desirable to carry out this Order.

c. Determine and publish, after proper investigation, such maximum prices, commissions, margins, fees, charges, or other elements of cost or price of materials or commodities, as the Administrator may from time to time deem fair and reasonable; and take all lawful and appropriate steps to facilitate their observance.

d. Advise and make recommendations to other departments and agencies, whenever the Administrator deems it appropriate, in respect to the purchase or acquisition of materials and commodities by the Government, the prices to be paid there—for, and in respect to such of their other activities as may affect the price of materials and commodities.

e. Inform the Office of Production Management of the amount, character, and relative importance of materials and commodities needed for civilian use; and advise and consult with the Office of Production Management with reference to its procurement, production planning, priority, and other actions the effect of which may be to diminish the supply of materials and commodities available for civilian use.

f. Establish and maintain liaison with such departments and agencies of the Government and with such other public or private agencies and persons as the Administrator may deem necessary or desirable to carry out the provisions of this Order.

g. Formulate programs designed to assure adequate standards for, and the most effective use of, consumer goods; stimulate the utilization of substitutes by civilians for consumer goods and commodities of limited supply; develop programs with the object of stabilizing rents; and promote civilian activities which will contribute to the purposes of this Order.

• • •

j. Advise upon proposed or existing legislation, and recommend such additional legislation as may be necessary or desirable, relating to prices, rents, or the increase in supply and the equitable distribution of materials and commodities for civilian use.

k. Keep the President informed in respect to progress made in carrying out this Order; and perform such other related duties as the President may from time to time assign or delegate to him.

3. The Administrator may provide for the internal organization and management of the Office of Price Administration and Civilian Supply, and may appoint such advisory committees as he finds necessary to the performance of his duties and responsibilities. The Administrator shall obtain the President's approval for the establishment of the principal subdivisions of the Office and the appointment of the heads thereof.

4. There shall be in the Office of Price Administration and Civilian Supply a Price Administration Committee consisting of the Administrator as Chairman, the Secretary of the Treasury, the Secretary of Agriculture, the Federal Loan Administrator, the Chairman of the Tariff Commission, the Chairman of the Federal Trade Commission, the Director General and Associate Director General of the Office of Production Management, or such alternate as each may designate, and such other members as the President may subsequently appoint. The Committee shall from time to time, upon request by the Administrator, make findings and submit recommendations to the Administrator in respect to the establishment of maximum prices, commissions, margins, fees, charges, and other elements of cost or price of materials or commodities as provided under paragraph 2c above.

5. Within the limits of such funds as may be appropriated to the Office of Price Administration and Civilian Supply or as may be allocated to it by the President through the Bureau of the Budget, the Administrator may employ necessary personnel and make provision for necessary supplies, facilities, and services. However, the Office of Price Administration and Civilian Supply shall use such statistical, informational, fiscal, personnel, and other general business services and facilities as may be made available to it through the Office for Emergency Management or other agencies of the Government.

DOCUMENT 81

"Price Control Panel Wants Two Women to Investigate Local Retail Price Ceilings," *Reading (Massachusetts) Chronicle*, August 13, 1943

Courtesy of the National Archives, Boston.

This article documents the Reading Ration and Price Control Board's attempts to recruit two women to check on local stores to determine if managers understand the requirements of price controls. The article concluded that it was difficult to recruit volunteers because women considered this kind of activity as "snooping."

Price Control Panel Wants Two Women to Investigate
Local Retail Ceiling Prices
Board Member Says Work is not Snooping if Properly Done—
Many Say it is, and Refuse the Job

The Reading Ration and Price Control Board this week is looking for two women who will serve voluntarily as investigators in the matter of price ceiling observance in Reading stores. "It is not 'snooping'," says Irving F. Jewett, chairman of the price control panel.

The board has for some time been trying to find helpers for this work and Mr. Jewett points out that it merely means checking up on all the stores—particularly food stores—to see if the managers understand the requirements of the price ceiling code. It in no way means that the local board is seeking to prosecute local storekeepers.

It has been carefully pointed out to several who have been offered the job that the investigator would upon entering the store, seek out the manager and inform him of the purpose of the visit. If there were any cases where the price ceilings were not being observed these would be called to his attention and he would be asked by the local board to make changes.

It would only be in the event of open defiance of board rulings that prosecution might take place.

In some instances local stores are not in accord on a matter of point values and there are stores where fewer points are asked for commodities that rate higher on the official scale. This is not allowable. Where prices are under the ceiling, the board does not attempt to bring prices up to a standard level but it is presumed by some that one result of the proposed plan would be to influence merchants to get higher prices if they found there was a chance. It may be generally supposed, however, that not many local merchants are selling much if any below price ceilings.

In spite of explanations of members of the board those who have been asked to take the job of price investigation have refused. Most of them felt that it was "snooping" and some would apparently have taken on the work if they could have been paid for it. It is required, however, that the service be voluntary, the only paid employees of the board being the office administrator and clerical staff.

Right now, the board wants two women who will undertake the task of consulting with merchants on ceiling prices. Mr. Jewett states that it will be a serve to the buying public and in many cases to the merchants.

If approached properly, the job need have no flavor of "snooping" and should require only the most friendly relations between the storekeeper and the investigator, the board declares.

Price panels in other towns are issuing public statements advising purchasers, with complaints against merchants over matters of prices, to take steps to bring about legal prosecution and redress. Mr. Jewett declares that such should not be necessary if the suggested plan of using investigators can be put into operation. The difficulty, however, is to find two women who will take on the duties.

DOCUMENT 82
Excerpt, *Volunteer Training Manual*, 1943

Courtesy of the National Archives, Boston, Records of the War Price and Rationing Boards, Office of Price Administration, Record Group 188.

This training manual provided information for volunteers who assisted the Office of Price Administration (OPA). The OPA's mission was to control money (price controls) and rents after the outbreak of World War II.

Volunteer Assistance Supervisor
TRAINING

This is TOTAL War. We are all in it together. We do not Persume [*sic*] to compare any Home Front job to the magnitude of the task demanded of the bombardier, the sailor, or the foot soldier. We can't help think of the job they are doing and how they are risking their lives to do it, while here at home none of us has come in direct contact with the real horrors of war. We have merely been personally inconvenienced in order to help prosecute total war.

The <u>war will</u> be won on the battlefield. Here at home a healthy economic system must exist to which sons, brothers, husbands, and friends may return—a place of peace and security, religion and love.

The preservation of this policy of Economic security for the post-war world is in large measure the responsibility of OPA Volunteers who aid in fighting inflation. . . . Inflation means a national catastrophe.

National security is guaranteed by community control. Each community has problems peculiar to itself, so by voluntarily solving its own problems, it stabilizes our nation's economy—safeguards our national security.

Role of Price Control:

Business as usual is impossible under conditions of total war. People have more money, but there is less for them to buy. As this greater amount of money bids for smaller quantities of goods, prices rise. It is the duty, then, of the OPA to keep the cost of living down so that everyone can have enough to eat, to wear, and a place to live—through price control.

Accomplishments of Price Control:

Ceilings have been established on the prices of 90% of what the average family buys. It protects business man and housewife alike.

Merchants have been able to replenish stocks.

Speculative buying has been prevented.

Hoarding has been made difficult.

Small business have been protected.

Installment buying has been made more economically sound.

The cost of living has shown comparitively [sic] little change.

World War I—up 64.6%

World War II—up only 27.2%

Home furnishings within 52 months increased

95% in War I

27% in War II

Investments are protected.

Role of Rationing:

Rationing is an American idea dating back to the days of the earliest settlers in this country, who, facing scarcities of food and clothing, pooled their precious supplies and apportioned them to everyone on an equal basis. When war upsets our regular economy, rationing is the one measure the government can take to insure equal opportunities for all citizens in obtaining the necessities of life. Rationing is a community plan for dividing fairly the supplies we have among all who need them. The first objective of our Rationing Program during this war emergency is to serve the welfare of the nation and the community. For example, a man with a million dollars cannot buy any more sugar than a person with one ration allowance.

Why Rationing?

Our Government, through the Office of Price Administration, is rationing only essential goods which have become scarce because of the war. Because of the detailed machinery necessary to administer the rationing program, the Government does not ration non-essentials when they become scarce. Each one of these items on the ration list today represents scarce goods, which, if not made available in the right place at the right time in sufficient quantity, would seriously impair our nation's war effort.

How Things Are Rationed?

When the supply does not permit a rationed commodity gereral [sic] distribution the individual's eligibility for the rationed goods is determined by his particular service to the war effort.

When the supply permits a general rationed distribution, everybody receives a share, the coupon and point system is used, with a change from time to time in the point values and validity of the ration period.

Who Rations:

The most strategic position of the Rationing Program is occupied by the 5500 Local War Price and Rationing Boards throughout the nation. Staffed with public spirited citizens of the community, volunteers who are giving their time and energies, without pay, to the administration of the Rationing Program.

DOCUMENT 83

Poster, "Rationing Means a Fair Share for All of Us," 1943, Office of Price Administration, 1943

Courtesy of the University of North Texas Digital Collection, Posters WW2, Roese 2.

The Office of Price Administration controlled prices and rationed scarce consumer goods during the war. Posters, such as this one, used cartoons to show that rationing meant "a fair share" for everyone. In the top scene, the woman on the left has purchased nearly all the meat in the butcher shop, leaving one small chop for the woman on the right. In the bottom, each woman has an equal share of meat purchased with their ration coupons.

RATIONING MEANS A FAIR
SHARE FOR ALL OF US

Document 83

DOCUMENT 84
Radio Clips to Be Used during January 1944

Courtesy of the National Archives, Boston, Office of Price Administration, Regional Department of Information, Record Group 188.

These radio clips were broadcast on behalf of the Office of Price Administration (OPA) during 1944. The clips served as reminders to everyone on the home front that adhering to the rules and regulations regarding price controls and rationing on the home front were vital to the United States' success on the battlefront.

OFFICE OF PRICE ADMINISTRATION
Regional Department of Information
55 Tremont Street
Boston 8, Massachusetts

While we sit in the comfort of our own homes, listening to the invasion news and of the brave deeds of our fighting men—we think more and more about our responsibility to these men. We think of the day when they will return home—and the kind of country they will return to. These men—who are doing our fighting—are dreaming of a world where peace and freedom mean prosperity and security. Are we doing our part to see that these dreams will come true? Our forces abroad are risking their lives to guarantee us peace and freedom. It's up to us at home to guarantee prosperity and security. We can do it by fighting and winning on the home front, just as our men are fighting and winning on the battlefield. We can do it by holding down our wartime living costs—by sticking to our ceiling prices—by preventing inflation and chaos—by keeping our economy stable. Then when our boys come marching home—they will find the security and prosperity they dream of—as they fight for peace and freedom.

As we sit near our radios, listening to the thrilling invasion reports how many of us can declare with patriotic satisfaction, "I've got a hand in the fight! The gasoline I didn't use is playing its part in the invasion!" Yes, the gasoline you didn't use—to drive to the country—or to go to the movies—or to the beach—together with millions of gallons we all saved—is playing an important part in winning the war. It's flying our planes—driving our jeeps and tanks—propelling our landing barges. Yes, that gasoline you <u>didn't</u> use—has gone to war on all <u>three</u> fronts—land, sea and air.

<u>We homefronters will continue our march</u> to victory in rationed shoes until there is a marked improvement in the supply situation. There is no indication that any such increased supply of civilian shoes will be coming this year. In 1943, there were 53 million fewer pairs of shoes on store shelves than usual. Our normal stock may be reduced by as many as 75 million pairs before 1944 is over. This would bring our national total of shoes down to the lowest point in years. Neither OPA nor the War Production Board can predict now when civilian shoe supplies will increase. But it is apparent that it will not be until the huge demand for GI shoes falls off . . . and we all know why those GI shoe orders are filled first these days.

<u>Your local Board can now issue</u> you a ration certificate for a coal-wood heating stove—if you are an eligible applicant—without regard to quota restrictions. A person is considered an eligible applicant if he has no stove to heat his living or working quarters—or if his stove is beyond repair. Production of coal-wood stoves during the summer usually exceeds demand and it is keeping pace now with the number of eligible buyers. For these reasons it is possible to remove quota restrictions on coal-wood heating stoves.

<u>WANTED! Your fuel oil tank!</u> Your government wants and needs your fuel tank for vital storage space, regardless of how small its individual capacity. A large percentage of industry tanks are storing the huge oil reserves necessary for our armed forces. There's not enough room to store civilian supplies, too. So, it's up to you to store as much oil as possible in your own home tank and now! Your next winter's fuel oil coupons can be used immediately. Don't wait. Order your fuel supply from your dealer today. Help ease the shortage of storage space—and at the same time, protect yourself—by making sure you'll have heat next winter. . . .

<u>Get your home-canning sugar as you need it</u>. That's the wartime watchword for you home-canners. Sugar is rationed because it is scarce. Sugar for home-canning is limited to 25 pounds per person for the same

reason. War has made us short on sugar. We must use it as carefully as possible. That is the reason you are asked to apply for home-canning sugar only as you actually need it. As you know, the canning season has been divided into two periods (GIVE DATES FOR YOUR AREA) for early and late canning. You can get up to ten pounds per person from now until _____ (DATE) for your early canning. When you put up later fruits, you can apply for whatever additional sugar you need—within your quota. None of us shall forget that the special provision for home-canning is such an important part of our total food supply. You, and every homemaker in the country, are urged to put up as much this wartime summer as you possibly can. Make every ounce of home canning sugar do its part for victory!

If any area where practically all fruits ripen early, home canners will be able to get their entire sugar allotments during the first period—if they need it. (FOR EXAMPLE: You home-canners here in _____ (LOCATION) will be able to get your full allotment of sugar—if you need it—right now. This exception is made because _____, _____, _____ and _____ (LIST FRUITS) are ready now and _____, _____, _____, _____, (LIST FRUITS) soon will be. Remember to apply for only as much sugar as you actually need. That's the wartime watchword of us home-canners.

You'll be finding a bigger choice of pies, cakes, puddings and other desserts when you pick up the menu at a restaurant, hotel or lunchroom, which does its own baking. They're able to offer more sweet rolls and desserts, because, they are getting about 25 percent more sugar for baking now. School and war-plant cafeterias—which do their own baking—are getting the same increase.

Your grocer can give you Red and Blue tokens in change for ration checks or certificates, as well as for stamps. OPA has made this provision especially for mail order refund cases. Mail order houses refund ration stamps with ration certificates or checks, when they cannot fill the order. Now you can use these ration checks or certificates, just as your ration stamps—even to getting tokens in change.

If you've been using oil for summer cooking in the past, then you're entitled to extra summer rations this year, according to word from the OPA. These extra rations are being limited only to those who switch to oil every summer and who already have the necessary oil-burning equipment.

FLASH!

<u>Housewives did you know</u> that you can now get your individual ceiling price lists for meats and groceries? Yes, the OPA has issued reproductions of the ones you've seen posted at your local grocer for home use. On them, you will find printed in clear type and in compact form, the ceiling prices for practically every food item you purchase. Many housewives jot down on their market pad at home, the ceilings for foods they intend to purchase that day. Those lists are yours for the asking. Just stop in at your local War Price and Rationing Board, or if you haven't the time—write or phone them and they will be pleased to send you a copy, in the mail.

<u>Would you like to get into the fight</u> to keep prices down? Well, here's your opportunity. The Office of Price Administration is conducting a drive to recruit thousands of more price panel assistants. There are more than 40,000 volunteers engaged in this work throughout the country—but thousands more are still needed. If you have a genuine interest in preventing living costs from rising—and I know you do—call your local War Price and Rationing Board and tell them you want to volunteer as a price panel assistant. Do it today—and help lick inflation!

<u>Here's an item for housewives</u> who are interested in profitable transactions. Your butcher is still accepting used kitchen fats. In return for each pound he receives, he will give you four cents and two red points. This is especially profitable now because those thirty red points we're getting have to last us four weeks. Now more than ever, your government needs those extra pounds of kitchen fats—for they are vitally important in the manufacture of explosives, drugs and other war materials.

<u>A local War Price and Rationing Board</u> at Port Arthur, Texas, recently got more information than they originally bargained for. When a woman, applying for additional sugar allotments for home-canning forgot to state the number of pounds sought for each family member, the Board promptly returned the application to her with instructions to specify exact weights. The woman, via return mail, wrote back that she weighed 210 pounds, her husband 145 and her mother-in-law 160!

DOCUMENT 85

Poster, "Save Waste Fats," War Production Board, ca. 1940s

Courtesy of the Library of Congress, LC-USZC4-4432.

The War Production Board, established by Executive Order 9024 on January 16, 1942, was empowered to "exercise general direction over the war procurement and production program." Among the responsibilities entailed in providing this general direction was promoting conservation on the home front, as illustrated in this poster produced by the War Production Board's Bureau of Industrial Conservation.

DOCUMENT 86
Aleut Women's Petition, October 10, 1942

Courtesy of the National Archives.

This petition was written by the Aleut women in the Pribilof Islands Program, in which US authorities evacuated Aleutians for fear that they would fall into Japanese hands. Native residents of this group from four volcanic islands off the coast of mainland Alaska in the Bering Sea were taken from their homes and crowded into "duration villages" like the Funter Bay Evacuation Camp in southeastern Alaska. Conditions, as this petition details, were deplorable. Many native peoples were forced to stay for more than two years in the camps. The editors have retained the grammatical errors contained in the original document.

We the people of this place wants a better place than this to live. This place is no place for a living creature. We drink impure water and then get sick the children's get skin disease even the grow ups are sick from cold.

We ate from the mess house and it is near the toilet only a few yards away. We eat the filth that is flying around.

We got no place to take a bath and no place to wash our clothes or dry them when it rains. We women are always lugging water up stairs and take turns warming it up and the stove is small.

We live in a room with our children just enough to be turn around in we used blankets for walls just to live in private.

We need clothes and shoes for our children how are we going to clothe them with just a few dollars. Men's are working for $20-month is nothing to them we used it to see our children eat what they don't get at mess house and then its gone and then we wait for another month to come around.

Why they not take us to a better place to live and work for our selves' and live in a better house. Men and women are very eager to work.

When winter comes it still would be worse with water all freezed up and grub short do we have to see our children suffer.

We all have rights to speak for ourselves.

(signed)

Mrs. Haretina Kochutin

Mrs. Alexandra Bourdukofsky

Mrs. Valentina Kozeroff

Mrs. Platonida Melovidov

Miss Anastasia Krukoff

Mrs. Alexandra Fratis

Miss Haretina Kochergin

Mrs. Sophie Tetoff

Mrs. Anna Kushin

Mrs. Anfesa Galaktionoff

Mrs. Olga Kochutin

Mrs. Juliana Gromoff

Mrs. Agafia Merculief

Mrs. Alexandra Kochutin

Miss Natalie Misikin

Mrs. Mary Kochutin

Mrs. Claude Kochutin

Vassa Krukoff

Anna Emanoff

Chionia K. Misikin

Heretina Misikin

Alexandra Melovidov

Marina Kozloff

Mary Kushin

Ifrosenia Rukovishnikoff

Mrs. Pelagia Krukoff

Mrs. Agrippa Tetoff

Mrs. Martha Krukoff

Mrs. Marva Stepetin

Mary Oustigoff

Agrippina Hanson

Alexandra Mandregan

Helen Mandregan

Alexandra Gromoff

Lubre Stepetin

Nina Oustigoff

Helena Krukoff

Miss Justina Stepetin

Antonia Stepetin

Francis Emanoff

Anna Stepetin

Kapetolina Buterin

Helen Kochergin

Prascodia Hapoff

Marina Sedick

Ludmilla Bourdukofsky

Mary Bourdukofsky

Alice Philemonoff

Virginia Kozloff

CHAPTER 5

The Secret War

American women served as spies and in resistance groups that engaged in sophisticated activities of deception and sabotage against the Axis powers during World War II. But the secret war also had different and in some cases darker connotations, as the US government turned on its own citizens, reflected in the internment of those of Japanese descent. The government also supported the Manhattan Project, the top-secret program to develop the atomic bomb, largely out of public view. Documents in this section illustrate the complex and often hidden roles that women chose or were forced to play during World War II.

DOCUMENT 87
Franklin D. Roosevelt, Executive Order 9066,
February 21, 1942

This executive order, signed in the midst of the hysteria of the first months of the United States' entry into World War II, gave the military authority to ban any citizen of Japanese descent from coastal areas. It also authorized the military to remove such people to assembly centers in California, Arizona, Washington, and Oregon. To a lesser degree, the order affected residents who were of Italian and German descent, and the government interned three hundred Italians and five thousand Germans.

Executive Order No. 9066
The President
Executive Order

Authorizing the Secretary of War to Prescribe Military Areas

Whereas the successful prosecution of the war requires every possible protection against espionage and against sabotage to national-defense material, national-defense premises, and national-defense utilities as defined in Section 4, Act of April 20, 1918, 40 Stat. 533, as amended by the Act of November 30, 1940, 54 Stat. 1220, and the Act of August 21, 1941, 55 Stat. 655 (U.S.C., Title 50, Sec. 104);

Now, therefore, by virtue of the authority vested in me as President of the United States, and Commander in Chief of the Army and Navy, I hereby authorize and direct the Secretary of War, and the Military Commanders whom he may from time to time designate, whenever he or any designated Commander deems such action necessary or desirable, to prescribe military areas in such places and of such extent as he or the appropriate Military Commander may determine, from which any or all persons may be excluded, and with respect to which, the right of any person to enter, remain in, or leave shall be subject to whatever restrictions the Secretary of War or the appropriate Military Commander may impose in his discretion. The Secretary of War is hereby authorized to provide for residents of any such area who are excluded therefrom, such transportation, food, shelter, and other accommodations as may be necessary, in the judgment of the Secretary of War or the said Military Commander, and until other arrangements are made, to accomplish the purpose of this order. The designation of military areas in any region or locality shall supersede designations of prohibited and restricted areas by the Attorney General under the Proclamations of December 7 and 8, 1941, and shall supersede the responsibility and authority of the Attorney General under the said Proclamations in respect of such prohibited and restricted areas.

I hereby further authorize and direct the Secretary of War and the said Military Commanders to take such other steps as he or the appropriate Military Commander may deem advisable to enforce compliance with the restrictions applicable to each Military area hereinabove authorized to be designated, including the use of Federal troops and other Federal Agencies, with authority to accept assistance of state and local agencies.

I hereby further authorize and direct all Executive Departments, independent establishments and other Federal Agencies, to assist the

Secretary of War or the said Military Commanders in carrying out this Executive Order, including the furnishing of medical aid, hospitalization, food, clothing, transportation, use of land, shelter, and other supplies, equipment, utilities, facilities, and services.

This order shall not be construed as modifying or limiting in any way the authority heretofore granted under Executive Order No. 8972, dated December 12, 1941, nor shall it be construed as limiting or modifying the duty and responsibility of the Federal Bureau of Investigation, with respect to the investigation of alleged acts of sabotage or the duty and responsibility of the Attorney General and the Department of Justice under the Proclamations of December 7 and 8, 1941, prescribing regulations for the conduct and control of alien enemies, except as such duty and responsibility is superseded by the designation of military areas hereunder.

Franklin D. Roosevelt
The White House,
February 19, 1942.

[F.R. Doc. 42–1563; Filed, February 21, 1942; 12:51 p.m.]

DOCUMENT 88
Photograph, *Marlene Dietrich Going over Radio Script,* 1942

Courtesy of the Library of Congress, LC-USZ62-104024.

German-born actress Marlene Dietrich was a staunch anti-Nazi and became a US citizen in 1939. During World War II, she helped sell war bonds and delivered speeches for the War Department. In 1944, she began overseas tours for United Service Organizations (USO), starting in North Africa and later in Europe. This photograph depicts her in the office of the Radio Branch of the Bureau of Public Relations for the War Department, which was housed in the Munitions Building. During World War II, Dietrich recorded albums in German for the Office of Strategic Services (the predecessor to today's Central Intelligence Agency) that helped create propaganda to lower the morale of German soldiers.

Document 88

DOCUMENT 89
Resume, Personnel Files, Julia McWilliams (Child), War
Department, Office of Strategic Services, December 14,
1945

*Courtesy of the National Archives, RG 226, Records of the Office
of Strategic Services, entry 224, OSS Personnel Files, box #514.*

Later well known as a chef and cookbook author, Julia (McWilliams)
Child served during World War II in an international spy ring over-
seen by the Office of Strategic Services. Child was an administrative
assistant in Chunking, China, and Washington, D.C. She was paid
$2,600 per year for her service. In April 2012, previously classified
files of twenty-four thousand spies, including many women, were
released by the Central Intelligence Agency. This resume, dated
May 17, 1943, reflects Child's background and business experience,
as well as her sense of humor and self-deprecating nature.

JULIA C. MCWILLIAMS   May 17, 1943

Washington, D.C.: The Brighton Hotel
2123 California St., NW
Residence Telephone: North 4430

Born: August 15, 1912, Pasadena, California

Height: 6 feet. Weight: 155. Health: Excellent (no major illnesses, operations, etc. No works days lost since employed with U.S. Gov't)

EDUCATION: Polytechnic Elementary School, Pasadena, California
The Katherine Branson School, Ross California. (3 yrs.)
Smith College, Northampton, Massachusetts. Graduated, B.A. 1934
Major Subject: History
Minor Subjects: Technique & Theory & History of Music.
French Literature.

LANGUAGES: French. Good reading knowledge. Fair writing knowledge. Am taking private lessons three times a week, reading &
conversation.
(Italian. A vague remembrance from two years at college.)

BUSINESS EXPERIENCE:

1. 10/1/35 to 5/1/37
W. & J. SLOANE, 575 Fifth Avenue, New York City.
Immediate Supervisor: Arthur W. Forester, Advertising Manager
My Position: Assistant to the Advertising Manager
Duties: General secretary & assistant. Copywriting, publicity, direct mail pamphlets. Making contancts [*sic*] with newspaper & magazine personnel for publicity, and keeping them interested in Sloane doings. Planning, setting up, & supervising photographic settings. Research on manufacturing methods. Doing anything at all that came up, and initiating new ideas, etc.
Salary: Started at $20.00 per week. Finished at $35.00.
Reason for leaving: Illness in family at home, had to return.

2. 11/1/37 to 6/1/39
THE COAST MAGAZINE, San Francisco, California
Position: Southern California Fashion Editor
Duties: Writing monthly fashion column. Started with first issue of magazine, so had to make all my own contacts with retail stores and wholesalers. Made up my own ideas about fashion trends, good buys, unusual finds, etc. Arranged and supervised photographs.
Salary: $25.00 per column.
Reason for leaving: Magazine bankrupt.

3. W. & J. Sloane: Beverly Hills, California
Position: Advertising Manager
Duties: Planning & preparing all store advertising, window and floor displays, and publicity. As there were no precedents to speak of when I took over, I had to start prectically [*sic*] from scratch, hiring good newspaper artists, typographer, printer, etc. Planning budget ($100,000.00 per year to spend), planning campaigns with store buyers, furnishing ideas, writing all copy, etc, layouts, etc.
Salary: $200.00 per month.
Reason for leaving: Fired, and I don't wonder. One needs a much more detailed knowledge of business, buying, markets, and more experience in advertising than I had for so much responsibility. But I learned a great deal, and did pretty well in establishing the mechanics of the office and the business personnel.

4. 8/22/42 to 11/16/42

U.S. INFORMATION CENTER, O.W.I., Washington, D.C.

Position & Duties: Senior typist in charge of Executive Index File, which was a card index with names of all the government executives in the various agencies above titles of Unit Chief, giving full name, home residence, past & present position in correct bureaucratic breakdown. Reading press releases, newspapers, etc. to catch names, checking with files or agencies for correct title. Sending out duplicates of cards to branch offices as well as putting them in master file. This was done with only slight supervision, and I made up my own system.

Salary: $1440.00.

Reason for leaving: Typed over 10,000 little white cards and put in for transfer to OSS.

5. 9/16/43 to present

OSS, Director's Office.

Immediate Supervisor: Marian O'Donnell.

Position: File Clerk.

Duties: Classifying & filing documents, improving filing system.

Salary: Came in at $1620.00. Raised to $1800.00.

Volunteer Work:

1. AMERICAN RED CROSS: Pasadena Chapter. 10/1/41 to 6/1/42

Position: Creating & supervising the volunteer stenographic services. Securing the help of the trained typists & stenographers. Instructing them in R.C. procedure, overseeing work. Typing, mimeographing, etc.

2. AIRCRAFT WARNING SERVICE, U.S. Army Interceptor Command, Los Angeles 3/8/42 to 6/1/42

Duties: Regular routine of the service, four 6-hour shifts weekly.

CIVIL SERVICE RECORD:

1. Passed Senior Typist Examination, June, 1942

2. Passed Junior Professional Assistant Examination, September, 1942

Graded: 91%

DOCUMENT 90

Photograph, *Civilian Exclusion Order #5*, Dorothea Lange, April 1942

Courtesy of the Library of Congress, LC-USZ62-34565.

Celebrated photographer Dorothea Lange photographed these posters that directed the removal of civilians of Japanese ancestry from the city of San Francisco by April 7, 1942. Lange (1895–1965) was hired the by War Relocation Authority to photograph Japanese communities, processing centers, and internment camps. Her earlier work during the Great Depression focused on displaced workers and migrants and provided her a unique perspective on what she deemed a civil rights crisis.

DOCUMENT 91
Letters to Clara Breed, 1942

Courtesy of the Japanese American National Museum.

Clara Breed was the children's librarian at the San Diego Public Library from 1929 to 1945. When many of her young of patrons of Japanese descent were interned, she remained in close contact with them, sending books and supplies. The museum has more than three hundred letters and cards sent to Breed that were passed on to Elizabeth Kikuchi Yamada, one of the children. Yamada donated them to the Japanese American National Museum, where they are now digitized. Visit http://www.janm.org/collections/clara-breed-collection/?page=1 for more information.

April 25, 1942

Dear Miss Breed,

Thank you very much for the book and the letter. I liked the book very much. We play all kinds of games in the playground. There is a recreation school for children from 5 to 11. I am 10 yrs. old, but I don't want to go, so I stay at home and play. Last night there was a picture show. There were 2 comic pictures, sports, sports in Africa, and a picture titled "The Gangs All Here." It was a gangster picture. There has been baseball games going on at one of the training tracks. San Diego won several times. My cousin Helen is working in the canteen, and day before yesterday she gave me a dime. She is very nice, and I wish you could meet her. You should have seen all the nice things Miss Fay sent me. She sent me a ball, some candy, a cute little boat, some nice cards, a 10 c. defense book, (with a stamp in it) and Fuzzy Wuzzy. Last week a friend sent me 2 funny books, and I still haven't read all of them yet, because everybody looks at it. Mother says "Hello." Say "Hello" to everybody for me.

Sincerely,
Katherine Tasaki

April 23, 1942
Dear Miss Breed,

I just received the two intensely interesting books which you so kindly sent. I was overwhelmed with joy to see the books when the postman opened the package for inspection. I cannot express in words my feeling of gratitude.

I want to thank you so much that I feel like writing pages and pages of "Thank you, Miss Breed, Thank you!" But I shall not for I must conserve on paper. Thank you from the bottom of my heart. The first thing I did after receiving the books was run to my parents and show them the nice books. Then I ran to Margaret Ishino and showed them to her. I was so happy I had to show them to someone.

Yesterday began my third week in Santa Anita. It is a beautiful place. It is the first time I have been here and I enjoy it very much. The weather differs greatly from San Diego. It is cold and rainy one day and the next day it is as hot as it could be.

Since I have been here I visited Seabiscuit's statue and have gone around the race track a few times.

We are fed three meals a day and the food is just fine. This is just like an army camp for the store is called a canteen and the cafeteria is called a mess hall. Everyday a line is, which people refer to as a bread line, formed leading to the mess hall when meal time is near. This line is blocks and blocks long. I often wait an hour or two before entering the mess hall. The mess hall is a huge room. The other morning I was the one thousandth person to enter it.

It took me a while to get use to my new home, but I am quite use to it now. I am sleeping where Seabiscuit used to sleep, I hope. "I am sleeping where Seabiscuit used to sleep" is a common saying around here.

School has not started yet and I am getting lonesome for homework. I heard we are going to have a library soon. It was the best news I have heard. I just love to read. By just looking at the books you sent, I recall the days when I use to walk to the library and have you help me find a nice book to enjoy.

The first week after we arrived, father, brother, sister, and I went every-day to the scrap wood pile to find wood to make our furnitures. We finally gathered enough wood to make a few tables and chairs. After looking at the results I thought of the primitive people who did what we did today.

But bitter feelings do not enter my head because I know we were sent to Santa Anita Assembly Center for our own protection. I am grateful to the Govt. for gathering us in such a nice place. If I am helping the Govt. by staying here, I am glad. I want so much to be of some use to the Govt.

My! all I have been doing is talking about myself. Now I would like to know how you are and all about San Diego. I imagine many students come to the library to get reference books. I wish I was still among them! I seem to be going on and on like the ticking of a clock, but the running out of ink has told me to stop. Before closing I would like to thank you again and I certainly would appreciate your correspondence.

Very sincerely yours,
Louise Ogawa
(over)

My address is:
Louise Yoshiko Ogawa
Santa Anita Assembly Center
Barrack 7 Avenue 7 Apt. #1
Santa Anita, California
Ps. I shall anxiously await your letter.

DOCUMENT 92
Photograph, *Japanese American US Naval Cadet Nurse, Kay Fukuda*, 1943

Courtesy of the Library of Congress, LG-DIG-ppprs-00267.

During World War II, noted photographer Ansel Adams created a series of photographs at Manzanar War Relocation Center, one of ten sites where Japanese Americans were interned during the war. In spite of being interned, some Japanese Americans served their country, including Kay Fukuda, shown in her US Naval Cadet uniform.

DOCUMENT 93
Photograph, *Baton Practice, Florence Kuwata, Manzanar Relocation Center*, 1943

Courtesy of the Library of Congress, LG-DIG-ppprs-00270.

Many children and teenagers were interned at Manzanar Relocation Center in California and sought to create as normal a life as they could, which often included sports. The first internees arrived in Manzanar on March 21, 1942. More than 90 percent of the evacuees were from the Los Angeles area. Sport was often an activity that helped the internees normalize their time in confinement. This image, by noted photographer Ansel Adams, captured Florence Kuwata's attempt to find joy in learning a new skill.

DOCUMENT 94

Excerpt, Interview with Amy Uno Ishii, Conducted by
Betty E. Mitson and Kristin Mitchell, July 9 and 20, 1973

*Courtesy of California State University, Fullerton Oral History
Program, Japanese American Project, Japanese American
Evacuation.*

In this interview, Amy Uno Ishii recounts the experience of her
family after the Japanese attack on Pearl Harbor on December 7,
1941, and the subsequent arrest of her family. Ishii was born in Salt
Lake City, Utah, on December 11, 1920, the fifth of ten children
born to her Japanese parents.

Mitchell: Do you recall the day of the Pearl Harbor attack? Do you
recall any special feelings you had?

Ishii: Well, of course. I think we all went through a terrible shock.
On that Sunday morning I was living as a domestic away from
home, and so I was not with my own family. By that time I was
almost twentyone [*sic*]. I was working as a domestic out in San
Marino, and I had just served breakfast to the family when the
news came on the radio that Japan had attacked Pearl Harbor. It's
hard to describe the shock. I know that the American people were
in great shock at the time of Pearl Harbor. And they were angry;
they were very, very angry at the Japanese for having been so dar-
ing as this. I remember that I asked my boss if I could make this
long distance call to Los Angeles to talk to my mother because of
the war having broken out. I asked him if I could have the day off
and if I could go home to find out what this was all about. I made
the call to my mother, and my mother was very, very upset. She
said, "I don't understand what is happening, but I am hearing the
news as you are hearing it on the radio there." She said, "I can't
understand Japan and what it's doing bombing Pearl Harbor." We
had no knowledge of anything like this happening, and it was just
an absolute shock.

We had mixed emotions about the bombing. We were thinking,
"Japan is committing suicide," because it is such a small country..

All of Japan could be laid right across the whole of California, and it would be all over with. "What is that small country doing coming this long, long distance to do such crazy things?" And at the same time we were very upset because the general public . . . Even the people that I worked for treated me and talked to me as though it was my own father who was piloting those planes out there at Pearl Harbor.

Mitchell: Oh, even the people you worked for treated you this way?

Ishii: Yes. I remember they told me that I could go home and how I had better stay at home until the FBI could clear me of any suspicion. I said, "Why should I be suspected of anything? I've lived in your home for many years now, nursed you when you were sick and fed you. And I never poisoned you once, and I'm not about to do it now." But they said, "You had better stay at home until we can get the FBI to clear you." And I thought, "Wow!" So I took the streetcar to my mother's. We got the news of Pearl Harbor's bombing just before noon, and it took me to three or four in the afternoon to get from the people's place in San Marino to my mother's.

Mitchell: Did you feel any animosity from some of the people you were riding on the streetcar with?

Ishii: No. I think everyone was in too much of a state of shock to point their finger at me and say anything. I felt like an ant. I wanted to shrivel up into nothing, and my mind was going a mile a minute, thinking, "What am I supposed to do, what am I supposed to say? All I know is that I am an American, and yet now, at a time like this, people are going to say, 'You are a Jap,' and that turns the whole picture around." I had never been called a "Jap" in my life. All of these things were going through my mind. By the time I got home the FBI was at our house.

Mitchell: What were they doing there?

Ishii: They were tearing out the floorboards, taking bricks out of the fireplace, and looking through the attic.

Mitchell: What were they looking for?

Ishii: Contraband.

Mitchell: Such as what?

Ishii: Machine guns, munitions, maps, binoculars, cameras, swords, knives, and what have you.

Mitchell: How was your family reacting to this invasion?

Ishii: Well, we just stood there—blah! What could we say with military police standing out in front with guns pointing at the house, and telling us to stay right there in a particular room while they went through the whole house? They tore part of the siding out on the side of our house to see if we were hiding things in between the walls. And all we could think was, "How ridiculous!" It was so nonsensical. They didn't have a search warrant. They didn't have any reason to be coming in like this and tearing up our house. And when they left, they took my father with them.

Mitchell: Did they conduct a general search of your neighborhood or was your house singled out?

Ishii: We were singled out. There were no Japanese in our neighborhood. We were living in a cosmopolitan area; it was mostly white. Our next-door neighbors were Germans and Italians. The people across the street were from England. We had a Korean living on the corner of our block who had a little Korean grocery store. I would say that there weren't any Japanese living within six blocks of our house. So we must have been singled out.

Mitchell: So on the very day that Pearl Harbor was bombed your father was taken away?

Ishii: Yes.

Mitchell: When did you hear from him next?

Ishii: Oh, we didn't hear from him for a long, long time. We were getting all kinds of phone calls from people who were very good to us and who knew us very well. Say, for instance, on a Saturday night we got a phone call saying, "It would be a very good idea if you drove down to Griffith Park tomorrow morning. Way inside of Griffith Park there is a CCC [Civilian Conservation Corps] camp, and this CCC camp is holding about three hundred men, and I think your father might be among them. So you might take a run down there and take a look." We really never knew who had called and told us.

On Sunday morning—instead of going to church—we all jumped in the car. We took toothpaste, soap, washcloths, underwear, pajamas, Hershey bars, chewing gum, and all kinds of things with us, and we took a ride out to Griffith Park. And sure enough, as we got way into Griffith Park, we found military police all around this encampment. All the men that had been picked up the first day of the war were rounded up in there; all were from this particular area. The people in the stockade, as we called it, were not allowed to converse among themselves because most of them didn't speak English.

Mitchell: Why didn't they converse in Japanese?

Ishii: If they did, the MPs couldn't have understood them, so they were threatened to be shot to death if they spoke Japanese. We were very brave, and very young, so we stood out there on the sidelines of this enclosure and yelled, "Dad, Dad, if you recognize us, put your hands up." All of us were yelling in unison at these men. Of course, these men were dumbfounded. They didn't expect a family of young kids to come out and look for them. Of course, my father realized immediately that this couldn't be anyone but his bunch of kids, so he was waving his hand, saying, "Great." So then all of us took turns pitching.

Mitchell: What were you pitching to him?

Ishii: Soap, toothpaste, his shaving kit and things. The MPs couldn't stop us.

Mitchell: Did they try to or did they just turn a blind eye to it?

Ishii: Well, they didn't realize what was going on, because everything was happening so fast. We laughed about the whole thing later. But this was our first encounter with Dad since he was taken from us.

Mitchell: What was the time span involved?

Ishii: About three weeks. I'm sure it was in January when we went to see him at Griffith Park.

Then another time we received a phone call saying, "It might be a good idea—if you know where the train station is in Glendale—for you to take a drive out there and just happen to be around."

This was on a Sunday morning again. So on Sunday morning we packed a lot of stuff again, goodies, clothes, foodstuff, and things, and we got into the car and drove out to Glendale. We had a problem locating the train station. It was right off San Fernando Road—practically under our noses—but we drove around and asked at a few gas stations. We parked a block away, and walked into the station there. It all looked very normal—like any Sunday morning when there is very little happening. But about ten minutes after we arrived there, here came all these Army trucks with canopies over the backs of them. And in all these trucks were all these men out of the compound at Griffith Park. So we knew that our dad must be in this group. So we hid, not letting the military police see us. But then we realized what was happening—they were going to be shipped away on a train. They got off the trucks and were lined up, but they were not handcuffed or anything like that.

Mitchell: Did the soldiers have guns?

Ishii: Oh, yes! When all of the men were lined up, our dad stood out like a sore thumb. He was very tall, and he had grown a beard. They were all looking so tired; all of those men looked so aged and tired, and when we saw our father, we just couldn't help but cry because the change in so short a time had been so drastic.

We didn't want Mother to see him like this because, I think, it probably would have just killed her on the spot. Fortunately, we hadn't brought Mother out with us. We figured that if we were going to get caught, at least we would be citizens being caught. Mother was an alien. If she got caught, we didn't know what they'd do with her, so we made her stay home. It was a long wait for her. We saw them line the men up and put tags on them with their I.D. numbers. They were all dressed in the same type of clothes—Army fatigues. We wondered where their regular clothes that they came in wearing were. A lot of those men were wearing suits when we saw them at Griffith Park.

Mitchell: How much time had elapsed since you saw them at Griffith Park?

Ishii: Maybe a couple of weeks. I don't think the men's heads were shaven or anything like that. All I remember is that all of the men were wearing the same type of clothing. The first thing that flashes into your mind is the movies where you see prisoners wearing prisoners' garb, so that really shook us up. The men were lined up to go on these trains, so we yelled at Dad.

Mitchell: Didn't you get a chance to talk to him at all?

Ishii: No, but he saw our faces, and he recognized each one of us. In fact, he hollered, "Hi, Hana. Hi, Mae. Hi, Amy. Be good, take care."

Mitchell: Did you have any idea where he was going?

Ishii: Oh, no. In fact, no one knew where they were taken until, I believe, we were in Santa Anita. After we were evacuated and were in Santa Anita, the Red Cross notified my mother that Dad was in Fort Missoula in Montana.

Mitchell: Was he in a camp set up specifically for aliens?

Ishii: It was a special camp for so-called hard core enemy aliens.

Mitchell: Was it just for Japanese?

Ishii: Oh, yes, all Japanese. These camps held the men who were fishermen out in Terminal Island and Long Beach and all along the West Coast from Washington to Mexico. These men were all pulled up out of their jobs because they worked on the West Coast. They could send signals and what have you. Oh, the American government thought these people were going to commit sabotage. So they categorized them as "hard core enemy aliens" and took these men away from their families—took them just like they took my father. There were approximately two thousand five hundred men taken from their families in this manner—Japanese language school teachers, judo teachers, kendo teachers, Buddhist priests, anyone who worked in the import and export business with Japan—rounded up and taken away.

Mitchell: So anyone who was considered dangerous in any sense was taken?

Ishii: Yes. They were not given due process or anything—they were just considered potentially dangerous. People say that families were not being broken up. That's a lot of malarkey; it happened to our own family. We know how badly the families were broken up. We've seen too many of our friends whose fathers were in the same situation as my father. A lot of the farmers up in Palos Verdes, Rolling Hills, Signal Hill, Dominguez Hills, and Huntington Beach areas were taken away. If they were suspected of anything at all, they were tagged "potentially dangerous enemy aliens," and taken. When you think of the number of Japanese people that were rounded up in this fashion, you've got to relate these numbers to the fact that each one of these men had a family—a wife, and so many children.

Mitchell: So that's at least two thousand five hundred families that were broken up.

Ishii: Exactly. So don't let anyone tell you that the families were not broken up or separated. It happened.

DOCUMENT 95
University of Wisconsin, "Alumni Who Touched Our Lives," *On Wisconsin*, July/August 1996, 19-20

Courtesy of the University of Wisconsin Alumni Association.

The University of Wisconsin's alumni magazine, *On Wisconsin*, began this series to recognize notable alumni. Mildred Harnack, who graduated with a bachelor's degree in 1925 and a master's degree in 1926, was included among this distinguished group that also included actor Don Ameche and psychiatrist Karl Menninger. Harnack was active in anti-Nazi resistance in Germany. She was executed by the Nazis in 1943 for her wartime activities.

Among the hundreds of thousands of students who have hiked up and down Bascom Hill since the University of Wisconsin's founding in 1848, an enormous number have gone on to distinguish themselves in their chosen careers. A smaller array of individuals transcend even the highest levels of distinction. These are the UW alumni who have directly or indirectly reached out and touched the very fabric of our lives. Here, in the first of what may become an ON WISCONSIN series—selected randomly and in purely alphabetical order—are a half a dozen whom we may never have met or known, but who have nevertheless carved an indelible place for themselves in our consciousness. . . .

Few, if any, University of Wisconsin alumni have risked and ultimately paid more in the cause of humanity than this literature major who also taught at the Madison campus during the flapper age. And few lives of the time departed so dramatically from the frivolity of the Roaring Twenties. Nearly two decades after receiving her degrees, Mildred Fish of Milwaukee died an unspeakably horrible death—after what no doubt was months of excruciating torture in a Nazi prison—on the direct orders of Adolph Hitler himself.

What led to her death is the stuff of a John LeCarre novel. She had discovered and developed a love for Germany and its philosophers during her years at the UW. Then, after meeting German scholar Arvid Harnack on campus, she married and returned with him to his homeland.

By the early thirties, Arvid Harnack was an official at the Third Reich's Ministry of Economics and Mildred taught American literature at the University of Berlin. Ironically, their American friends seem to have wondered how these two people could accept or acquiesce to, let alone live under, the extremes of Nazism. Neither Mildred Fish Harnack nor her husband could afford to openly address such a question. For they had established an anti-Nazi underground resistance group with access to sensitive military information.

The group eventually became known as "The Red Orchestra" (the implication being that it was a Communist espionage cell, when in fact it was made of up anti-Nazi's of every stripe) because of its clandestine broadcasts to the USSR. Somehow, for almost a decade, the Harnacks and their co-conspirators managed to evade detection while helping dissidents and Jews escape the country. They published illegal newsletters and a newspaper as well as *verboten* speeches by Franklin Roosevelt. As if that were not perilous enough, the group also committed sabotage, fomenting slave labor revolts, hung anti-Nazi posters, and passed both military and economic intelligence to the U.S. and the Soviet Union.

With the Gestapo about, their luck couldn't last. In 1942, more than one hundred members of "The Red Orchestra" were rounded up and summarily tried. Mildred's husband was sentenced to death and executed on Christmas Eve that same year. Days before, he'd written to her: " . . . I feel part of all that is good and beautiful in the world. . . . Despite everything . . . the darkness was outweighed by the light. And this is largely because of our marriage. . . . "

Mildred's life at first seemed about to be spared. A chaplain visiting her at Plotzensee Prison noted her blonde hair had turned white, that she was so emaciated, so broken by six months of "interrogation," she could not stand upright. Looking twice her age, she had been sentenced to six years of hard labor. But that changed suddenly and stunningly when her case came to Adolph Hitler's attention. Enraged at what Mildred Fish Harnack had done and setting an example, he ordered her beheaded in early 1943. She was the only American to receive such an execution.

DOCUMENT 96
Report, Field Name: Diane, September 30, 1944

Courtesy of the National Archives, ARC Identifier: 595661.

Virginia Hall (1906–1982) was born in Baltimore, Maryland, and educated at Radcliffe and Barnard Colleges. Fluent in French and German, she worked at several US embassies, was an ambulance driver in the French Army, served in Britain's Special Operations Executive, and then joined the US Office of Strategic Services. In this document, she describes sabotage efforts, the political situation in France, and those among her group who were arrested by the Gestapo. Hall served as an undercover spy in German-occupied France and worked to arm and train the French resistance during World War II. She sometimes used the name Diane Heckler and was well known to the Gestapo. This report is incomplete, pages are missing, and the typing was so faint that it is difficult to ascertain some of the words.

I. Briefing—Scope of mission.

II. Activities in the Field.

III. Fulfillment of mission.

IV. Engagements with the enemy.

V. Sabotage activities.

VI. Protection against destruction by the enemy.

VII. Information on various [illegible].

VIII. Political situation.

   IX. Members of the group arrested.

   X. Members of the group killed in action.

   XI. Prisoners captured.

   XII. People in the circuit recommended for American decoration.

   XIII. French civilians or Allied officers deserving awards.

   XIV. Names of collaborators.

   XV. Were you decorated in the Field?

OSS (SO)
WE SECTION

September 30, 1944

Activity Report of Virginia Hall

Field Name: Diane
Circuit: Heckler

I. Briefing—Scope of the Mission

Arrived in Field on March 21, 1944.
Left field September 26, 1944.
Returned London September 26, 1944.

II. Activities in the Field

Arrived on the Brittany coast on March 21, 1944. Aramis and I went straight to Paris by rail where Madam Long, 59 Rue do Babylone, an old friend of mine, found a room for Aramis in a nearby pension where the landlady was Gaulliate and he made out no registration forms and would be in the greatest comparative security. Mme. Long placed her own flat completely at my disposal but, after talking to Aramis for a while, considered him too talkative and indiscrete and [told] me that he should never come to her flat again.

   Next day Aramis accompanied me to the Creuse, in spite of a very painful knee which he had sprained during his landing on the coast. At Maisons near Crozant in the Creuse I saw farmer Eugene Lopinnt who found a little house with one room, no water or electricity, but the road for me and arranged to have me work and eat at his own house in the far end of the village. Aramis returned to Paris to start his work and arrange couriers to come to me at Maisons.

I did the cooking for farmer Lopinnt, his older mother and his hired hand, on an open fire as there was no stove in the house, and took the cows to pasture.

Charles Montagno arrived on the 8th to tell me that he, Louis, and Pierre had arrived safely and that Louis had gone to the Nievre and to Paris and would see me on his return.

I found a few good fields for receptions and farmers and farm hands willing and eager to help. Aramis [came] once to Maison; twice, but with nothing to report except having found Madame Rabut, an old family friend, whose flat he might use as a safe house. He did not seem to understand using couriers or the advisability of doing so doing and fiercely resented any suggestions. Aramis was very tired by the three trips. In spite of his robust appearance he is not very strong, can not carry parcels or packages of any weight, because his has no strength in his arms, and he was ill for a few days after each strenuous trip that he made.

III. Gevold, Fayelle, Hulot, Andre, and Naudet of the FFI, of whom I disapprove as men.

Ferannd of the FTP who was most sincere.

Commandant Mare of the FTP who seemed very efficient but then I did not know well enough to know whether he was really a Moscow trained or not, although I suspect as much.

Dodo Zurbach, my man Friday, who had perhaps the hardest job of all working for a slave driver and who acquitted himself most ably.

Lt. Bob (Le Boulicaud) in command of the Maquis at Villengro, who has done a well job, and stood by me like a brick through any amount of trouble. You might read his report for enlightenment.

Commandant l'Ancien, commanding the coup de main forces—a very grand person.

Monsier Ruollo, near Froconot, who helped on receptions, and was part of the milice patriotique and had one hundred and fifty men at my disposition for reception or any other work I might wish them for.

Monsier Bornard—milice patriotique—came to receptions. A very able man indeed, but he had been side tracked by Fayloolo and company and shelved.

Commandant Therond, who acted able honest, and, who unfortunately resigned as soon as I left.

Edmond Lobrat, cousin of Loah, who did heroic courier work for me on his bicycle.

c) My life in the Creuse consisted of taking the cows to pasture, cooking for the farmers on an open fire and doing my WT work.

In the Cher and the Nievre, I was again milkmaid, took the cows to pasture, milked them and the goats and distributed the milk and was able to talk with a lot of people in the very normal course of my activities.

Life in the Haute Loire was difficult in that I spent my time looking for fields for receptions, spent my day bicycling up and down mountains, seeing fields, visiting various people, doing my WT work and then spending the nights out waiting, for the most part in vain, for deliveries. Pectoral and Marcel of the Ardecho were exceedingly kind and helpful to me, in my earliest difficulties.

IV. Engagements with the Enemy.

I personally took part in no engagements.

V. Sabotage Activities—Excerpts from Telegrams, 27 July to 12 August

a) Bridge blown at Montagne cutting road Langogne Le Puy.
b) 4 cuts in railroad Langogne—Brausse.
c) Freight train derailed in tunnel at Brausse.
d) Bridge blown on railway between Brioude—Le Puy.
e) Freight train derailed in tunnel at Monistrol d'Allier and fifteen metres of track blown up behind wrecking train and crew after it had gone into tunnel to clear up the wreckage.

DOCUMENT 97
Citation for Perseverance and Ingenuity for Virginia Hall, Recipient of the Distinguished Service Cross, 1945

Courtesy of the National Archives, ARC Identifier: 595152.

A civilian, Virginia Hall worked for the US Office of Strategic Services in France for seven months, from March through September of 1944. She helped train three battalions of French resistance forces. After the war, President Harry S. Truman wanted to recognize her work, but Hall declined because she wanted to continue her work and protect her secret identity. To honor her wishes, the OSS hosted a private ceremony on September 27, 1945, where Hall was awarded the Distinguished Service Cross award. She was the only American woman and the first civilian to be awarded this honor during World War II.

THE WHITE HOUSE
WASHINGTON

Miss Virginia Hall, an American civilian in the employ of the special Operations Branch, Office of Strategic Services, voluntarily entered and served in enemy occupied France from March to September 1944. Despite the fact that she was well known to the Gestapo because of previous activities, she established and maintained radio communication with London Headquarters, supplying valuable operational and intelligence information, and with the help of the Jedburgh team, she organized, armed and trained three battalions of French Resistance Forces in the Department of the Haute Loire. Working in a region infested with enemy troops and constantly hunted by the Gestapo, with utter disregard for her safety and continually at the risk of capture, torture and death, she directed the Resistance Forces with extraordinary success in acts of sabotage and guerilla warfare against enemy troops, installations and communications. Miss Hall displayed rare courage, perseverance and ingenuity; her efforts contributed materially to the successful operations of the Resistance Forces in support of the Allied Expeditionary Forces in the liberation of France.

/s/ Harry S. Truman

A true copy:

Frank L. Bull, Jr.
Major, AUS

DOCUMENT 98

Memorandum from William J. Donovan to President Harry S. Truman, May 12, 1945

Courtesy of the National Archives, ARC Identifier: 595672.

In this memo, William J. Donovan, the head of the Office of Strategic Services, notified President Truman that Virginia Hall had been given the Distinguished Service Cross.

SECRET

12 May 1945

MEMORANDUM FOR THE PRESIDENT:

Miss Virginia Hall, an American civilian working for this agency in the European Theater of Operations, has been awarded the Distinguished Service Cross for extraordinary heroism in connection with military operations against the enemy.

We understand that Miss Hall is the first civilian woman in this war to receive the Distinguished Service Cross.

Despite the fact that she was well known to the Gestapo, Miss Hall voluntarily returned to France in March 1944 to assist in sabotage operations against the Germans. Through her courage and physical endurance, even though she had previously lost a leg in an accident, Miss Hall, with two American officers, succeeded in organizing, arming and training three FFI Battalions which took part in many engagements with the enemy and a number of acts of sabotage, resulting in the demolition of many bridges, the destruction of a number of supply trains, and the disruption of enemy communications. As a result of the demolition of one bridge, a German convoy was ambushed and during a bitter struggle 150 Germans were killed and 500 were captured. In additional Miss Hall provided radio communications between London Headquarters and the Resistance Forces in the Haute Loire Department, transmitting and receiving operational and intelligence information. This was the most dangerous type of work as the enemy, whenever two or more direction finders could be turned in on a transmitter, were able to locate the transmittal point to within a couple of hundred yards. It was frequently necessary for Miss Hall to change her headquarters in order to avoid detection.

Inasmuch as an award of this kind has not been previously made during the present war, you may wish to make this presentation personally. Miss Hall is presently in the European Theater of Operations.

William J. Donovan
Director

DOCUMENT 99
Excerpt, Oral History Interview, Lilli Hornig, Interviewed by Cynthia C. Kelly, November 4, 2011

Courtesy of the Atomic Heritage Foundation's Voices of the Manhattan Project, available at manhattanprojectvoices.org.

A native of Czechoslovakia, Lilli Schwenk came with her family to the United States after her father was threatened with internment by the Germans. In 1943, Schwenk married scientist Don Hornig, who was invited by George Kistiakowsky (the Ukrainian-American physical chemistry professor at Harvard University who participated in the Manhattan Project and later served as President Dwight D. Eisenhower's science advisor) to come to Los Alamos to work on a secret project. A chemist by training herself, Lilli Hornig worked first on plutonium chemistry and then with the explosives group, when concerns were raised that radiation might damage reproductive organs. In this interview, she discusses the Trinity test and her decision to sign the Los Alamos scientists' petition to have a demonstration of the bomb's destruction rather than dropping it on Japan. This interview is part of the Voices of the Manhattan Project, a joint project by the Atomic Heritage Foundation and the Los Alamos Historical Society to create a public archive of our oral history collections of Manhattan Project veterans and their families.

Lilli Hornig: I'm Lilli Hornig and that's spelled L-I-L-L-I; H-O-R-N-I-G.

Cindy Kelly: Terrific. Now we have to start at the next question, is—can you give us your birth day?

Hornig: I can; it's March 22, 1921. I was born in what is now the Czech Republic; a little town about—probably about fifty miles north and slightly east of Prague, and I lived there until I was eight. My father was a scientist. He was a chemist working in the big dyestuffs plant there. Dyestuffs was still big business in the '20s. And we left there in 1929. I was eight years old and moved to Berlin.

We lived there for four years and when Hitler—after Hitler came to power, my father was actually being threatened with being taken off to a concentration camp. And he spent several weeks sleeping at friends' houses so he wouldn't be found, and he left for America. And my mother and I had to wait for quite a long time, well, several months. So we came in on Election Day in 1933. And LaGuardia had just been elected Mayor that day and there was this huge celebration in Times Square, a million people all yelling and screaming, and so we went to see that. I remember that day well.

My mother was actually an MDO, she's in practice, and so I was sort of introduced to science early on. My father took me occasionally, very occasionally, on a Sunday to his lab, and I just loved all the glassware, and he gave me some micro-sized glassware for my doll house. I always assumed I would—well, they assumed—to I think that I would be either a chemist or a physician. And I was kind of squeamish at the time, so I went for chemistry. I was pretty determined on that.

We ended up living in Montclair, New Jersey. I went to high school there, junior high and high school. And I was talking to a friend yesterday and remembering my first day of school when I spoke very little English and I had to take placement tests, and I'd never seen a test like that before, you know, where you check things or circle things or whatever. And the first class I actually went to was cooking, which I basically wasn't even allowed in the kitchen. And I remember the first—that—what they were doing that day was making creamed carrots, and I'd never heard of a creamed vegetable, nobody in Europe ever creams carrots. And I remember coming home and telling my mother about it, she was equally astonished. I never cooked creamed—anything since then.

But I, you know, Montclair was not then what it is now. I've met someone recently who lives there, and I hear it's very sort of loose and full of artists and writers and that sort of thing. That was not true at the time. It was a business place most—my father largely commuted to New York and I didn't find it particularly a great place to be growing up, so I was delighted to go to college. I went to Bryn Mawr and I had a marvelous, marvelous time; marvelous education, I think. And when it came to graduate school there wasn't much question I wanted to go to Harvard. Little did I know how women were treated at Harvard, I might say, but I found out very soon.

One of the first things I learned was there wasn't a ladies' room in the building. I had to go to another building to find the ladies' room and I had to get a key for it, which was very unusual back then. And that sort of gave me a message. And then I had to meet with the department. It was called the "Division Room" for some reason. The usual thing was portraits on the wall, the wall of past chairmen and other notables, and long polished table. They were all sitting around one end and I was alone at the far end and very much under scrutiny. And the first thing they said was, "Well, the girls always have trouble with physical chemistry, so you'll take Harvard undergraduate physical chemistry."

And I said, "I'm a grad student, I didn't come here to take undergraduate courses." And they were quite upset by that idea and I proposed that if I could pass the qualifying exam, which I didn't know ahead of time we had to take, they would let me take the graduate course. So I studied Don's notes; I met him the first day I was there, and aced the exam. But unfortunately I really didn't know enough math and so I had to take a graduate thermodynamics and statistical mechanics course and I absolutely blew the thermodynamics. I just didn't—I didn't know what the notation meant.

And I was trying to catch up but of course fell behind, so I flunked the first semester and then I got an A the second semester, but they made me retake the first semester. And that was all the time I actually spent at Harvard; that plus the war work because when we came back Don was—had disappointment here—and at Brown, Brown was—the department was very nice and offered me lab space so I could do my experimental work here, and then I commuted to Harvard once or twice a week for seminars and such. And that worked out very well. I also had our first daughter that year.

And just after she was born, a few months after—she was born the end of May. The chairman of the Chemistry Department dropped dead at his desk in his office. And it was very hard to hire faculty then because there were so many guys coming back and making huge classes, men graduating or getting their graduate degrees during the war; they'd all been doing other stuff. So they were desperate and they asked me if I would teach his courses, he was an organic chemist, I was an organic chemist. So here I was with a brand new building, with a Master's Degree, teaching 250 guys, and I think there were six girls in the first class. Students used to come—they had separate classes and a lot of the humanities because that's where most of them were majoring, and the others were sent to the Brown campus for their coursework. It was sort of an awkward arrangement.

One of them actually was a very good student; the others I don't remember much about. But then I also had to teach a senior course and that was much more fun. They were—it was a small group. I actually saw a couple of them at one of the reunions some thirty years ago now, I think. But those were good years. And then I finished my—we came back from Los Alamos in '46, and I finished my degree in 1950 and had my second daughter later that year, and then I had Chris after that, and then we moved to Princeton and I had Leslie there. And we did a lot of moving.

So yeah, Don—that story has been told many times and I wasn't there but, I mean, I was home. But he—Rob Wilson, who had been his Ph.D supervisor, very good friend, was also his boss there [at Harvard] and the story is that he was a very sort of careful person. And very sensitive about classified matters; all what they were doing was all classified. They were developing ways to measure air; explosions in air. It was actually called "Underwater," but that was a different group. They were working underwater and so Don—his thesis had ended up being on blast measurement, and he went down there. And they worked out on Nonamesset Island and went out there no matter what the weather, sometimes it was very rough, and set off blasts and tried to measure how well they were doing.

And I was just getting settled—we were able to rent, well, a house really. It was a carriage house on one of the big estates and it had, I don't know, three or four garages that went in to lots of storage space upstairs, and I had this little caretaker's apartment where we lived. It had been flooded in the '38 hurricane and still had all the high water marks all over the walls. And an incredible furnace that produced masses of carbon monoxide. If you opened the door carelessly it would all burst out and flare up, but—and I knew next to nothing about housekeeping, but I learned slowly.

And anyway, Rob Wilson called—asked Don one day to—said he would like him to come up to the attic, I think, in the lab and he needed to talk to him. Don had no idea what that might be about. And when they got there Rob said, "How would you like another job?"

And Don's response was, "What have I done wrong?"

He said, "Nothing, but how would you like another job?"

Don said, "Well I can't—unless you tell me something about it I can't make a decision."

And Rob said, "Well I can't tell you much about it." He's a very slow speaker and very low voice.

And Don said, "Well tell me where it is."

And he said, "No I can't tell you."

"Well, can you at least tell me is it north, south, west?"

"No, couldn't tell you."

And so on, a certain amount of detail, and then it was all over. Rob said, "Well I want you to think it over very carefully and go talk to Lilli and let me know your decision in the morning."

So Don came home with this story. We agreed that this was not sufficient information to make a decision on, and so Don went back and said, "No," he didn't think he would do it.

The next thing that happened was, the PA system comes on and says, "Dr. Hornig, Dr. Kistiakowsky is calling you from Sante [Santa] Fe."

And I guess in between, Conant had called him, James Bryant Conant, and Don was very angry about that because he actually sent him—have you seen those posters on the mailboxes that said, "Uncle Sam is pointing his finger at you?"

And Don said, "Well I don't know anything about this," and Conant didn't tell him much either. But then when Kistiakowsky called, he—and with a few curses, which was very much his style—he said, "Dammit, you come out here." And so Don brought that news home, and that sounded pretty interesting to me and did to him too, obviously.

But I had one reservation. I said, "What am I going to do there?"

And so Don talked to George some more, and after that George said, "Oh we're scouring the country for people—anybody with a

Master's in chemistry, especially from Harvard, is going to be more than welcome." So I was looking forward to that, but of course, no commitment of any kind. And so we bundled up our small household and drove. We had to turn in our house and a lovely sailboat in order to buy a car, which we had never owned before. And we had an old '37 Ford coupe that proved to be very useful later, because somebody had knocked out the board between the trunk and the seat so there was a clear six foot space back there. And it became an ambulance for the ski slope. I took two people, including Klaus Fuchs to the hospital, when they had skiing accidents.

But anyway, back to getting out there. Don of course went straight to work, and I went to the personnel office. And the first question was, "How fast can you type?"

And I said, "I don't type." And I actually didn't—not in the usual sense; I've learned a lot since. So anyway that presented a problem to them, but they scouted around, and then I had to fill out a security questionnaire in quint-duplicate and they looked at it. I had at the time had relatives in Ireland, Argentina, Spain, and maybe Switzerland, I don't know, they all moved around so much I had no idea anymore.

And so they looked at this and said, "Oh, this can take weeks to come back." But it turned out they had already investigated my father quite thoroughly. And so BSQ came back in three days, and I had a job in the chemistry department doing what was called "fundamental wet research," which was involved—working with plutonium, determining the solubility of various plutonium salts. It was essentially nothing known about plutonium chemistry at the time. And there was one other woman in the division, she and I worked together and we had our little cubby hole and did our little procedures and put them under the Geiger counter. It wasn't terribly inspiring and nobody actually really spoke to us.

Our boss was Don Wall, who came from Berkley, and they were pretty much a closed society anyway. So we clunked along there for a couple months. And then they got the first results from Hanford with the bad news about 240, plutonium-240, which was much more active than 239. And the first response was to fire both of us instantly. And I complained a bit about that, and they were worried obviously about reproductive damage. I tried delicately to point out that they might be more susceptible than I was; that didn't go over well. But I guess I wasn't very good at handling things like that.

So I went back to the personnel office and they said, "Well they need people in X division," which was Kisty's division. So I went to see him and he was by then a good friend, but this was strictly business and he gave me several choices, which I explored. And then I ended up with Henry Linschitz, Walter Koski, measuring shock fronts from potential implosions trying to get a perfect segment of the sphere on the shock front, which we never quite managed. And they were very interesting actually, because in the end all they had was empirical stuff. There was no theory that explained what was happening in the shock front, and basically Kisty took a huge gamble at the same time as he was taking a gamble on Don's firing unit. So that's what I did then for most of the rest.

I quit after the [Trinity] test and was planning to go back to graduate school early and get my hands into it really, well, but I would still finish out there. But as it turned out I came down with hepatitis—during the war a lot of people had hepatitis from food. I ate one raw oyster in my entire life and that was it. I was very, very sick for weeks and weeks, so I didn't go back to school but I did go back to work eventually. At the time in the summer of—early summer or late spring of '46 they were starting to move stuff to Sandia and everything that our group had done was going down there, that Don's group had done.

I suppose my previous one had already been dissolved. I was going to mention what Don was doing which was probably more—is better known, surely. He was very discouraged the first few months we were there because there really wasn't anything for him to do. There were no blasts to measure except stuff that he already knew how to do. And so he was pretty discouraged about that and bored, but we all went to—all the people with white badges could go to any meeting they wanted to. And he went to one on initiating a blast, I think there were only a few people there. And they were working on synchronizing a bunch of thirty-two detonators with primacord, which you know well I assume. Primacord is—looks like a piece of rope, and it's an explosive and you can time the moment of the explosion by how much primacord you use, how far the distance is, and connect it to a detonator and set it off with a little charge.

So that was what they were working on, hoping to synchronize all this. I do not remember all the technical details but I think the thirty-two points had to detonate within something like a millionth of a second. And I think it was no hope at that point that you could do that with primacord and detonators. And so Don would think about this, and he thought the trigger spark gap, and don't ask me to explain it, was the way to go. And he took that idea to Oppenheimer and Oppenheimer said, "Let's see you work on it." So that's what he worked on, he designed these spark gaps that were—I've forgotten how they were charged up, with condensers, I guess. I'm sure you probably know more details about it than I do. So that's what Don ended up doing, and that's how he came to be on the tower of babysitting the bomb of Trinity.

And Ben Bederson was one of the SED's in the group. Whereas I dealt with David Greenglass. He was a tech sergeant in the shop—machine shop, and I used to take our designs to him to be made up—plates we used for the explosions. And Klaus Fuchs used to come to our section—we had a weekly section meeting where we reported little bits of information—and Klaus Fuchs came to every one of those. I always wondered why, he was very silent man and he—I don't recall him ever asking a question, but he took notes all along, and so between him and Greenglass I probably contributed some information unwittingly.

Kelly: Would you have thought either one was a spy?

Hornig: Not Greenglass; no, he was just a Brooklyn kid. He was a lot like Ben Bederson, you know, irreverent and fresh. But Klaus Fuchs I was very suspicious of. I didn't think of it as spying, I mean, I was uneasy; he made a lot of people uneasy, I think. He was so sort of closed in himself. And I remember he asked me to dance, as the British Mission gave a huge party after the end of the war, and—well maybe it was before then—but anyway we danced. And I knew he was coming from Germany and having come from there myself, so I thought we might have something in common. But he was very silent about his own background. He very, very—well his—some of his family were there and some weren't. The whole thing sounded odd to me and I think I remember talking to Don about it afterward and saying, "I think—really sort of creepy, I think." But I certainly didn't follow up in any way.

Kelly: I understand a lot of people used him as a baby sitter, including the Teller's?

Hornig: I've heard that. Well the Teller's, they were nuts anyway. I shouldn't say that. He was—they were both very vigorous people. He was kind of a loud mouth. I think he had few friends here, but there was this whole "Hungarian mafia," Wigner at Princeton, who also came to Los Alamos, and Teller, and who was the other one? Yes, John von Neumann was one of that group, and Leo Szilard. But the only—well, I remember John very well. He spent quite a bit of time at Los Alamos and then we used to see him in Princeton as well. I never met Szilard, but Teller was the sort of loud mouth in the group—Wigner was a very quiet guy.

As I remember very well arriving in Sante [Santa] Fe because we had a miserable trip. We drove through a thunderstorm coming up 285, I think it was, from Tucumcari to Sante Fe, and the road just went over the hills, there were no road cuts. It went up and down and there was a huge thunderstorm that we could watch it sort of stitching across hill tops, and then it hit our car. It was a terrific jolt and a blue white flash, but it was raining so hard that being on rubber tires, we would otherwise possibly not have survived that. But it just—that grounded through the rain.

So that was all right but we were a little bit shaken, and we arrived late in the afternoon in Sante Fe. We went to 109 East Palace where the office was and they were already closed, so we went to La Fonda and settled in there for the night. And it was just an enchanting place, I mean, it was nothing like it is now. It was, you know, lots of interesting stuff everywhere. I'd never been in the southwest; I've been in Colorado, but not this kind of thing at all, and we were both just enchanted.

And the next morning, we checked out of the hotel and went to have breakfast in the coffee shop down on the plaza. And there were a couple and I looked at them and said, "You know, he looks like a physicist to me." And it turned out to have been Bob and Ruth Marshall—Marshak, excuse me. But we didn't find that out until later, and the reason they come into the store was—we left breakfast and went on up to—went to 109 East Palace and met Dorothy McKibbin, and I think she was the only person there. And she was just a wonderful person, everybody adored her. She was sort of Mommy to everybody and invited people to her house for dinners and various things. So she told us where we were going and that sounded like great fun.

So off we went. I think we stuck to the main road and went up through Espagnola. But the road up the hill was under construction at the time but people were still using the old dirt road, one car wide. And in fact we found out later the week before we got there a truck had gone over the side and the driver was killed, of course. And it was a hazardous drive, but so exciting.

And Dorothy had said, "When you get there"—she'd given us passes of course—"Go through the gate and go into the center of town and head for the water tower because that's where the housing office is." So we did that. Didn't know it was going to be as easy as it turned out to be, to find the water tower, and I hadn't been to town, which it certainly wasn't at the time. And what was her name? Vera Somebody who ran it—I might think of her last name but I can't right now, assigned us to T54, which was a little house right next to the PX. And two apartments, one on each end, single story, that awful green color, but in front was a lovely pond, the fire pond and grassy meadow going down to it, and I thought that was a nice place to live. Well it turned out later that that place had actually been assigned to the Marshak's, but they hadn't shown up yet because they were sightseeing. Ruth insisted she had to see Sante Fe. So we lucked out and they didn't because they ended up in one of the—I think it was McKay Housing, little pre-fab sorts of places, and it was terrible. She was—I don't think she ever forgave us because they had been sent the floor plan and so they were established and so they had chosen furniture to bring and had it shipped and it, of course, didn't fit where they were. I don't know what they did about it, but that was sort of a funny sideline on the whole thing.

And although—the place we were assigned was filthy, and so the first thing it needed was a good scrub. And we had—they gave us two GI bunks and a table and two chairs and that was it. Our furniture supposedly was coming by freight and should have been there a week or two later. We didn't yet have it two months later so we called up the mover and he said, "Oh, I'm so glad you called. I jotted down your address on an envelope somewhere and I can't find it." So he hadn't shipped anything yet. He finally did and it arrived in August; we got there the middle of May.

But the next morning there was all kinds of machinery out front. They were putting up a ten-foot chain link fence and painting over the meadow for a parking lot for the GI vehicles. So that was our view for the rest of our time at Los Alamos. But other than that it was lovely; we looked right across the valley at the mountains, and it was a beautiful place.

We did a lot of camping and hiking. We were both hikers and I don't know—on a good day it was thirty-five miles a day with a full pack, how's that? Oh, Sawyer's Hill was the ski hill, and we did ski there. I sort of learned to ski; I never really liked it. When I turned fifty I said, "That's it, no more skiing." And then we rode often with Kisty and his soon-to-be wife, Irma Shuler.

And then we had one interesting ride with the two of them. We had several, but this particular one we were going to a ranch on the other side of the Rio Grande, so we went down. We used horses from the cavalry stables, they rented them out, they liked to have them exercise. And the reason they had cavalry was to ride, to guard the fences. And so we went over to this ranch—that was kind of a long ride too, it was thirty or forty miles. And we got there, and it turned out the woman who owned it and ran it—it was a guest ranch—was Russian. Apparently had been a Duchess but I wouldn't swear to that. And the other—there was one woman staying there who said she was Swiss, she had a very strong German accent, and she was traveling with a male guide. She was planning to film bears in the mountains, she said; that seemed a funny thing to be doing in the middle of the war actually. And for dinner this Russian Duchess had a friend there staying with her, a woman friend, and for dinner they'd invited a guy who was a rancher in the valley somewhere. And I will never forget him because he came on a white horse with a black cloak floating behind him and he had bright white hair and a very handsome guy, I might say, and a huge silver belt; just a character.

As the evening went on we realized that Don and Irma were the only two native-born Americans in this whole crowd. And I was quite sure the so-called Swiss lady was a spy; she may well have been, I don't know. I don't remember now who this spectacular male was. But he made quite a picture galloping across the dessert.

Well, George Kistiakowsky was a character, and we thought a great person. There were people who hated his guts, I think, and Teller may have been one of them; I'm not sure about that. But he was a fine scientist and had a great deal of experience that was suitable for the project. He had been an officer in the White Russian Army in the first war as a kid of eighteen, I think, and fought his way out to Odessa, I believe, and they—I think they commandeered a ship somehow. In between he was—he's written this up, there's an article—I think it was in the New York Times Magazine, where he recalled some of that era. But the story was that he was interned by the French in Odessa—I can't vouch for this—and that they were so dirty that he escaped and went to an English camp.

But anyway, eventually he and his crew apparently commandeered this ship and none of them had ever been to sea before but they figured out how to run it. Then they discovered that they were actually in the middle of a mine field in the harbor, or as they came out of the harbor, but they made their way. And he ended up at that point in Berlin and made a living as a glass blower. He was this fabulous glass blower, which is not an easy skill to learn, and he could blow quartz spirals, and that was fairly esoteric kind of thing. Almost nobody ever used—was able to do that. So he made a living that way, and at the same time or shortly after began his graduate work with [inaudible] at the university in Berlin, and I assume that's when he married his first wife; I've never met her. And they eventually came here—I'm not—I don't know about the timing. In fact, I think it was in the late '20s, and he went to Princeton for a bit, I believe, before coming to Harvard, where he spent the—well except for Los Alamos and being science advisor to Eisenhower, he spent the rest of his career at Harvard. I see his wife every Tuesday, we go to lunch together in Cambridge.

During the war he went to a place called "Boosten," which was an explosive research place in or near Pittsburgh, I don't know exactly. And so he was leading expert on explosions, and that's why he was at Los Alamos. And he was, I think, probably as frustrated as Don a good part of the time with, you know, having to wait so long before they could actually do what they were asked to do, which is measure explosion. But he was a very gregarious sort; he was either friends or enemies with lots of people and a great charmer, as you have undoubtedly have heard. Very good friend.

Oppenheimer was universally admired. I think his wife Kitty probably wasn't; she was a difficult person, is my impression. I barely knew her and really didn't know him well at all; I had no occasion to be close with them. We were half their age. I mean, we were twenty-three and twenty-four when we got there, and he was in his forties. There were more people our age than his; very youthful crowd. I remember General Groves getting very annoyed at the fact that there were so many women having babies in the hospital there. Apparently most of the cases were maternity cases and he didn't think the U.S. Army should be paying for all that, but they did.

During the Trinity test—I knew it was coming up and in fact, two days before they'd had a malfunction down there, an early misfire on the X unit. And at two o'clock in the morning our group leader, Lewis Fussell, was knocking on my bedroom window saying, "You have to get up, we have some work to do." And he and I went off to the Tech Area at two o'clock in the morning with a list of equipment that we had to replace down there. And neither of us had ever been in the stock room before, mind you, so we had quite a time finding it, but by about five o'clock I think we had everything together and it got shipped off on a truck and they had it in the morning down there.

But anyway, I had planned to drive up to Sandia Mountain, which had a nice road to the top and a clear view 110 miles down to the Trinity site. Some friends came with me, Earl and Betty Thomas—no I guess Earl was—it was just Betty Thomas, I think Earl may have been at Trinity, and David Anderson who was also part of the X group. I'm not quite sure what his job was, but he was a friend that we hiked with and did other things with. And so the three of us—our car couldn't have taken more than three—were up there, and we knew it was—the shot was scheduled to go off before sunrise in order to—for all the cameras to function properly.

And so there we sat at ten thousand feet and we slept a little, we put sleeping bags on the ground. None of us slept very well and so we got up about three o'clock, I guess, and started waiting for the shot, keeping our eyes glued on the site. And we waited and waited and at 4:30 the sun rose. And we were so crushed and disappointed and said, "Well, I guess it's not going to go today," and we had to go back up through the hill and get to work. And so we packed up our sleeping bags and got in the car. It didn't take long, I mean, it was quick decision, and I was sitting in the car reaching for my ignition key—and the thing bloomed in front of us. And of course we had neglected the fact that at ten thousand feet the sun rises earlier then it does at two thousand or three thousand down in the dessert. So we blamed ourselves for not being good scientists there, but we did see it and it was just incredible.

Just a couple of nights ago I saw a film on PBS of the superbomb tests and it reminded me very strongly, and of course the scale is far bigger, but the pictures are much like what I remember in my mind as the—these sort of boiling clouds and color—vivid colors like violet, purple, orange, yellow, red, just everything. It was fantastic. And we were all kind of shaken up but—and we waited for the shock wave to come, which it did, requisite, I don't know—fifteen, eleven, twelve, fifteen minutes later.

And then we backed up and started down the mountain, and we stopped at a diner somewhere near Albuquerque for breakfast. And the guy behind the counter said, "You guys know anything about that explosion they had down at the proving grounds?" We said, "What, no, we didn't know about that?"

Yes, I remember the petition to—not to use the bomb as a weapon came around just after the test. And I don't know—I think it may have originated in Chicago or maybe in Oak Ridge, but I think Chicago was right. And some of my friends in the same group, whatever it was, X something, were signing it. And I thought about it and I thought that was a good idea. I think many of us had really worked on it—on the bomb with the thought that it might deter Hitler. Once the European war was over with, well, a lot of the people left right away, Kisty left for instance soon after that. I don't—there wasn't certainly among the scientists the same gut feeling about using it. And we thought in our innocence—of course it made no difference—but if we petitioned hard enough they might do a demonstration test or something like they later did at Bikini and Enewetak, and invite the Japanese to witness it. But of course the military I think had made the decision well before that they were going to use it no matter what. And so we had very mixed feelings about that.

I think Don was still at Trinity when I signed it; I'm not sure about that. Actually he came back the next day from after the test. He and George drove up in a jeep with no top, and the jeeps in those days didn't even have side straps. And they were both so exhausted of course. They took turns driving apparently, and then I remember one of them veered off the road, the other one said, "Time for you to take a nap, let me drive." And they came—Irma was at our house waiting for them. They came over—they came late in the day around dinnertime and George literally fell asleep sitting in a straight chair. So Irma took him home and Don had a good long nap. But they were quite exhilarated; it had been a success.

But when the bomb was dropped we were—Don and I were actually in Milwaukee visiting his family because his brother was in the Navy and was slated to be shipped out and this was his leave, just a few days before showing up at the West coast. And we knew damn well he wasn't going to be going anywhere, much at least not into danger, and we knew that the drop was imminent. We didn't know the precise moment. Certainly Don's parents didn't have TV at the time and I don't know if there were ever any news on, but Don and I went downtown. There were all the papers with the headlines, so we knew it had gone off.

That was an odd mix of feelings. I mean, certainly some triumph and the destruction was just so incredible. I think we've all been a little haunted by that over the years.

But we had an interesting experience several years ago. Don was asked to come and speak at the University of Colorado Science Policy Program that was working on a volume of all the science advisors they could find to talk about how science policy gets made, how the president makes those decisions. And while we were there we talked to and sat in various seminars and also went to an undergraduate class in physics and spoke briefly and then stayed for the rest of it.

Afterwards a student came up to us, a young man probably about thirty and clearly half Japanese. And he said, "I'm going to tell you something that's rather hard for me because you know in Japan we're very, very close in the family and we don't talk much to other people about our feelings." But he said, "My grandmother was in Hiroshima when the bomb was dropped and she survived and so did my mother. And she got engaged to an American serviceman later and was coming here." He said, "My grandmother told her that she should be glad she's going and that"—I'm trying to think of the precise words—but basically that the atom bomb had been a blessing for Japan because it got rid of the old government and the war like—well, the utter destruction that was taking place which was actually worse then what these bombs did. It all happened in a flash, one moment.

But I was very moved by that, that he told us that. He had been a Marine—he'd done a stint in the Marines and then he decided to get an education when he came out. So I've thought back about that a number of times.

It was a fabulous time in our lives, that's really the answer; you know we were so young. When I look now at our grandchildren, the youngest ones are about the age we were then and they're so not yet really adult in some ways, and they don't think of themselves as having adult responsibilities. It's very striking to me because we had no doubt that we were grown up, but the, you know, we weren't the only people. There were lots of other people who were our age with very responsible jobs, massive social life—we've never had a busier one. Everybody had—got together for dinners or hikes or go camping or go riding. It was a theater group and Don was in and I did scenery for them and there was lots of music, but somehow we weren't in that much. Don is very musical, he used to play the violin, but somehow he just didn't there.

What else did we do? Well, we went off to Indian Pueblos for dances and that kind of thing. I remember—of course we had Indian women who were assigned as house cleaners. And one I had came from San Ildefonso and we went down one Sunday, we were up buying pottery, actually and ran into her and she invited us into her house. And I saw a papoose board with a baby on it, it was swinging from the ceiling, and everybody who went by gave it a little shove and that baby was happy as a clam. And then she said, "Oh the christening is next Sunday, will you come?"

And we said, "Yes, we'd love to" and so we came down there with a little present and all that sort of thing. There wasn't any christening, nothing ever happened. That was kind of funny.

But yeah, there was an awful lot of sightseeing to do and you know, we did all we had time for. Some complained and some loved it. It depended a lot, I think, on how housebound they were with little kids. It was kind of hard work, not a clean place. There were a lot of dust storms and that sort of thing and you know, you came in from a dirt road directly into your living room. So if you were a good housekeeper, which I wasn't, you'd probably fret about that.

Some of them—I had one friend who—her husband worked in the group and they had a one year old and a two year old and two dogs, two Dalmatians, and then she had twins and the dogs had eleven puppies in a two-bedroom apartment. It was a real zoo.

DOCUMENT 100

Photograph, *Library in Jackson Square Commercial District, Oak Ridge, Tennessee*, ca. 1940s

Courtesy of the National Archives, Atlanta, RG 326, Atomic Energy Commission, box 160.

Boomtowns were created during World War II in support of industrial production, including aircraft production and shipbuilding. During the Manhattan Project, the US government fenced in a secret city in Tennessee, now known as Oak Ridge, that supplied local shopping, food, and entertainment to the workers engaged in building the atomic bomb. This image shows a library in Oak Ridge.

DOCUMENT 101
Letter from Lousie E. Remeik to President Franklin D. Roosevelt

Courtesy of the National Archives, Atlanta, RG 225, Records of the Committee on Fair Employment Practice, Regional Files, Region VIII, box 3, Folder Clinton Engineer Works, Louise E. Remeik, 7-BN-116.

In this letter, Louise Remeik pleads with President Franklin D. Roosevelt for assistance with an employment issue. Born in New York City, Remeik and her sister were adopted by a Latvian couple after the death of their mother. The two girls were raised in Latvia before returning to the United States during the Great Depression. Latvia was invaded by Nazi Germany on July 10, 1941, and Remiek mentions that she has not had any word of her adopted mother. Although she was an American citizen by birth, her adoption by the Latvian couple disqualified her for work at Clinton Engineering Works in Oak Ridge, Tennessee. The plant, which manufactured explosives, was managed by Eastman Corporation from January 1943 to May 1947. The editors have preserved the original spelling and grammatical errors in the letter.

---

607 Maynard Avenue
Knoxville 17, Tennessee

Mr. President
White House
Washington D.C.

Dear Mr. President:

I am appealing to you in hope that you will be kind enough to consider my case and help me get my job back.

I will try to put my case before you as simple as possible.
I was employed by the Clinton Engineer Works Tennessee Eastman Corporation, Clinton Tennessee as a trainee. I was trained by them for seven weeks. The sevent [*sic*] week we where advenst [*sic*] in confidential

matters. We where show [*sic*] secret machinery, machins [*sic*] and blue prints what we had to memorize. I was doing very nicely as my trainee record will show, than I was terminated by request <u>of the army</u>. After two week of waiting I received my release reading "Unable to obtain clearance." I didn't know what it was all about, so I asked my husband (who works for Stone and Webster on the same project) to go to the Army Intelligence Department to find out.

My husband was told by Captain Leonard (who is the head of the Intelligence Dep.) that I was terminated because I have a mother by adoption in Latvia and that the <u>Army have a rule not to employ people with</u> relatives in foreign country.

I think it is very unfair ruling, special in my case. I will give you Mr. President my racial background so you can see how unfair it is:

I was born in New York City my mother died when I was about two years old, and I with my sister was adopted by Mr. and Mrs. G. Zarin. They then moved us to Latvia (1920) in Europe to live. My real father stayed in America (he is living in Milwaukee, Wisconsin). My brother was raised in orphanage [*sic*] in U.S.A.

When I was of age I was given a choice: to stay in Latvia and become their heiress or to keep my American rights and go to America and make my own future. I choose to come to America as an American citizen (1934) also my sister returned to America.

My father by adoption died in Latvia (1935). The only living person I could call a relative is my mother by adoption, and even from her I haven't heard or received any word for the last three and half years (since Latvia is invadet [*sic*] by germans).

So this is my case Mr. President. Now I would like to ask you if you think it is fair for a [*sic*] American citizen to be terminated from a important position just because it [*sic*] <u>maybe</u> have a relative in foreing country? I said maybe because I don't know if she is still living.

I was adopted by Mr. and Mrs. G. Zarin because I was to young to have my say. If I would have my choice I would have stayed in the orphanage with my brother. My brother now is in the U.S. Navy Coast Guard over sees [*sic*] fighting for our country, my husband is working in a defence project, and I was so proud when I was employed by the Clinton Engineer Works, Tenneesse, Eastman Corp. Clinton, Tenn. I felt that at last I have found a possession where I could do my part for my country.

Mr. President I am a good wife and mother to my family and as far as I know ther is not a single blackening ting in my record. But then to be reliest of a job because of now fault of my, it is unbearable!

Ther [sic] is now [sic] other place to appeal Mr. President so you are my last hope. I know if you could only find time to look in to my case, you could find a way to help me get my job back.

Hoping I haven't taken up to much of your time Mr. President.

I remain hopeful to hear from you.

Yours respectfully
Louise E. Rimeik
Thank you.
My address:
Mrs. L. Rimeix
607 Maynard Ave.
Knoxville 17, Tennessee

DOCUMENT 102

Excerpt, Mary Barbara B. Dannaher, Veterans History Project Interview, February 24, 2010, by James Lyko

Courtesy of the Elihu Burritt Library at Central Connecticut State University.

A native of Boston, Mary Barbara B. Dannaher served in the Navy Women's Reserve (WAVEs) as a cryptographer in Washington, D.C. She worked specifically on JN-25, the main, and most secure, command and control communications scheme used by the Imperial Japanese Navy. For a full transcript, see the Library of Congress's Veterans History Project website: http:// lcweb2.loc.gov/diglib/vhp/story/loc.natlib.afc2001001.74608/ transcript?ID=mv0001.

Mary Barbara Brennan Dannaher: When we arrived—when I arrived in Washington, I was assigned, first of all, to go to the Navy Yard. They never said we would go straight to our office. We were to go to the Navy Yard. So we went to the Navy Yard and there we expected to be reimbursed for the trip that we took from Waterloo—Cedar Falls, Iowa, home. And then back down to Washington. Well, come to find out the government never pays for train trips over certain parts of the country that is designated as: Land grants. And so by the time we got reimbursed it was not quite what we expected.

James Lyko: Oh, my. Surprise. Surprise. Yes.

Mary Barbara Brennan Dannaher: So, anyway, that was one of the things that we sort of said: Uh-oh. Well, now we're on the Navy case for our travel. Anyway, it was fine. But then there were some of us who were assigned to Nebraska Avenue—not Nebraska Avenue. I'm sorry. We were assigned to the Navy Department on—right downtown Washington. I think it was—I'm not sure. I don't know whether it was on Pennsylvania Avenue or one of those. But, anyway, that's where our assignment was. But before that our billet would be at the national—at the Capitol Park Hotel. And that was on South Capitol Street right across from Union Station, which was a great central place to be—and—but because we were walking everywhere or taking mass transport. So the next day we were to arrive at the Navy Department ready to go to work. Before we were even allowed to go to the office, our desk, anyplace, we had to take an oath because we were going to be working on top secret materials.

James Lyko: So you're hearing this for the first time, right?

Mary Barbara Brennan Dannaher: Yes.

James Lyko: Your assignment?

Mary Barbara Brennan Dannaher: Yes. So we swore not the divulge any information, to the grave. This has changed since then. But I'll explain that later. We were sent to offices. And the offices were very crowded. These buildings were put up during World War I. And the Navy Department really didn't have any place like the Army did at the Pentagon. So they were sort of spread out all over the city. And, but, this was the main office. We worked there for several months right into the spring. I had two room-mates. Very interesting young ladies. One was Natalie Fiske, F-i-s-k-e. Her grandfather was president of the Metropolitan Life Insurance Company. And she was assigned to Nebraska Avenue as I was. And she was instrumental in introducing me around town. And we were taken out to lunch one time at the National Press Club. And the man who was manager of the Metropolitan, evidently—in Washington—had visited with Eleanor Roosevelt, previously. And, of course, he had a lot to tell us about that. And she was a very interesting girl, herself. She was brought up not in the United States. She was brought up in Paris. I don't know why. Her father was evidently employed there. My other roommate was very active in France with the State Department. She was a clerk. But she ended up, before she came to the United States, a secretary to Admiral Leahy's wife. And she was a good friend of Robert Murphy. And I don't know if you are familiar with the situation. But Robert Murphy and Mark Clark did a lot of under-cover work in France before the—oh, what's the word I want to use—before we went into Normandy.

James Lyko: Yeah. Going across the Channel.

Mary Barbara Brennan Dannaher: Yes.

James Lyko: The invasion.

Mary Barbara Brennan Dannaher: Yes. The invasion. And so she would not—she was not cleared to work with us at—

James Lyko: Okay.

Mary Barbara Brennan Dannaher: Nebraska Avenue. Well, she had a lot of friends. And it was one of those things. We didn't know. No one told us anything. Nor did we really want to know.

James Lyko: Yeah.

Mary Barbara Brennan Dannaher: We were very, very aware of secrecy and how it could be very dangerous for all of our military, all of the people involved in the war effort, if anyone divulged anything. And just discussing things in public, like a restaurant or a soda fountain or someplace, you knew enough to just keep your mouth shut about anything that went on when it was related. So we were—Natalie and I on occasion did travel, because we had a long way to travel once they—in the spring when they transferred our offices up to Nebraska Avenue.

James Lyko: Yeah.

Mary Barbara Brennan Dannaher: We took over the—the Navy was able to procure the beautiful buildings that had belonged to the Mount Vernon Young Ladies' Seminary. And it was a gorgeous building. Lovely grounds. And an attached chapel where we used to have our religious—we had Protestant and Catholic services there. And I'm not sure if the Jewish didn't have services there also, in the chapel. So that was very convenient, because then our WAVE quarters were built across the street from work. And they started with three buildings. Ended up with 25. That is the number of WAVES that were working on codes and ciphers for the United States Navy. And, of course, this building and the work we were doing was with the Vice Chief of Naval Operations. And so, actually, we were working for that effort—that part of the Navy.

James Lyko: And how many were you, did you say? Twenty-five?

Mary Barbara Brennan Dannaher: Twenty-five—well, I showed—

James Lyko: You said twenty-five buildings?

Mary Barbara Brennan Dannaher: Twenty-five buildings.

James Lyko: Okay.

Mary Barbara Brennan Dannaher: Yeah. Filled with WAVES.

James Lyko: Filled? Okay. So that's a lot?

Mary Barbara Brennan Dannaher: So thousands—

James Lyko: Yes.

Mary Barbara Brennan Dannaher: of women worked on these. And, of course, there were some men also. As a matter of fact, our office, we had mostly officers from the University of Ohio. The whole—the head of the whole Nebraska Avenue program there was—he wasn't a Captain. I can't remember exactly. But his name was Ford. And, of course, he was Navy. And he later became an editor of the Heritage Magazine after he got out of the service. So I wish I could remember his title but I don't. We were very, very aware of the fact that this was an important job.

First of all, we worked around—we didn't—we worked—first of
all, when we went there, we used to work watches. Eight hours
for two days—well, eight hours each day. Say, 8:00 to 4:00. Then
we were off until the next day at 4:00. We worked 4:00 to 12:00
for two days. Then we were off until late watch started at 12:00.
And we worked 12:00 to 8:00 for two days. Well, this was not
a very healthy situation. All we did was sleep and eat and go to
work. So then they changed it. And we worked five-day watches.
So we were on watch from 8:00 to 4:00 for five days and so forth.
So that worked out. And since we were right across the street
and living in the WAVE quarters, it was easy because our mess
hall was there. A huge mess hall. And we even fed the Marines
who were stationed over at American University. And when they
would come to eat in our mess hall, they fed us as women should
be fed. Smaller portions and so forth. And, of course, the Marines
would go back with their tray and the bread would be piled up.
Like half a loaf of bread for each meal. But the food was excellent. The food was just wonderful. And we had Navy cooks. And
when we went—visited other Naval bases, like to go to a dance or
something like that and they invited us for their meal, we were—
we were inundated with food. And we realized that the men ate
differently than we did.

James Lyko: They still do.

Mary Barbara Brennan Dannaher: Yes. Well, we were doing very,
very well at Nebraska Avenue and—at the WAVE quarters—until
summer came. And, of course, there was no air-conditioning
in either the places where we slept or in the mess hall. And the
mess hall, sometimes I think—well, if you have ever been in
Washington in the summertime, you know it can get very hot
and humid. And we were all—we had to eat with our uniform.
Full uniform. That meant wool suits. Long sleeved shirts and ties.
Hats. So as the women started passing out in line—

James Lyko: Yeah. Yeah.

Mary Barbara Brennan Dannaher: they knew something had to be
changed. So we received a new uniform for summer. And it was
a nice—very nice uniform. Very cool. We still had to wear our
tie. We still had to wear our hat. But it was cool. It was a dress.

Yes. And so it was a lot happier. And lots of times WAVES would just not go to mess. They just wouldn't go because they knew it was just too hot there. So they would pay for their own food and go down to the local restaurant to eat. But it wasn't convenient because there wasn't usually—it was a long walk to go down to the center where we were and to find any place to eat. But it turned out very well at the mess hall. And there were—we had so many things. We had a pool. We had dancing lessons. We had sports. We put on plays, if anyone was interested. The Warrant Officer in our unit that worked with us became quite famous as a TV actor. And he appeared with Eve Arden in that show that she was in.

James Lyko: Miss Brooks?

Mary Barbara Brennan Dannaher: Yes. Miss Brooks.

James Lyko: Is that so?

Mary Barbara Brennan Dannaher: And he was her boyfriend. Right.

James Lyko: Really?

Mary Barbara Brennan Dannaher: Yes. And we didn't have shredding machines then. We had what we called burn bags. And so any materials that we worked on we had to put in these burn bags—we had to discard—we had to put in the burn bags. And then once every so often, the burn bags would have to go down to a place where they burned them. So they always had to have an escort. And the poor young man that worked with us, like the fellow who was our Warrant Officer, had to have a side arm. And, of course, we would always kid them and say, please, don't shoot yourself in the foot because—have you ever been taught how to use a gun to begin with? Nothing—we didn't have any accidents anyway. But during that time I worked on JN-25, which was a very important Naval code. We did not compromise 25 when I went into the service and went to work on it. JN-25 was compromised long before that. And there were people in Hawaii, a group of intelligence officers—a small group—who were working on it and were doing a very good job, as a matter of fact. But, unfortunately, at that time, the Navy only had 42 people in the whole Navy—

James Lyko: Who could speak Japanese?

Mary Barbara Brennan Dannaher: Who could speak Japanese fluently.

James Lyko: Yeah.

Mary Barbara Brennan Dannaher: And so that was a drawback. However, we must have been very cautious about how we reacted to the code when we did compromise it, because the Japanese continued to use it right through the war. And they may have changed things so that we would have to go to work and figure out what the change—how the change was made. At one time they were using—in a message they would put—I can't say it was a graph—they put a piece—I don't know. It was almost like something that was cut out of a piece of paper so that it would be cut out in certain places. And you would put it down over the message.

James Lyko: Oh. A mask?

Mary Barbara Brennan Dannaher: And you just—a mask. Yes. And so then we had to figure out, with the mask, you know—it wasn't our job to figure it out. We were still doing additives. Adding five numerals to five numerals. Getting a sum. And that sum always had to be divisible by three. There was never any carrying. In other words, if you said 9 plus 5, the answer was 4. And so, but three was a superstition, evidently, with the Japanese.

James Lyko: Oh, really?

Mary Barbara Brennan Dannaher: Because it did limit them, somewhat, in the use of numbers. We were very successful, but we were always cautioned if we were successful. And that was a secret. Almost—it was almost body language when you saw other people from other sections in the cafeteria that things were good that day.

James Lyko: Oh. Okay.

Mary Barbara Brennan Dannaher: It was maybe more smiles on a face or something like that. But we were always cautioned that when we left the building, poker face.

James Lyko: Don't indicate anything?

Mary Barbara Brennan Dannaher: Don't indicate by your expressions that something good was going on inside. So we took secrecy very seriously. And it was all—we met some wonderful people. I stayed with JN-25 for about a year and a half, almost two years. And then I was transferred with my Section Head to weather codes. And in the weather codes we had a job—and it—we kept getting these messages, and we didn't know how to classify them. So we would say, well, we have—already have top secret. So, and we already had top secret ultra. So we got so we would say, well, we'll classify this as top secret ultra ultra. When we got to the third ultra, we had one of the officers coming in and he said to the group—and we worked in a very small space. I don't think we even had a window. And he said, look—he said, regarding classification—he said, pretty soon it's going to get to the point where nobody is going to be able to read this message. And he said, and we do have to read it. So, he said, let's cut it down to one ultra. And so that was the way it was. But it was a lot of—it was very interesting to work with the meteorologists because we found out so much about weather.

Timeline

1941

- October: The United Services Organization (USO) was founded.
- June: President Franklin D. Roosevelt signed Executive Order 8802, which banned racial discrimination in defense industries.
- December: Japanese bombers attacked the US Naval Base at Pearl Harbor, Hawaii.

1942

- February: President Roosevelt signed Executive Order 9066, giving military officials the authority to detain 120,000 Japanese Americans in assembly centers and, later, internment camps.
- May: Congress created the Women's Army Auxiliary Corps (WAACs), and Oveta Culp Hobby became its first director.
- June: President Roosevelt established the Office of Strategic Services (OSS) to coordinate US overseas intelligence.
- July: Congress authorized the Women Accepted for Voluntary Services (WAVES).
- July: WAAC training schools opened.
- July: Congress authorized the use of $6 million for child-care facilities for children of women in defense work.
- September: Gas rationing went into effect across the nation.
- September: The Women's Air Force Service Pilots (WASPs) was established.

1943

- Artist J. Howard Miller published his now-iconic image of "Rosie the Riveter."

- February: Mildred Harnack-Fish, an American member of the resistance group the Red Orchestra, was executed by Nazi Germany.

- April: Meat, canned food, and cheese became rationed goods

- April: Congress passed the Sparkman Act, which allowed for women physicians to be commissioned into the armed forces.

- May: Normal Rockwell's "Rosie" illustration was published on the cover of the *Saturday Evening Post*.

- July: WAAC was officially changed to the Women's Army Corps (WAC) after Congresswoman Edith Nourse Rogers worked to drop "auxiliary" from the organization's name.

- July: WACs left for duty overseas, arriving in London first, before being deployed throughout the European Theater.

1944

- June: President Roosevelt signed the Serviceman's Readjustment Act (known as the GI Bill). The housing and education benefits that would serve male veterans did not extend to female veterans.

- June: Four days after D-day, army nurses landed at Normandy.

1945

- January: The only all–African American WAC unit, the 6888th Central Postal Directory Battalion, deployed for Europe.

- February: Nurses from the US Army Nurse Corps and the US Navy Nurses Corps who were captured at the fall of Bataan and Corregidor (1941–1942) were released by the Japanese.

- May: Germany officially surrendered to the Allied powers.

- August: The United States dropped nuclear bombs on Hiroshima, Japan, on August 6 and Nagasaki, Japan, on August 9.

- September: The first class of women entered Harvard Medical School on an equal basis with men.

- September: Japan formally surrendered to the Allied powers, thereby ending World War II.

1946

- February: The War Department announced a retention and re-enlistment program to encourage active-duty WACs with specialized skills to remain in the service and former WACS to reenlist; 80 percent did so for another year.

- February: General Dwight D. Eisenhower approved the creation of the Women's Medical Service Corps. Congress passed the bill in 1947 and combined it with a bill that gave regular status to women of the Navy Nurses Corps.

1947

- April: The Army-Navy Nurses Act became public law.

- October: The Women's Service Integration Act was approved by the Senate. General Eisenhower hand-delivered a letter of support to the chairman of the House Armed Services Committee urging quick approval. The bill was postponed until 1948.

1948

- June: President Harry S. Truman signed the Women's Armed Services Integration Act (Public Law 625), allowing women into the military on a full-time basis, though not in combat positions.

- June: The first Regular Army WAC Training Center at Fort Lee, Virginia, was established three days after integration of the woman's armed services into the regular armed forces of the United States.

- July: President Truman signed Executive Order 9981, which banned racial discrimination in the US military.

- December: Lieutenant Colonel Mary Hallaren was sworn in as director of the WAC, replacing Colonel Westray Battle Boyce.

1949

- Military officials terminate the WAC, Army of the United States. Women who were honorably discharged reenlist in the WAC Regular Army (the WAC disbanded in 1978).

- The first African American women enlisted in the Marine Corps.

Discussion Questions and Assignments

1. How did women balance the expectations of gender roles with the needs of the government and industry to put them to work?

2. How were African American, Hispanic, and immigrant women treated during World War II?

3. What role did propaganda play in bringing women into the workforce?

4. How does the iconic image of "Rosie the Riveter" shape or obscure the diversity of women's experiences during the war?

5. In what ways did class shape women's experiences during the war?

6. What kinds of stereotypes about women were prevalent in industry and government documents during the war?

7. How did the presence of women in industry challenge traditional views of women's work?

8. What do the letters and oral histories included in this collection reveal about women's daily lives and personal struggles?

9. What motivated women to support the war effort?

10. How did women's participation in auxiliary services during the war shape their postwar access to the military?

11. What did women's participation in resistance activities reveal about their contributions to the war?

12. How did women balance their patriotism with their desire for financial independence during the war?

13. How did women's working lives differ during the war?

14. In what ways did women resist limitations placed on them during the war? To whom did they protest?

15. What role did women play in resistance activities in Europe?

16. What role did female celebrities such as Marlene Dietrich and Margaret Mitchell play in the war?

17. How did sports and popular culture depict women's experiences during the war?

18. How did highly educated women, such as physicians and scientists, contribute to the war effort?

19. How did the war shape gender and family relationships during and after the conflict?

20. What role did children play during World War II, and how was that shaped by their mothers' experiences?

Classroom and Research Activities

The assignments included in this section are intended to span a week-long unit focused on women and World War II, but this could be easily modified.

Activity 1: Quotable Quotes

In a short paper (500 to 750 words), respond to one of the following quotations. In your paper, select at least five primary documents from this collection to help shape your argument.

Quote 1: "There is one front and one battle where everyone in the United States—every man, woman, and child—is in action, and will be privileged to remain in action throughout this war. That front is right here at home, in our daily lives, and in our daily tasks."—President Franklin D. Roosevelt, April 28, 1942

- What does this quote from President Franklin D. Roosevelt reveal about women's role in the war effort?

- Review chapter 4 and consider what this quote and these documents reveal about the expectations of Americans at home.

Quote 2: "The war gave a lot of people jobs. It led them to expect more than they had before. People's expectations, financially, spiritually, were raised. There was such a beautiful dream. We were gonna reach the end of the rainbow. . . . I remember a woman saying on the bus that she hoped the war didn't end until she got her refrigerator paid for. An old man hit her over the head with an umbrella. He said, 'How dare you!' (Laughs.)"—Peggy Terry, a woman who worked in a munitions factory

• What does Terry's quote reveal about how women viewed their war-time work?

• Compare this quote to the documents in chapter 1 and reflect on how the war reshaped women's lives and expectations?

Quote 3: "We came back to Los Angeles at the end of the war, believing that there was no other way but to be American. We were discouraged with our Japanese culture. My feeling at the time was, I had to prove myself. I don't know why I had to prove myself. Here I am, an ex-GI, born and raised here. Why do I have to prove myself? We all had this feeling. We had to prove that we were Americans."—Peter Ota, a Japanese American veteran whose family was interned during the war.

• What does this quote reveal about the postwar experience for Japanese Americans?

• Compare this quote to the documents related to Japanese internment in chapter 5.

Activity 2: Hollywood Goes to War

Prior to the US entry into the war, the movie industry, centered in California, produced films that condemned Axis aggression and supported the Allied powers. After the bombing of Pearl Harbor, the US government depended on Hollywood directors and stars to influence the tens of millions of American moviegoers. Hollywood played a critical role in producing propaganda films that championed stories of patriotism, duty, and sacrifice for audiences in the United States and abroad. The film industry supported the war effort, and the success and continued popularity of many wartime movies, such as *Casablanca*, reflect the continued influence that this era has on the American cultural landscape.

Step 1: View the online exhibition created by the Kennesaw State University Museum of History and Holocaust Education: http://marb.kennesaw.edu/hollywoodandwar/exhibits/show/hollywoodgoestowar.

Step 2: Select and view two films that reflect the diversity of women's experiences during the war. Possible options include *Four Jills in a Jeep* (1944), *Cry Havoc* (1943), or *Two Girls and a Sailor* (1944).

Step 3: Compare women's roles in these films with the documents presented in this collection and consider the following questions:

• How was women's work portrayed in the various films, and how did that differ from the documents in this collection?

• How were women presented as contributors to the war effort in the films and in the documents?

• In what ways were immigrant or minority women included in this conversation in films and in the documents?

• How was humor used to present women's experiences in film. Was this humor reflected in the primary documents?

• Did Hollywood glamorize the war and women's roles in it?

Activity 3: Curate an Exhibition on Women at War

Step 1: Review all of the images in this documentary collection and discuss how as a group they tell a story about women's diverse experiences during the war.

Step 2: Using the entire collection of images, invite groups of students to curate an exhibition by creating:

• A title

• An introductory panel (100–200 words)

• Label copy for each image (50 words or less)

Step 3: If each group would like to include additional images, visit the online prints and photographs catalog at the Library of Congress, available at http://www.loc.gov/pictures/, or the digital photography collection at the National Archives, available at http://www.archives.gov/research/alic/reference/photography.html.

Step 4: Have each group present its final exhibition project to the larger group.

Activity 4: In Their Own Words

Oral history is an important source of information about women's experiences during World War II. In this activity, select three to five oral history interviews focused on one of the following topics. Each student will write a three- to five-page research paper (not to exceed 1,250 words) using both primary and secondary sources.

Option 1: Japanese Internment

Step 1: Review the section on internment in chapter 5 of this documentary collection.

Step 2: Select an additional three to five oral histories focused on women's experiences during internment. The Densho project (available at http://www.densho.org/densho.asp) has collected the testimonies of Japanese Americans who were interned during World War II and is an excellent resource for students and teachers.

Step 3: Identify four to six secondary sources. Densho provides a good link to resources: http://www.densho.org/resources/default.asp.

Step 4: Craft a research paper that considers the following questions: What factors shaped women's experiences during internment? How were traditional gender roles undermined in the camps? What did women do to cope with the stress and humiliation of their incarceration?

Option 2: The Manhattan Project

Step 1: Review the section on the Manhattan Project in chapter 5 of this documentary collection.

Step 2: Select an additional three to five oral histories focused on women's experiences while working on the Manhattan Project. Voices of the Manhattan Project (available at http://www.manhattanprojectvoices.org/oral-histories) is a joint project by the Atomic Heritage Foundation and the Los Alamos Historical Society to create a public archive of oral history collections of Manhattan Project veterans and their families. It provides a wealth of information on women's experiences.

Step 3: Identify four to six secondary sources. Voices of the Manhattan Project provides a good list of links to resources. Visit http://www.manhattanprojectvoices.org/resources.

Step 4: Craft a research paper that considers the following questions: What factors shaped women's work on the Manhattan Project? How did traditional gender roles shape that work? What did women do to cope with the stress of working on the atomic bomb?

Activity 5: The Double V Campaign

Step 1: Review the documents in this collection focused on African American women's experiences.

Step 2: View the online exhibition *Patriotism Crosses the Color Line: African Americans in World War II*, available at the Gilder Lehrman Institute of American History, at http://www.gilderlehrman.org/history-by-era/world-war-ii/essays/patriotism-crosses-color-line-african-americans-world-war-ii.

Step 3: Review the "Suggested Sources" section on the exhibition website.

Step 4: Prepare a thirty-minute presentation on women's roles in fighting for victory abroad and civil rights at home.

ANNOTATED BIBLIOGRAPHY

Books

Adkins Covert, J. Tawna. *Manipulating Images: World War II Mobilization of Women through Magazine Advertising.* Lanham, MD: Rowman & Littlefield Publishers, 2011.

As part of the Lexington Studies in Political Communication Series, this volume focuses on how the media shaped women's experiences during World War II. The author draws much of her research from the National Archives and presents a brief but useful introduction on the role propaganda played in mobilizing women.

Anderson, Karen. *Wartime Women: Sex Roles, Family Relations, and the Status of Women during World War II.* Westport, CT: Greenwood Press, 1981.

Anderson's book examines the short-term changes of the war years and how this temporary transformation shaped the economics of American families. The monograph addresses topics such as wartime jobs, union responses, and women in the workforce. The final chapters focus on how the postwar United States denied women equal entry into the workforce.

Bérubé, Allan. *Coming Out under Fire: The History of Gay Men and Women in World War II.* New York: Free Press, 1990.

This groundbreaking study of the experiences of gay men and lesbian women during World War II is essential reading for anyone interested in the history of gender in the United States. Bérubé integrates the experiences of both men and women into the chapters to describe the barriers and prejudice they faced as they sought to serve their country.

Brown, Carrie. *Rosie's Mom: Forgotten Women Workers of the First World War.* Boston: Northeastern University Press, 2002.

This volume examines how women in 1917, a full generation before Rosie the Riveter, entered the workforce and served the war effort. The first chapter offers important context and is followed by a highly readable and well-illustrated history of women who are often forgotten in women's and labor history.

Campbell, D'Ann. *Women at War with America: Private Lives in a Patriotic Era.* Cambridge: Harvard University Press, 1984.

This volume examines the significant changes in American life during the war, with particular emphasis on how the war disrupted women's lives and in some cases threatened their values. The author divides the book into eight chapters, with the final one focused on how the war reshaped women's roles in American life. It is a slim but useful volume for students interested in this era. Pay particular attention to the introduction, "Rediscovering the Women of the 1940s."

Colman, Penny. *Rosie the Riveter: Women Working on the Home Front during World War II.* New York: Crown Publishers, 1995.

This brief but immensely readable book is divided into nine chapters, complete with illustrations. Pay particular attention to the items at the end, including a useful list of women's wartime jobs, facts and figures about women war workers, and a chronology.

Dombrowski, Nicole Ann, ed. *Women and War in the Twentieth Century: Enlisted with or without Consent.* New York: Garland Publishing, 1999.

This edited volume documents women's experiences in war in a wide range of conflicts. The book is divided into three parts, and each part contains essays focused on topics as diverse as French Catholic women during World War I to Mayan women in Guatemala. Part 2 is devoted to World War II, and the essay on sexuality and the Women's Army Air Corps deserves special attention.

Escobedo, Elizabeth R. *From Coveralls to Zoot Suites: The Lives of Mexican-American Women on the World War II Home Front.* Chapel Hill: University of North Carolina Press, 2013.

This monograph, focused on Mexican American women, shows how wartime work shaped their labor, their home lives, and their communities. The necessities of war helped women exercise some measure of control over their public lives and reshaped gender and ethnic roles that had been so carefully circumscribed. Escobedo presents a little-known story, "Greatest Generation," that recovers the lives of these women and enriches our understanding of the war.

Frank, Lisa Tendrich. *An Encyclopedia of American Women at War: From the Home Front to the Battlefield.* Santa Barbara, CA: ABC-CLIO, 2013.

This two-volume set presents a comprehensive view of women's experiences during the war. The more than three hundred entries cover a range of topics, from individual biographies to legal cases, military policies, military branches, and wartime organizations. The introductory essay presents a useful overview about women's roles at home and abroad. The bibliography is especially valuable to anyone interested in World War II.

Gluck, Sherna Berger. *Rosie the Riveter Revisited: Women, the War, and Social Change.* Boston: Twayne Publishing, 1987.

This volume is one of the most useful overviews of the period, reflecting the voices of those who lived through the war. Gluck has presented a well-organized, thoughtfully written, and important collection of oral histories that reflect the range of women's experiences.

Greenwald, Maurine Weiner. *Women, War, and Work: The Impact of World War I on Women Workers in the United States.* Westport, CT: Greenwood Press, 1980.

There is a great deal of scholarship on women and World War II, but less on women and the "Great War." This book offers context in which to understand

Rosie the Riveter's mother's generation and how labor evolved in the early twentieth century. The book is accompanied by an excellent bibliography.

Gregory, Chester W. *Women in Defense Work during World War II: An Analysis of the Labor Problem and Women's Rights*. New York: Exposition Press, 1974.

This brief book examines the challenges women faced working in defense industries during World War II. The book is divided into sixteen chapters, some focused on specific industries such as shipbuilding, steelmaking, or agriculture. Others focus on the experiences of African American women, comparisons between male and female workers, and the status of women after the war. The book includes useful tables on a wide range of topics.

Harris, Mark Jonathan, Franklin D. Mitchell, and Steven J. Schechter. *The Homefront: America during World War II*. New York: G. P. Putnam's Sons, 1984.

This oral history collection focuses on the remembrances of what the authors call "homefront survivors of World War II." The book is divided into thirteen chapters, focusing on a wide range of topics, including "Women Alone" and "Homecoming." Though not specifically focused on women, there are plenty of female voices that reflect the war's impact.

Hartmann, Susan M. *The Home Front and Beyond: American Women in the 1940s*. Boston: Twayne Publishers, 1982.

This volume, part of a series entitled American Women in the Twentieth Century, focuses on various aspects of women's lives on the home front during the war. Each chapter is devoted to a different theme, from the law, politics, and education to labor unions, the family, and popular culture. In the introduction, Hartmann explains, "The Second World War transformed the economy, made unprecedented claims on women and men, and disrupted social arrangements on a broad scale."

Honey, Maureen, ed. *Bitter Fruit: African American Women in World War II*. Columbia: University of Missouri Press, 1999.

Honey corrects the distorted view of women's history during World War II by focusing on the experiences of African American women. While Rosie the Riveter has become the iconic female figure of the war, her experiences obscure the broader role of black women in wartime industries, on the home front, and in auxiliary services. Honey draws from *Negro Digest*, *The Crisis*, *Opportunity*, and *Negro Story*, the most influential periodicals of the time. An important contribution of the volume is the attention on how the war shaped the civil rights movement and women's roles in it.

———. *Creating Rosie the Riveter: Class, Gender, and Propaganda during World War II*. Amherst: University of Massachusetts Press, 1984.

Divided into four sections ("The Creation of the Myth," "Middle-Class Images of Women in Wartime," "The Working-Class Woman and the Recruitment Campaign," and "Class Differences in the Portrayal of Women War Workers"), this volume addresses why the war failed to transform women's working lives. Two of the most compelling questions Honey addresses are these: How did

Rosie become transformed into the post-1945 model of femininity? Why did the war fail to improve women's status in the United States?

Kiernan, Denise. *The Girls of Atomic City: The Untold Story of Women Who Helped Win World War II*. New York: Touchstone, 2013.

This *New York Times* bestseller recounts the story of the top-secret World War II town of Oak Ridge, Tennessee, and the young women who helped built the atomic bomb. Nearly seventy-five thousand residents called the town home, a community that was not listed on any map. Kiernan recounts the experiences of these women and presents what *Publishers Weekly* calls an "intimate and revealing glimpse into one of the most important scientific developments in history."

Knaff, Donna B. *Beyond Rosie the Riveter: Women of World War II in American Popular Graphic Art*. Lawrence: University of Kansas Press, 2012.

Knaff's book focuses on the visual culture of women during the war and how posters, cartoons, comic strips, and advertisements were intended to shape women's behavior. Knaff examines the tension between femininity, wartime work, and patriotism and provides a unique window into the lives of American women during the war.

Lewis, Brenda Ralph. *Women at War: The Women of World War II—at Home, at Work, on the Front Line*. Pleasantville, NY: Reader's Digest Association, 2002.

This richly illustrated and highly readable book tells the story of women at war. The short introduction is accompanied by ten chapters and a section at the end on further reading. The book is especially useful for the diversity of experiences it depicts and the clever sidebars that illuminate important, often unknown stories of the war.

Litoff, Judy Barrett, and David C. Smith. *American Women in a World at War: Contemporary Accounts from World War II*. Wilmington, DE: Scholarly Resources, 1997.

This volume focuses on trying to "reconstruct the worldview of the 1940s for modern readers" by selecting documents from the time period. The editors divide the book into six sections: "Preparing for War," "In the Military," "At Far-Flung Fronts," "On the Home Front," "War Jobs," and "Preparing for the Postwar World." Readers might enjoy the suggested reading section at the end of the book.

———. *Since You Went Away: World War II Letters from American Women on the Home Front*. New York: Oxford University Press, 1991.

This dense collection of letters, many of them quite short, illustrates the fears, hopes, and frustrations associated with war. The editors have divided the volume into nine chapters, focused on topics such as courtship by mail and war brides. The timeline at the end is especially helpful.

Merryman, Molly. *Clipped Wings: The Rise and Fall of the Women Airforce Service Pilots (WASPs) of World War II*. New York: New York University Press, 1998.

This volume "examines the accomplishments and struggles of the Women Airforce Service Pilots (WASPs) of World War II—their service, their premature disbandment, and how they finally got some of the recognition they deserved." The book is divided into nine chapters, with a rich bibliography at the end.

Milkman, Ruth. *Gender at Work: The Dynamics of Job Segregation by Sex during World War II*. Chicago: University of Illinois Press, 1987.

Milkman's classic work on gender during World War II is essential reading for anyone interested in this period in history. Her work focuses on the roles that women played during the war and how labor history, including the history of unionization, was shaped by women. This concise volume is richly illustrated and offers a nice overview of this topic.

Parker, Pauline E. *Women of the Homefront: World War II Recollections of 55 Americans*. Jefferson, NC: McFarland & Company, 2002.

This useful oral history collection is organized by themes and provides a rich record of the American experience during World War II. There is a particularly interesting section entitled "Voices from Abroad." The author describes the book as "a small tribute to those women who by themselves raised the children, kept their families together, kept industry going, served in the military and kept alive the faith and hope of those abroad in war."

Poulos, Paula Nassen. *A Woman's War Too: U.S. Women in the Military in World War II*. Washington, DC: National Archives and Records Administration, 1996.

This book grew out of a conference by the same name that was hosted by the National Archives, March 3–4, 1995. The book is divided into seven sections: "Setting the Stage," "Making History: Women, the Military and Society," "Contributing to the War Effort," "Confronting the Realities of Service Life," "Documenting Women's Service: Memoirs, Museums, Historical Collections," "Documenting Women's Service: National Archives and Records Administration," and "Leading the Way." There is a useful appendix regarding sources at the National Archives as well.

Putney, Martha S. *When the Nation Was in Need: Blacks in the Women's Army Corps during World War II*. Metuchen, NJ: Scarecrow Press, 1992.

This slim volume documents in great detail the experiences of African American women in the WACs. The text is complemented with a number of rare photographs, and the tables in the appendices are particularly useful in understanding the scope and scale of women's participation in the war.

Rupp, Leila J. *Mobilizing Women for War: German and American Propaganda*. Princeton: Princeton University Press, 1978.

This useful comparative history focuses on how government propaganda campaigns before and during World War II affected women's wartime contributions. Two chapters, "Occupation: Housewife" and "Rosie the Riveter: American Mobilization Propaganda," would be of particular note to those interested in American women.

Sigerman, Harriet, ed. *The Columbia Documentary History of American Women since 1941*. New York: Columbia University Press, 2003.

> This rich documentary history focuses its first chapter on women during World War II. Readers will find fourteen documents that illustrate the complex and varied experiences of women during the war. Eleanor Roosevelt is represented here, as is Yoshiko Uchida, who was interned during the war, like so many Japanese Americans. Those interested in women's lives after the war will be rewarded by this dense volume. Pay particular note to the section at the end titled "Further Reading about Twentieth-Century Women."

Stevens, Michael E., ed. *Women Remember the War, 1941–1945*. Madison: State Historical Society of Wisconsin, 1993.

> As part of series entitled Voices of the Wisconsin Past, this slim volume presents the war from the perspective of women in Wisconsin. It is divided into seven chapters, with a biography of each interviewee at the end. The oral histories offer a rich record of the various roles that women played in a single state.

Thomas, Mary Martha. *Riveting and Rationing in Dixie: Alabama Women and the Second World War*. Tuscaloosa: University of Alabama Press, 1987.

> This short volume focuses on the women of Alabama and the various contributions they made to the war effort. The book offers a useful regional perspective and provides a thorough essay on sources at the end.

Weatherford, Doris. *American Women and World War II*. New York: Facts on File, 1990.

> Weatherford's comprehensive treatment of women during World War II is essential reading. Her book is divided into four sections: "Be a Nurse and See the World," "The Military Woman," "The New Industrial Woman," "The Home Front," and "Afterward." Each section presents a dense, yet readable history of the period.

Wise, Nancy Baker, and Christy Wise. *A Mouthful of Rivets: Women at Work in World War II*. San Francisco: Jossey-Bass Publishers, 1994.

> This volume focuses on women in manufacturing jobs, but also includes women in white-collar professions. The authors explain that the "book provides readers with touching and inspiring examples of the courage, determination, and sense of humor these women demonstrated as they performed their jobs, cared for their families, coped with marginal housing and transportation, moved great distances, and rarely thinking they were doing anything special, survived physical and emotional challenges."

Yellin, Emily. *Our Mother's War: American Women at Home and at the Front during World War II*. New York: Free Press, 2004.

> This collection presents a thorough view of the war and women's role in it. The book is divided into three parts, focused on the home front, the front lines, and on unknown stories of women (from prostitutes to anti-Semitic mother's groups). Yellin has a thorough bibliography that would be useful to students and scholars of the era.

Online Resources

Digital Vaults, National Archives, http://www.digitalvaults.org.

> These digital vaults include documents, photographs, and other primary sources related to women and World War II. Highly searchable, the database is especially useful for locating obscure materials.

Partners in Winning the War: American Women in World War II, National Women's History Museum, http://www.nwhm.org/online-exhibits/partners/exhibit entrance.html.

> This online exhibition, created in 2007, is divided into five sections: "Changing Images of Women's Roles," "Women in the Military," "Women Serving the Military," "Women in Production," and "Women at Home and in the Community." The site is lavishly illustrated and examines women's varied roles.

"Rosie the Riveter: Women Working during World War II," National Park Service, www.nps.gov/pwro/collection/website/rosie.htm .

> This website focuses on women's work during World War II, with particular attention to factory labor.

Rosie the Riveter: Real Women Workers in World War II, Library of Congress, http://www.loc.gov/rr/program/journey/rosie.html.

> This online exhibition focuses on women's varied roles during World War II, presenting diverse experiences that go beyond the common Rosie the Riveter icon.

World War II and the American Home Front, National Park Service, http://www.nps.gov/nhl/themes/homefrontstudy.pdf.

> This teacher's guide, created by the National Park Service, provides a wide range of useful information for high school and university faculty members; it is focused on the home front during World War II.

Women Come to the Front, Library of Congress, http://www.loc.gov/exhibits/wcf/.

> This online exhibition focuses on women who served on the front lines during World War II.

ABOUT THE MUSEUM OF HISTORY AND HOLOCAUST EDUCATION

The Museum of History and Holocaust Education (MHHE) at Kennesaw State University, in Georgia, presents public events, exhibits, and educational resources focused on World War II and the Holocaust in an effort to promote education and dialogue about the past and its significance today. The MHHE seeks to work with the local community, schools and faculty, and students at KSU to meet these goals.

The Museum of History and Holocaust Education is funded in part by the Marcus Foundation and is housed at the KSU Center on Kennesaw State University's extended campus.

The MHHE hosts numerous traveling exhibitions, including *Beyond Rosie: Women and World War II*. For information about this exhibition, please call 470-578-2083 or visit http://historymuseum.kennesaw.edu/.

INDEX

A

Abercrombie and Fitch, xxii
academic professions, xx, 55
accountants, xxiii
Adams, Ansel, 185, 187
African Americans: aircraft manufacturing plants, 44–48; auxiliary services, xxv; employment status, 56–57; flag-making, 106–7; low-status jobs, xvii, xxv; trailer camps, 125–26; workplace discrimination, xvii, 4–5, 56, 64–66
agriculture, 56, 57, 130
aircraft manufacturing plants, 14, 15–16, 44–48, 57–58
Air Evacuation School, 109, 110
Albuquerque, New Mexico, 215
Aleut women, 173–74
All-American Girls Professional Baseball League, 72–74
All-American Girls Softball League, 73
Allied powers, xiii, xxii–xxiii
aluminum cans, xxviii
Ameche, Don, 194
American Merchant Marine Academy, 90
American Women's Hospitals, 85–86
American Women's Voluntary Services (AWVS), xxvii
Anderson, David, 214
anti-Nazi underground resistance, xxviii, xxx, 194, 195, 196–202
appointed women officers, 119–22
Arden, Eve, 226
Arkansas State University, 84
Arlington, Vermont, xvi
Arlington, Virginia, 125
Army Air Forces, 115–16
Army Medical Corps, xxi, 83–85, 86
Army Nurse Corps, xxiii, xxiv, 108–10
Ashe, B. F., 116–17
Atlanta, Georgia, 65–66, 156–57

atomic bomb, xiii, xxxi, 150, 209, 214–17, 218. *See also* Manhattan Project
Atomic Heritage Foundation, 202
auditors, xxiii
auxiliary services: background information, 89; Cadet Nurse Corps, 101–2; Coast Guard Women's Reserve (SPARS), xxiii, xxvi, 104–6; female pilots, 99–101; importance and functional role, xxiii–xxvii; navigational tool instruction, 90; Navy Women's Reserve (WAVES), xxiii, xxvi, 64, 91, 97–99, 103, 111–13, 221–28; personal surveys, 108–13; sexual orientation, 97–99; Uncle Sam's Nieces (photograph), 96; Women Airforce Service Pilots (WASPS), xxiii, xxv, xxxii, 89, 99–101; Women's Army Auxiliary Corps (WAACs), xxiii, xxiv, xxvi, xxxii, 89, 90–91, 93–95, 113–14
Axis powers, xii, xiii, xiv

B

Bacon, Antoinette Frissell. *See* Frissell, Toni
bacon grease, xxviii
Baltimore, Maryland, 196
bank tellers, xxiii, 55
Barringer, Emily Dunning, xxi, 82–85
Barry, J. L., 41
baseball teams, 72–74
batteries, xxvii
Beckman, Trish, 101
Bederson, Ben, 209
Belgium, xii
Bell Aircraft Corporation, 14, 44–48
Bell Bomber plant, 14, 44–48
Berry College, 130
Berry Farmerettes, 130–32

Beyond the Home Front: Women's Autobiographical Writings of the Two World Wars (Klein), 97
bicycles, xxvii
Bikini Atoll, 215
blitzkrieg (lightning war), xii
Bloom, Ada Glasser, 66–72
blue collar jobs, 56
bond drives, xxviii, 156–58
Bonney, Thérèse, 79–81
bookkeepers, xxiii
bouchon assemblies, 2
Bourke-White, Margaret, xxii–xxiii
Bowman Field, Kentucky, 109
Boyer, Kate, xxiii
Breed, Clara, 183–85
Bressler Editorial Cartoons, Inc., 37
British Special Operations Executive (SOE), xxix, xxx, 196
Brotherhood of Sleeping Car Porters, 4
Brousse, Charles Emanuel, xxix–xxx
Brown, John Mason, 106
Brown University, 204–5
Bubley, Esther, 62
Buck, Pearl, 140
Bull, Frank L., Jr., 200
Bureau of Industrial Conservation, 172
Bureau of Public Relations, 177
burn bags, 226
business administration, 55
Business Week, xxvii
butter, xxvii

C

Cadet Nurse Corps (poster), 101–2
Cammermeyer, Gretta, 97
Campbell, Ely, xviii
canned foods, 126, 129, 169–70
casualties: executions, xxx, 194, 195–96; industrial jobs, xviii; Pearl Harbor attack, 7, 148; Pearl Harbor widows, 11; war casualties, 147
ceiling prices, 159–66, 168–71
celebrity advocates, 156–57, 177–78
censorship, 148–49
Central Intelligence Agency (CIA), 179
Cerasale, Ethel Carlson, 108–10

Chalker, Lloyd T., 105
Chapelle, Dickey, xxiii, 81–82
Chappel, Owen, 99–101
Chicago, Illinois, 215
child care facilities, xviii–xix, 23–24, 133–37
Child, Julia McWilliams, 179–81
children's questions about war, 132–33
Christmas message, 105–6
Chunking, China, 179
Churchill, Winston, 153
Citizens Defense Corps, 123
City College (New York), xxviii
civil defense activities, xxviii, 123
Civilian Conservation Corps (CCC), 190
Civilian Exclusion Order #5, 182
civilian occupations, xx–xxiii, 17
civil rights campaign, xvii. *See also* workplace discrimination
Civil Service Commission, 65–66
civil service jobs: African American women, 64–66; employment opportunities, xxi, xxiii, 55, 61–62; women's rights, 60–61
"Civil Service" (poem), 64–65
Civil War era, xiv
Clark, Mark, 223
Cleaver, June, xxxiii
clerical work: African American women, 64–66; aircraft manufacturing plants, 57–58; employment opportunities, 55, 63–64; Japanese Americans, 59; post-World War II era, xxiii; temporary federal employees, xxi, xxiii, 55, 61–62; women as proportion of all workers, 56
Cleveland, Ohio, 142, 145–46, 151
Clinton Engineering Works, 219, 221
coal-wood heating stoves, 169
Coast Guard Women's Reserve (SPARS), xxiii, xxvi, 104–6
Cochran, Jackie, xxv
code breaking, 221, 224–28
coffee, xxvii
Collins, Eileen, 101
Collins, Marjory, xxi, 125
Colman, Penny, xix

commissioned women officers, 119–22
Committee for the Care of Young
    Children in Wartime, 135
commodity shortages, xxvii, 123, 159–
    62. *See also* rationing programs
Comprehensive Interpretive Plans, 51
Conant, James Bryant, 206
Conover, David, xvi
conservation efforts, xxviii, 123. *See also*
    home-front support efforts
Converse, Mary, 89–90
Cook, Constance, xx
cooking oil, 170–71
Cornell University, xx
Corpus Christi, Texas, 11
cost of living, 165
Cowden, Violet, 99–101
craftsmen, 56
Craig, May, 78
Crane, Clare Marie Morrison, 142–54
Crawford, Joan (photograph), 75
Creuse, France, 197–99
Crile Hospital, 146, 154
cryptographers, 221, 224–28
Czechoslovakia, 202

D

Dachau concentration camp, xxiii
Daley, Richard E., 115–16
Dannaher, Mary Barbara Brennan,
    221–28
Davis Monthan Air Base, 144
Davis, William H., 21–23
day care centers, xviii–xix, 23–24,
    133–37
D-Day, 150, 151
deception activities, xxviii, 6–7, 175. *See*
    also espionage; sabotage operations
defense industries: female employees,
    8–10, 15–17; workplace discrimina-
    tion, xvii, 4–5, 65–66, 126, 219–21.
    See also wartime jobs and services
Denmark, xii
Department of Labor, xxxiii, 3, 15,
    55–57
Department of the Treasury, xvi, 156
detonation research, 208–9

Dietrich, Marlene, 177–78
discrimination: African American
    women, 56, 64–66; auxiliary ser-
    vices, xxv; defense industries, 4–5,
    126; gender inequality, xvii–xviii;
    sexual orientation, 97–99; war cor-
    respondents, xxii; workplace dis-
    crimination, xvii, 64–66. *See also*
    workplace discrimination
Distinguished Service Cross award,
    199–201
documentary photographers, xxi, 62
Dodd, Martha, xxx
Dodd, William E., xxx
Domby, Lucy Lovett, 118–19
domestic ideals, xxxii–xxxiii, 1, 49
domestic service, 56, 57
Donahue, Virginia, 147
Donna Reed Show, The, xxxiii, 1
Donovan, William J., 201–2
Doolittle, Jimmy, xxii, 149
"double shift" work, xviii
Double V campaign, xvii
Dougherty, Norma Jeane Baker, xvi
Doyle, Geraldine, xvi
Doyle, Mary, xvi
drafting aides, 58
Dugan, Dorothy L., 38–41
Duran, Evelyn, 12–14
duration villages, 173–74

E

Eaker, Ira C., xxxii
Eastman Corporation, 219, 221
Eisenhower, Dwight D., xxiv, 89, 202
employment and hiring tips, 41–43
employment opportunities: aircraft
    manufacturing plants, 14, 15–16,
    44–48, 57–58; civil service jobs, xxi,
    xxiii, 55; clerical work, 55, 57–58,
    63–64; factory work, xiii–xix, 1;
    middle-class women, 62–64
employment status: African American
    women, 56–57; aircraft assembly
    plants, 57–58; women as proportion
    of all workers, 55–56
end of the war, 118–19, 151

Enewetak Atoll, 215
engineers, 55, 58
England, Kim, xxiii
Enigma codes, xxix
enlisted women, 119–22
enlistment controversies, xxv–xxvi
enlistment efforts, 91–93
Enright, Marion R., 96
equal wages, xviii, xxv, 19–23, 83
Erickson, Ethel, 57–58
Espanola, New Mexico, 211
espionage, xxviii, xxix, 179, 195
European Theater, xiii, 201–2
Evans, Redd, xv, 18
executions, xxx, 194, 195–96
Executive Order 8734, 159–62
Executive Order 8802, xvii, 4–5, 126
Executive Order 9024, 172
Executive Order 9066, 175–77
Executive Order 9163, 90–91
Executive Order 9328, 21

F

factory work: African American
    women, 44–48, 57; aircraft manu-
    facturing plants, 14, 15–16, 44–48,
    57–58; clerical jobs, 57–58; defense
    industries, 15–17; employment
    opportunities, xiii–xix, 1; women
    as proportion of all workers, 56
Fair Employment Practices Committee,
    4, 5, 56, 65–66
Falter, John Philip, 103
Farewell to Manzanar, xxxi
Farm Security Administration (FSA),
    xxi, 125–26
Federal Bureau of Investigation (FBI),
    63, 177, 189
female journalists, xxi–xxiii
female physicians, xx–xxi, 55, 82–87
female pilots, xxv, 16, 99–101
female veterans, xxvi
Ferrying Command, xxv
film librarians, 66–71
Fisher, Mary Shattuck, 132
Fish-Harnack, Mildred, xxx, 194, 195–96

Fiske, Natalie, 223–24
flag-making, 106–7
flight nurses, 81–82
Follow the Band (1943), xv
food shortages, 126
Ford, Gerald, 78
Fort Missoula, Montana, 193
France, xii
French resistance, 196–202
Frissell, Toni, 76–77
Fuchs, Klaus, 207, 209
fuel oil tanks, 169
Fukuda, Kay, 186
Funter Bay Evacuation Camp, 173
Fussell, Lewis, 214

G

Gander Field, Newfoundland, 150
gasoline, xxvii, 123, 168–69
Gattus, Ottilie Juliet, xxxii–xxxiii
gender inequality, xvii–xviii
gender relationships, 137–42
gender stereotypes, 25–36
General Management Plans, 51, 53
General Motors Corporation, 19–23
Georgia College for Women, 112
German Americans, 175
Germany, xii, xiii, xiv
Gestapo, xxx, 195, 196, 200, 201
GI Bill (1944), xxvi, 154
*Girls of Atomic City: The Untold Story of
    the Women Who Helped Win World
    War II, The* (Kiernan), xxxi
Glendale, California, 191–92
gold stars, 150
goods and staples scarcities, xxvii, 123,
    159–62. *See also* rationing programs
"Good Work, Sister" (poster), 37
Goolrick, Faye, 50
Gorham Manufacturing Company, 2
Government girls, xxi, xxiii, 55, 61–62
Great Britain, xii
Greenglass, David, 209
Griffin, Georgia, xxviii
Griffith Park, California, 190–92
groceries, 152, 171

Groves, Leslie Richard, Jr., 214
Grumman Aircraft Engineering
    Corporation, xxxiii
Guadalcanal, xiii

H

Hall, Virginia, xxx, 196–202
hand grenade assembly, 2
hard core enemy aliens, 193–94
Harnack, Arvid, xxx, 195
Harnack, Mildred. *See* Fish-Harnack,
    Mildred
Harpers Ferry Interpretive Planning
    Center, 50, 51–52
Harper's Weekly, xiv
Harvard Medical School, 87
Harvard University, xx, 204, 213
Harven, Betty, 110
Haute Loire Department, 197–99,
    200, 201
heating oil, xxvii
heating stoves, 169
Heckler, Diane. *See* Hall, Virginia
Henderson, Elizabeth, 142–54
Herbert Kerkow Productions, 25, 36
high-paying defense jobs, xvii
Hill, Mary E., 96
hiring tips, 41–43
Hiroshima, Japan, xiii
Hitler, Adolf, xii, xiii, xvi, xxxii, 8,
    195, 196
Hobby, Oveta Culp, xxiv, xxv
Hobby, William P., xxiv
Holdsworth, Alberta M., 96
Hollem, Howard, 11
Hollis, Florence, 137–42
home-canning, 129, 169–70
home-front support efforts: Berry
    Farmerettes, 130–32; community
    service, 142–54; day care centers,
    xviii–xix, 23–24, 133–37; Farm
    Security Administration (FSA)
    trailer camp, 125–26; marital rela-
    tionships, 137–50; parental advice,
    132–33; poster campaigns, 123–24;
    price controls, 159–66, 168–71;

rationing programs, xxvii–xxviii,
    123, 126, 152–53, 165–71; victory
    gardens, 123–24, 126–29, 147, 152;
    V-mail, 148, 155–56; war bonds,
    156–58; waste fats, 172
Homer, Winslow, xiv
homosexuality, xxv, 97–99
Hornig, Don, 202, 204–9, 215–16, 217
Hornig, Lilli Schwenk, 202–18
housing communities, xvii–xviii
Houston Post-Dispatch, xxiv
Hughes, Eileen, xiv
Hulick, Anna Marie, 93–95
Hungerford, Cy, 43
Hunter College, 112
Huntsville Chemical plant, xviii
Hyde, Doris, 96

I

identification cards (photograph), 77
"I Gave a Man!" (poster), 156, 157
immorality, xxvi
Imperial Japan, xii
industrial casualties, xviii
inflation, 159, 164, 171
insurance, 55, 83
internment camps, xxxi, 175–77,
    182–87, 193
Inwood Community Day Nursery, 136
Iowa State College for Women, 112
Ishii, Amy Uno, 188–94
isolationist policies, xii
Italian Americans, 175
Italy, xii, xiii, xiv
"It's a Woman's War Too! Join the
    WAVES" (poster), 103
Iwo Jima, xiii, xxiii

J

Japan, xii, xiii, xiv, 6–7, 147–48, 188–89,
    227
Japanese American National Museum,
    183
Japanese Americans, xxxi, 59, 175,
    182–94

Jefferson Barracks, Missouri, 109
Jensen, J. Hans D., xxxi
Jewett, Irving F., 163, 164
JN-25 code, 221, 226–28
John Carroll University, 154
Johns, Herbert G., 142, 143
Johnstone, Thomas A., 21–23
journalists, xxi–xxiii, 69–70, 76–81

K

Kaiser Shipyard, xviii
Kelley, Kathryn A., 44
Kelly, Cynthia C., 202, 209
Kerkow, Herbert, 25, 26, 36
Kiernan, Denise, xxxi
King's Point, New York, 90
Kistiakowsky, George, 202, 206–7,
    208, 212–13, 215–16
kitchen fats, 171, 172
Klein, Yvonne M., 97
Klinefelter, C. F., 36
Koski, Walter, 208
Kuwata, Florence, 187

L

labor organizations, xvii–xviii, 19–23
labor regulations, 38–41
labor shortages, xiv, xvii, xxvii, 1
Lange, Dorothea, xxi, 182
Latina women, 12–14
Latvia, 219, 220
law firm jobs, xx, 55
League of Their Own, A (film), 74
Leave It to Beaver, xxxiii, 1
lebensraum (living space), xii
legal professions, xx, 55
Lend-Lease Act (1941), xii–xiii, xiv
lesbians, xxv, 97–99
letter-writing, 148
Lewis, Brenda Ralph, xiv, xxv, xxix
Libby, Leona Woods Marshall, xxxi
librarians, 66–71, 183
Life magazine, xxii
Linschitz, Henry, 208
living conditions, xvii–xviii

Lockheed Corporation, 14
Loeb, John Jacob, xv, 18
Long-Range Interpretive Plans, 51,
    52–54
Los Alamos Historical Society, 202
Los Alamos, New Mexico, 205, 210,
    211–12. *See also* Manhattan Project
Love, Nancy Harkness, xxv
Love, Robert, xxv
low-status jobs, xvii, xxv
Luce, Henry, xxii
Luxemburg, xii
Lyko, James, 222–27

M

"make do and mend" spirit, xxvii, 123.
    See also home-front support efforts
male coworkers, xviii, xxv
Management-Labor Appeals
    Committee, 38–41
managerial work, xxiii, 56, 58
Manhattan Project, xxviii, xxxi, 202–18.
    See also Hornig, Lilli Schwenk
Mann, Ethel, 11
Manzanar War Relocation Center, xxxi,
    185–87
March on Washington Movement, 4
Marietta, Georgia, 14, 44
Marine Corps Women's Reserve, xxiii,
    xxvi
marital relationships, 137–50
married women, xvii, xviii–xix
Marshak, Bob and Ruth, 210, 211
mathematical skills, 58
Mayer, Maria Goeppert, xxxi
McDowell, Beulah V., 65–66
McKibbin, Dorothy, 210, 211
McNutt, Paul V., 25
McWilliams, Julia. *See* Child, Julia
    McWilliams
meat, 123, 152–53, 166–67, 171
Medical Corps, 83–85, 86
medical professions, xx–xxi, 55, 82–87
Meigs, Mary, 97–99
Mein Kampf (Hitler), xvi
Menninger, Karl, 194

Merchant Marines, 90

Metropolitan Life Insurance Company, 223

Meyer, Georgette Louise. *See* Chapelle, Dickey

middle-class women, 62–64

Midway Atoll (1942), xiii

Mildred Pierce (film), 75

military auxiliary services: background information, 89; Cadet Nurse Corps, 101–2; Coast Guard Women's Reserve (SPARS), xxiii, xxvi, 104–6; female pilots, 99–101; importance and functional role, xxiii–xxvii; navigational tool instruction, 90; Navy Women's Reserve (WAVES), xxiii, xxvi, 64, 91, 97–99, 103, 111–13, 221–28; personal surveys, 108–13; sexual orientation, 97–99; Uncle Sam's Nieces (photograph), 96; Women Airforce Service Pilots (WASPS), xxiii, xxv, xxxii, 89, 99–101; Women's Army Auxiliary Corps (WAACs), xxiii, xxiv, xxvi, xxxii, 89, 90–91, 93–95, 113–14

military rank, xxii

military service, xxxii, 89, 119–22. *See also* specific military organization

military uniforms, xxii, 93, 225

Miller, J. Howard, xvi, 17, 18

Milwaukee, Wisconsin, xxx

"Minimum Standards for Employment of Women in Industry" (poster), 3

misconduct, xxvi

Mitchell, Kristin, 188–94

Mitchell, Margaret, 156

Mitson, Betty E., 188

Mobile, Alabama, xvii, 8–10, 116–17

Mocas Tolis, Effie, 111–13

model postwar family, xxxii–xxxiii, 1, 49

Monahan, Evelyn, 108, 111

Monroe, Marilyn, xvi

Montclair, New Jersey, 203

Morley, Burton R., 116–17

Mount Vernon Young Ladies' Seminary, 224

movies, 149

Mulcahy, William, xix

munitions plants, xiv, xviii, 2, 15–17

Murphy, Patricia, 62–64

Murphy, Robert, 223

"My Day" (Roosevelt), 60–61

N

Nagasaki, Japan, xiii

Nancy, France, 109

Narragansett, Rhode Island, xiv

National Conference of Social Work, 137

National Geographic, xxiii

National Park Service, 50–54

National Press Club, 223

National War Labor Board (NWLB), 19–23

National Women Veterans Foundation, Inc., 108, 111

native peoples, 173–74

Naval Air Base (Texas), 11

Naval Reserve Act (1938), 91–92

navigational tool instruction, 90

Navy Department, 222–28

Navy Nurse Corps, xxiii

Navy Women's Reserve (WAVES): employment opportunities, 64; government legislation, 91; importance and functional role, xxiii, xxvi; personal surveys, 111–13; recruitment efforts, 103; secret assignment, 221–28; sexual orientation, 97–99

Nazi Germany, xii, xxix–xxx, 194, 195, 219

Nelson, Donald, xiv

Netherlands, xii

Neuman, Charlcia, xxvii–xxviii

neutrality legislation, xii–xiii

Newfoundland, Canada, 62

Newport, Rhode Island, xiv

newspapers, xxviii

newsreels, 66–71, 149

New York Post, xxx

New York Times, xviii

New York Vassar Club, xxviii

Nichols, Constance C., 64–65
non-military occupations, xx–xxiii, xxvi–
    xxvii, 17, 57–58
Normandy (1944), xiii
North Africa (1943), xiii
Norway, xii
nuclear weapon development, xxxi
nursery schools, xviii–xix, 23–24, 133–37

O

Oak Ridge, Tennessee, 215, 218, 219
oath of service, 113–14
Office for Emergency Management,
    159, 162
Office of Civilian Defense, xxviii, 135,
    136
Office of Price Administration and
    Civilian Supply (OPACS), xxvii,
    159–62, 164–71
Office of Production Management, 161
Office of Strategic Services (OSS), xxix–
    xxx, 177, 179, 196, 199–202
Office of War Information (OWI), xv,
    xxi, 66–71, 90, 125, 129, 181
Officer Personnel Act (1947), 121
officer's identification card (photo-
    graph), 77
Ogawa, Louise, 184–85
oil: cooking oil, 170–71; fuel oil tanks,
    169
Olds, Robert, xxv
On Wisconsin, 194–96
Opa-locka, Florida, 72–73
Oppenheimer, Kitty, 213–14
Oppenheimer, Robert, 209, 213–14
organized labor, xvii–xviii, 19–23
Our Army (magazine), 115–16

P

Pacific Theater, xiii, xxiii
pacifism, xii
Paramount Music Corporation, xv
parental advice, 132–33
Parents' Magazine, 134
Parker, Alfred, 129
Parma, Ohio, 146

Pathe Films/Pathe News, 66–71
pay adjustments, 19–23
peace time military service, 119–22
Pearl Harbor attack, xiii, xiv, 6–7, 147–
    48, 188–89
Pearl Harbor widows, 11
Perkins, Frances, 15, 55
permanent status, 119–22
personal surveys, 108–13
Petrovic, Ann, 73–74
Photo Fighter (comic book), 79–81
photographers/photojournalists, xxi,
    62, 69–70, 76–77, 79–82, 125
photographs: All-American Girls
    Professional Baseball League,
    73; Bell Bomber plant, 14; Berry
    Farmerettes, 131; child care
    facilities, 134; child care facilities
    cartoon, 24; Civilian Exclusion
    Order #5, 182; Farm Security
    Administration Trailer Camp for
    Negroes, 125; female Harvard med-
    ical students, 87; flag-making, 107;
    flight nurse with wounded soldiers,
    82; Florence Kuwata, 187; Japanese
    American woman, 59; Joan
    Crawford, 75; Kay Fukuda, 186;
    Marlene Dietrich, 178; Mary
    Converse, 90; Mary Withrow,
    14; May Craig, 78; Oak Ridge,
    Tennessee, 218; Pearl Harbor wid-
    ows, 11; Sheriger Family Planning
    Their Victory Garden by Reading
    Up on the Subject, 128; telephone
    operators, 62; Uncle Sam's Nieces,
    96; war bond rally, 158; woman in
    kitchen, 49; women assembling
    hand grenades, 2
Pidgeon, Mary Elizabeth, 15
pilot training, 99–100
Plotzensee Prison, 196
plutonium chemistry, 207
Polish invasion, xii
Port Arthur, Texas, 171
Portland, Oregon, xviii
poster campaigns: Cadet Nurse Corps,
    101–2; canned foods, 129; female
    factory workers, 43–44; "Good

Work, Sister", 37; home-front support efforts, 123–24; minimum standards for employment of women in industry, 3; pin-up girls, 43–44; rationing programs, 166–67; recruitment efforts, xvi, 17–18, 103; Rosie the Riveter, 17–18; "Service on the Home Front", 123–24; victory gardens, 126, 127; V-mail, 155–56; war bonds, 156, 157; waste fats, 172; Women Accepted to Voluntary Emergency Services (WAVES), 103
postwar family ideals, xxxii–xxxiii, 1, 49
post-World War II opportunities, xx–xxiii, 154
Pribilof Islands Program, 173
price controls, 159–66, 168–71
primacord, 208–9
prisoners of war, 146
Problems in Supervision: Supervising Women Workers (film), 25–36
professional baseball teams, 72–74
professional work: African American women, 57; aircraft manufacturing plants, 57–58; employment opportunities, 55; librarians, 66–71, 183; post-World War II opportunities, xx–xxiii; women as proportion of all workers, 56
propaganda campaigns, xv–xvi, xxviii, 43–44, 69–70, 101–3
Providence, Rhode Island, 2
Publicity Bureau (US Army), 155–56
Public Law 554, 90–91
Public Law 625, 119–22
Public Law 689, 91–93
public nurseries, xviii–xix, 23–24, 133–37
Purple Heart awards, xxvii

R

racial prejudice, 56, 64–65, 126
Racine Belles, 73
radio broadcasts, 177
radio clips, 168–71
Radio Corporation of America (RCA), 41
Rake, Denis, xxx

Randolph, A. Philip, xvii, 4
rationing boards, xxi, 162–66, 171
rationing programs, xxvii–xxviii, 123, 126, 152–53, 165–71
razor blades, xxviii
Reader's Digest, xviii
Reading Ration and Price Control Board, 162–64
recruitment efforts: controversies, xxv–xxvi; government legislation, 91–93; poster campaigns, 103; recruit characteristics, 116–17; Women's Army Corps (WAC), 115–16
Red Cross, xxvii, 150, 193
Red Orchestra, xxx, 195
Regular Air Force, 119–20
Regular Army, 119–20
Regular Marine Corps, 119–22
Regular Navy, 119–22
relocation camps, xxxi, 59, 173–77, 182–87, 193
Remeik, Louise E., 219–21
resistance movements, xxviii, xxx, 194, 195, 196–202
retail price ceilings, 159–66, 168–71
Richards, Elizabeth A., xxvii
Richmond, California, 50–54
Rockford Peaches, 73
Rockwell, Norman, xvi, 17–18
Rogers, Edith Nourse, xxiv, 90
Rome, Georgia, 130
Roosevelt, Eleanor, xviii–xix, xxi, 60–61, 223
Roosevelt, Franklin D.: declaration of war, xiii, 6–7; enlistment controversies, xxv; Executive Order 8802, xvii, 4–5, 126; Executive Order 9066, 175–77; Executive Order 9163, 90–91; Executive Order 9328, 21; Lend-Lease Act (1941), xii–xiii, xiv; National War Labor Board (NWLB), 19; Office of War Information (OWI), 66–67; Sparkman Act (1943), xxi; war bonds, 156; workplace discrimination, xvii, 4–5, 56, 65–66, 126, 219–21
Rorke, Harold B., 76–77

Rosenkotter, Judith, 93–95
Rosie the Riveter, xi, xv–xvi, 17–18
Rosie the Riveter (1944), xv
"Rosie the Riveter" (song), xv, 18
Rosie the Riveter/World War II Home
    Front National Historical Park,
    50–54
Royal Army Medical Corps, 85–86
rubber, xxvii, 123
Russell, Clifton, 130, 132

S

sabotage operations, xxviii, xxix, xxx,
    195, 196–202
Salazar, Margarita, xvii
Salt Lake City, Utah, 143–44, 188
salvage efforts, 123
Sandia Mountains, 214–15
Sandia National Laboratories, 208
San Diego Public Library, 183
Santa Anita, California, 193
Santa Fe, New Mexico, 210
Saturday Evening Post, xvi, 18, 103
"Save Waste Fats" (poster), 172
Scherbius, Arthur, xxix
Science News Letter, 132–33
Science Service, 132
scientific aides, 58
scientific and technological research,
    xxxi–xxxii
Scott, Anne Firor, xx
Searles, David, xxiv
Secretary of War, 176–77
secret war: background information,
    xxviii–xxxii, 175; cryptography, 221–
    28; espionage and sabotage opera-
    tions, xxviii, xxix, xxx, 195, 196–202;
    internment camps, xxxi, 175–77,
    182–87; Japanese Americans, xxxi,
    59, 175, 182–94; Manhattan Project,
    202–18
segregation, xvii, 125–26
separated families, 188–94
Servicemen's Readjustment Act (1944),
    xxvi, 154
"Service on the Home Front" (poster),
    123–24

service organizations, xxiii–xxvii
sexual misconduct, xxvi
sexual orientation, xxv, 97–99
Sheriger Family Planning Their Victory
    Garden by Reading Up on the
    Subject, 128
Shevenell Company, 39
shoes, xxvii, 39, 169
Shuler, Irma, 212, 216
silk stockings, xxviii
Silvas, Rosa, 12–14
Simpkin, William E., 20
skilled labor, 56
Slade, Ernestine J., 44–48
Social Security Administration, xxi
Society for Science and the Public, 132
Soviet Union, xiii
Sparkman Act (1943), xxi, 82–85
Sparkman, John J., 82–85
SPARS. *See* Coast Guard Women's
    Reserve (SPARS)
Special Operations Executive (SOE),
    xxix, xxx, 196
Speer, Albert, xxxii
sports activities, 187
spying. *See* espionage
Stalingrad (1942–1943), xiii
stars, gold, 150
stereotypes, gender, 25–36
Stimpson, Henry L., xv, xxv
Stimson, Barbara, 85–86
St. John, Newfoundland, 150
Stratton, Dorothy C., 104, 105–6
Studenbacker, J. W., 25
student-based agricultural work pro-
    gram, 130
sugar, xxvii, 123, 169–70
supervisors, xxiii, 58
Sweetwater, Texas, 99, 100
Szilard, Leo, 210

T

Tariff Act (1930), 160
Tasaki, Katherine, 183
Taylor, George W., 21
Taylor, James B., Jr., 62–64
tea, xxvii

telephone operators, 61–62
Teller, Edward, 209, 210, 212
temporary federal employees, xxi, xxiii, 55, 61–62
Terry, Peggy, xviii
"Their Real Pin Up Girl" poster, 43–44
Thomas, Earl and Betty, 214
Thorpe, Amy, xxix–xxx
timeline, 229–32
Time magazine, xix
tin cans, xxviii
tinfoil, xxviii
toys, xxvii
trailer camps, 125–26
training films, 25–36, 70
training manuals, 164–66
Treasury Department, xvi, 156
Trinity test, 209, 214–15
Tripartite Pact (1940), xii
Truman, Harry, xxx, xxxii, xxxiii, 89, 119, 200–201
Tucson, Arizona, 143, 144–45

U

Uncle Sam's Nieces (photograph), 96
union organizations, xvii–xviii, 19–23
United Automobile, Aircraft and Agricultural Implement Workers of America–C.I.O., 19–23
United Electrical, Radio and Machine Workers of America–C.I.O., 19–23
United Service Organization (USO), xxvii, 145–47, 177
University of Arizona, 144
University of Arkansas, 84, 85
University of Colorado Science Policy Program, 216
University of Wisconsin alumni, 194–96
unmarried women, xvii
uranium hexafluoride gas, xxxi
US Army Air Corps, xxii
US Army Nurse Corps, xxiii, xxiv, 108–10
US Army, Publicity Bureau, 155–56
US Cadet Nurse Corps (poster), 101–2
US Department of Labor, xxxiii, 3, 15, 55–57

US Department of the Treasury, xvi, 156
US Employment Service, 9–10, 17, 38–41
US Marines, xxiii
US Naval Cadet Nurses, 185–86
US Office of Education, xxxii, 25, 36
US Quartermaster Corps, 106–7
USS *Atlanta*, 157
US State Department, xxx

V

vacuum cleaners, xxvii
Vatudrip, 2
V-E Day, 150, 151
venereal disease rates, xxvi
veterans, female, xxvi
Veterans History Project, 142, 221
Vichy government, xxix–xxx
victory gardens, xxviii, 123–24, 126–29, 147, 152
V-mail (Victory mail), 148, 155–56
Voices of the Manhattan Project, 202
volunteer services, xxvi–xxvii, xxviii
von Neumann, John, 210

W

waffle irons, xxvii
wages and benefits, 19–23, 38–41, 61–62, 71, 83, 92–93, 139–40
Wakatsuki, Jeanne, xxxi
Wall, Don, 207
War Advertising Council (WAC), xv
war bonds, xxviii, 156–58, 177
war casualties. *See* casualties
war correspondents, xxi–xxiii, 78
War Department, xxi, xxiv, 177
War Gardens for Victory (poster), 126, 127
War Labor Board, xviii
War Manpower Commission, 8, 116–17, 133
War Price and Rationing Boards, 166, 171
War Production Board (WPB), xiv, xxviii, 169, 172

warrant women officers, 119–22

War Relocation Authority, 59, 182

Wartime Civilian Control Agency, 59

wartime jobs and services: aircraft manufacturing plants, 14, 15–16, 44–48,
57–58; defense industries, 8–10,
15–17; employment and hiring tips,
41–43; labor disputes, 19–23, 38–41;
Latina women, 12–14; munitions
plants, xiv, xviii, 2, 15–17; post-war
legacy, xxxii–xxxiii; training films,
25–36. *See also* employment opportunities; factory work

wartime labor disputes, 19–23, 38–41

wartime production, xiii–xv, xix, 1

waste fats, 171, 172

weather codes, 228

"We Can Do It!" poster, xvi, 17–18

"We'll Have Lots to Eat This Winter,
Won't We Mother?" (poster), 129

Westinghouse Company, xvi

white collar jobs, 56, 57

Wigner, Eugene, xxxi, 210

Wilson, Rob, 205–6

window signs, 149–50

Withrow, Mary, 14

Woman in Kitchen (photograph), 49

Women Accepted for Voluntary
Emergency Services (WAVES):
employment opportunities, 64; government legislation, 91; importance
and functional role, xxiii, xxvi; personal surveys, 111–13; recruitment
efforts, 103; secret assignment, 221–
28; sexual orientation, 97–99

Women Airforce Service Pilots
(WASPS), xxiii, xxv, xxxii, 89, 99–101

Women as Proportion of All Workers,
by Occupational Status (1940-1947),
55–56

Women Assembling Hand Grenades
(photograph), 2

women doctors, xx–xxi, 55, 82–87

Women's Armed Services Integration
Act (1948), xxxii, 89, 119–22

Women's Army Auxiliary Corps Oath,
113–14

Women's Army Auxiliary Corps
(WAACs)/Women's Army Corps
(WAC): Anna Marie Hulick, 93–95;
end of the war, 118–19; establishment, 90–91; importance and functional role, xxiii–xxiv, xxvi, xxxii, 89;
Lucy Lovett Domby, 118–19; misconduct charges, xxvi; oath of service, 113–14; recruitment efforts,
115–17; secret war, xxxi

Women's Auxiliary Ferrying Squadron
(WAFS), xxv

Women's Bureau, Department of
Labor, xxxiii, 3, 15, 55–57

Women's National Press Club, 78

Women's Reserve Act (1942), 91–93

women's rights, 60–61

"Women Want to Get It Over!" brochure, 41–43

workplace discrimination: African
Americans, xvii, 4–5, 56, 64–66;
defense industries, xvii, 4–5, 126,
219–21; gender inequality, xvii–xviii;
women doctors, 82–85

Work Projects Administration (WPA),
123–24

World War I, xiv, 2

World War II: auxiliary units, xxiii–xxvii;
Rosie the Riveter/World War II
Home Front National Historical
Park, 50–54; women's legacy,
xxxii–xxxiii

Wormeley, Katharine, xiv

Y

Yamada, Elizabeth Kikuchi, 183

Yank magazine, xvi

Young, Virginia, 11

Z

Zarin, Mr. and Mrs. G., 220

zippers, xxvii

ABOUT THE EDITORS

DR. JULIA BROCK holds a PhD in public history from the University of California, Santa Barbara, and is the director of interpretation at the Museum of History and Holocaust Education, Kennesaw State University. Previously, she has served as the assistant reviews editor at the *Public Historian* and as a consulting historian for the National Park Service. In addition to curatorial duties at the MHHE, she was the coordinator for a Museums Connect grant, funded by the US State Department and the American Association of Museums, that joined students at KSU and at Hassan II University in Casablanca, Morocco, in a project to build an online exhibit based on themes of identity, migration, and the experiences of Muslims in the US South and in Morocco. Brock served as co-curator for KSU's traveling exhibit, *Beyond Rosie: Women in World War II.*

DR. JENNIFER DICKEY is an assistant professor and the coordinator of public history at Kennesaw State University. She holds a BS with honors in business administration from Berry College, a master's degree in international business from the University of South Carolina, a master's degree in heritage preservation from Georgia State University, and a PhD in public history from Georgia State University. She has worked for the Historic Preservation Division of the Georgia Department of Natural Resources and for the National Park Service. Her research focuses on the cultural impact of Margaret Mitchell's *Gone with the Wind*, and her book, *A Tough Little Patch of History: Gone with the Wind and the Politics of Memory*, was published by University of Arkansas Press in 2014. She is coeditor of *Museums and Globalization*, published by the American Alliance of Museums in the spring of 2013. She has curated dozens of exhibitions and is a well-known public historian and preservationist.

RICHARD J. W. HARKER is the education and outreach manager at the Museum of History and Holocaust Education at Kennesaw State University. He completed an MA in modern history with honors at the University of St. Andrews, Scotland, and an MA in history at the University of Durham, England. He is completing his PhD in public history at Georgia State University. He co-curated *Beyond Rosie: Women in World War II* for the Museum of History and Holocaust Education and edited teacher's guides, curriculum packs, and a catalog for the exhibit.

DR. CATHERINE M. LEWIS is assistant vice president of Museums, Archives, and Rare Books, the director of the Museum of History and Holocaust Education, and a professor of history at Kennesaw State University. She is also a guest curator and special projects coordinator for the Atlanta History Center. She completed a BA in English and history with honors at Emory University and an MA and PhD in American studies at the University of Iowa. She has curated more than twenty-five exhibitions throughout the nation and has authored, co-authored, or edited eleven books, including *The Changing Face of Public History: The Chicago Historical Society and the Transformation of an American History Museum* (Northern Illinois University Press, 2005), *Don't Ask What I Shot: How Eisenhower's Love of Golf Helped Shape 1950s America* (McGraw-Hill, 2007), and three similar documentary collections with the University of Arkansas Press.